Cesar M. Rodriguez and W. Charles Sawyer
The Economies of Latin America

Cesar M. Rodriguez and W. Charles Sawyer

The Economies of Latin America

DE GRUYTER

ISBN 978-3-11-067490-3
e-ISBN (PDF) 978-3-11-067493-4
e-ISBN (EPUB) 978-3-11-067499-6

Library of Congress Control Number: 2021936059

Bibliographic information published by the Deutsche Nationalbibliothek
The Deutsche Nationalbibliothek lists this publication in the Deutsche Nationalbibliografie;
detailed bibliographic data are available on the Internet at http://dnb.dnb.de.

Sadly, W. Charles Sawyer passed away when we were at the final stages of this project. Charlie was a great economist and a dear friend. This book is dedicated to him. Thank you, Charlie.

Acknowledgments

We wish to sincerely thank both Nathan Gamache and Jeffrey Pepper. One of us had worked with Nathan during a stint as a journal editor and been put into initial contact with Jeffrey. Jeffrey understood immediately what we were trying to accomplish and then let us do just that. In this industry, that is a level of freedom that is not common. As is frequently the case in book publishing, Jeffery has moved on to other opportunities. Fortunately, Jaya Dalal did great work in getting the final manuscript into the finished product that you are reading. The production of this book has involved more than the usual amount of luck and this final smooth editorial transition was just one of many instances. More specifically, Alejandro Murillo-Segura produced some of the tables and graphs, and Claudia Gonzalez helped us with the final details. Last but not least, we would like to thank Portland State University and Texas Christian University for providing the environment and resources for us to write this book.

https://doi.org/10.1515/9783110674934-202

Contents

Preface

Why a new book on the economies of Latin America? Roughly speaking, the literature on Latin American economics can fall into three groups. First, there is the book/journal format that is mostly accessible to academics. Second, there are a collection of textbooks, which are both "long" and based on the assumption that the content is being supplemented by lectures. Finally, there is a small number of books aimed at the general reader about the economies of Latin America. However, these books usually assume some previous familiarity with the region and are focused on government policy choices. Faced with this context, the purpose of this book is to provide the non-specialist reader with a usable introduction to the economies of Latin America. Our task here is to strike the right balance between the general and the specific, such that both the general reader and instructors of courses on Latin America can find usable information on the region.

In order to get this done, the book is informally split into two parts. The first part consists of the first three chapters and the final chapter. The second part offers country-specific details that supplement the overall information contained in the first section. Chapters 1 through 3 introduce the region, explaining its economic history, and describe the central economic challenges of Latin America. Chapters 4 through 7 walk the reader through specific economic details for (i) Argentina and Brazil (Chapter 4), (ii) Chile, Colombia, Peru, and Uruguay (Chapter 5), (iii) Bolivia, Ecuador, Paraguay, and Venezuela (Chapter 6), and (iv) Mexico and Central America (Chapter 7). Although the grouping of countries might look arbitrary, we hope to convince the reader how strikingly homogenous those groups are in economic terms. The final chapter deals with the economic future of the region. After setting up some of the constraints on the region, the discussion centers on what a version of success would look like for Latin America.

One issue that always comes back when discussing the economies of Latin America is where to find current information on the region. Regardless of preferences, the weekly section "The Americas" in *The Economist* is probably a must read. However, in many cases, these articles tend to assume that the reader has a certain background level of knowledge and understanding of the region that most non-specialist readers do not have. With this book, we also hope to provide the necessary information to make the material presented in *The Economist* more accessible to the general reader.

https://doi.org/10.1515/9783110674934-204

Chapter 1
An Introduction to the Economies of Latin America

> For much of Latin America's history, the world economy has treated the region as a basket of natural resources that have been packaged and shipped to satisfy the consumption of richer foreign nations.
> Shawn William Miller

Everyone has their own impressions of the different regions of the world. It is probably safe to say that in most cases these impressions may shape an imprecise view of each region. Perhaps no other region of the world is less well understood than Latin America. What may be missing is why Latin America as a region is distinct. Put another way, why does Latin America matter? The first part of this chapter details Latin America's place in the world with respect to land, population, resources, and gross domestic product (GDP). In these aspects, Latin America is important. In another sense, there is a perception that something might not be working well in Latin America. Unfortunately, this intuition might be correct. The second part of the chapter discusses Latin America as a relative economic "underperformer." The origins of this disappointing performance can be traced back hundreds of years to colonial Latin America and subsequent events following the break with Spain. The third section of the chapter begins our discussion of this history. As in any situation, it is one thing to face drawbacks but it is more complex if those challenges persist. In the fourth part of the chapter, we start detailing some of these issues. A flip answer to what still is pending in Latin America frequently is answered with two words: education and infrastructure. That is too simplistic, but it also is a partial truth. The whole story is more complex and unraveling that complexity will provide the reader with a better understanding of this story. We will begin by discussing the levels of business regulation and taxes that have contributed to a large informal sector in the region. With some background information about Latin America in hand, the final part of the chapter introduces the economic geography of the region and how the middle section of the book is laid out.

The Promise of Latin America

Let us start here with a theme that will permeate the book. Most of us are probably familiar with a certain type of person. What we are referring to here is the sort of person who naturally has all of the characteristics necessary for success. However, despite all of their natural ability, they are never very successful. Of course, they

https://doi.org/10.1515/9783110674934-001

are not absolute failures, as their performance may be average or even above average. The point is that they can be considered *relative* failures in the sense that they were never able to get their performance to match their potential. Analogously, Latin America as a region could be classified as a relative economic failure. By global standards, Latin America is in the middle of the pack. However, it is like the talented person stuck in middle management. As we will discuss, Latin America has plenty of land. It is endowed with an incredible array of natural resources, full of talented people. However, the people of the region are telling the rest of us that Latin America has deep problems. A lot of people with high levels of education may move to another country. It is when the painters, plumbers, car mechanics, and other highly skilled people are leaving that one suspects that something is not working properly.

In Latin America, land is not a problem. The region contains 14 percent of the land mass of the world. Unlike some countries or regions, most of the land is usable and the climate varies from tropical to temperate. However, there is a catch: arable land. In this regard, looking at Latin America on the map can be deceiving. In the world, 21 percent of the land is arable. In Latin America, it is about 10 percent. While the region is a noticeable force in many agricultural products, the base of that is not as large as one might think. In the neighborhood, so to speak, Latin America looms much larger. It contains half of the land in the Western Hemisphere. This is conservative as much of the land mass of Canada does not have a temperate climate. There is an interesting twist on the climate of the Western Hemisphere. The reversal of the seasons above and below the equator creates a natural potential for trade between North America and Latin America. Since some products are inherently seasonal, there is the possibility that freer trade in the Western Hemisphere could lead to gains from trade that are larger than would usually be the case.

Notice that the use of the word "land" is different than its conventional use. In economics, land is not just what one stands on. Land in this context also includes any resources associated with the land, such as minerals and agricultural products, that can be produced on the land. In this regard, Latin America always has been exceptionally lucky. The modern story of resources in Latin America began more than 500 years ago. In a failed attempt to get to the Far East from Europe, Christopher Columbus ran into the Western Hemisphere. In his first encounters with the region, he literally found gold. This was the beginning of a quest for resources that continues into the 21st century. The first 150 years of Latin American history was marked by the quest for gold and silver. Even today, Latin America produces 16 and 29 percent of the world's gold and silver, respectively. Lesser mineral booms occurred periodically down through the centuries in gold, diamonds, and guano. While the latter is no longer important, it was the source of a major war in the 19th century. The borders of modern Chile, Peru, and Bolivia are a result of that conflict. The strained relationship among these three countries can be traced back more than a century.

Moving past historical considerations, Latin America currently is a major source of both major and minor minerals. The distinction between the two is a bit arbitrary as all of these minerals are of some importance in the world economy. The list of "minor" minerals is bauxite, iron ore, lead, nickel, tin, and zinc. For each of these minerals, Latin America is responsible for 10 to 20 percent of world output. As will be shown later, some of these minor minerals are extremely important for particular countries. For example, iron ore is an important mining industry in Brazil. The three "major" minerals that are produced in the region are oil, copper, and lithium. Oil was discovered in Latin America in the early 20th century. Historically, Mexico and Venezuela have been the two major producers. Brazil is in the process of becoming another major producer. Argentina has significant resources that have yet to be exploited. Colombia rounds out the countries producing oil in the region. In the world oil industry, Latin America is not the Middle East, but production is not trivial. It could be far higher because Venezuela has the world's largest reserves. As a result, the future of oil production in Latin America is quite important for the global oil industry. This is another example of the unfulfilled potential of the region.

Copper and lithium are a different matter. Chile and Peru account for more than half of the world's production of copper. In Chile, copper accounts for more than 60 percent of exports and is nearly 20 percent of GDP. The comparable numbers for Peru are 16 percent and 48 percent. Lithium is the quintessential commodity of the 21st century. Obviously, it is used in batteries, but it has other industrial and medical uses. Currently, Chile and Argentina rank as the world's second and fourth largest producers, respectively. This could change in the near future. The term "lithium triangle" is now part of the vernacular use to describe the industry. Like copper, Chilean reserves of lithium dwarf that of any other country of the world. It has more than twice the reserves of the second country, Australia. Together, Argentina, Bolivia, and Chile have more than half of the world's reserves of lithium. As one can see, the age-old story of mineral wealth in Latin America continues.

To a lesser extent, there is a similar story concerning agricultural products and Latin America. As will become clearer, the story of agriculture in Latin America is one of relative success. Recall from the above that Latin America has less than 10 percent of the world's arable land. Despite this, it uses that land exceptionally well. Latin America accounts for 25 percent of the world's agricultural output. Perhaps a part of this relative success can be attributed to a long agricultural history. Less than a century after the easy gold and silver wealth had been "extracted" from the region, significant agricultural production started. The two earliest examples were cochineal and indigo. The former is a natural red dye, and the better-known indigo is a blue dye. These were small, specialty products relative to what was to follow. The 17th century saw the increasing production of sugar and tobacco. The expanded production of these two products transformed them from luxuries to ordinary consumption items for the people of Europe. The 18th century saw similar results through the production of coffee. While these products are now staples of consumption in high-income countries, they are still luxury goods in much of the world. As a result, there is still a substantial amount of growth left in these commodities. The development of steamships in the late 19th century transformed the agricultural sector of the region. The tall sailing ships were beautiful but terribly expensive to operate. As a result, only cargoes with a high value to weight ratio such as coffee, sugar, or tobacco could be profitably transported in these ships. Steamships were what we now call a *disruptive technology*. The dramatic lowering of transportation costs meant that bulk commodities like wheat could now be transported cheaply over long distances. This led to a surge of agricultural exports from the region that fostered rapid economic growth. Ships with the capacity to carry refrigerated cargo were developed shortly thereafter. The result was a surge in exports of beef and pork. All of these products are still important exports from a number of countries in the region, especially Argentina and Brazil. In the second half of the 20th century, further reductions in transportation costs have led to large increases in exports of fresh fruits and vegetables from Latin America. More recently, the region has begun exporting a number of specialty agricultural products such as chia and quinoa. Like the older staple commodities, a product that starts out as a luxury good can quickly become something with a much larger base of consumption. Quinoa is just a modern version of an old cycle. These may well not be the last of these products. A little known fact is that Latin America is one of the most biologically diverse regions of the world. Of the top 10 countries of the world in terms of biodiversity, Latin America contains 6. While measures of biodiversity are not precise, any listing of it always contains Latin American countries in the region at either near or at the top. The point is that these new specialty products quite probably are not the last.

Having land and resources is important, but having a population to use the land is essential. The population of Latin America is approximately 644 million. This is no doubt a conservative estimate, as a considerable percentage of the economy is in the *informal* sector. The informal sector includes informal residential communities such as the *favelas* of Brazil. The UN estimates that there are 130 million squatters living in Latin America. While the population is large, it is no longer growing very fast. In the second half of the 20th century population growth was high, as Latin America was passing through the demographic transition. In general terms, as economies move from low to middle income a combination of lower death rates and unchanged birth rates produces a rapidly expanding population. In the 1960s the population of Latin America was growing at nearly 3 percent per year. The change in the last 50 years has been dramatic. The population is now growing by less than 1 percent, which is only marginally higher than the 0.7 percent for the United States (US). Further, the population is increasingly urban. In the mid-1970s half of the population of the region still lived in rural areas. Today, more than 80 percent of the population lives in urban areas. As will be discussed in more detail, the population is relatively well educated. Literacy is universal and increasing numbers of students are moving past primary schools into secondary schools and universities. While the quality of these schools is uneven, the overall educational level of the people of the region keeps rising. The point that is being made is that Latin America has changed. In fact, the region has changed more in the last several decades than perhaps the perceptions of people outside the region have changed. This is just another example of what economists call adaptive expectations. The perception of things changes with a lag. Things change but it takes a while for perceptions to catch up with the change.

Latin America as a Relative Failure?

The section above highlights some obvious facts about Latin America. It has a large land mass with predominantly temperate climates. It has a stunning abundance of resources associated with that land. Some countries of Latin America rank in the top twenty in terms of working hours per worker, according to Giattino et al. (2013). With all of these advantages, the relative economic position of the region could be better. In this section, we present some data to quantify what the problem is and show just how the region has underperformed since World War II. To start, one needs to make the distinction between absolute and relative failure. In an absolute sense,with the exception of the 1980s, Latin America always makes economic progress. Rather, the challenges come in relative terms. Economic progress in the region has struggled to keep up with global averages. With such an abundance of land, resources, and people this relative underperformance is a long-standing puzzle. Our immediate task is to show this in numerical terms.

We can begin to do this by referring to Table 1.1. The table presents population, GDP, and GDP per capita for all of the countries of Latin America. It also presents analogous data for Latin America, low-, middle-, and high-income countries, as well as the world. For the sake of comparison, it might be useful to keep a couple of pieces of US data in mind. The GDP of the US is more than $20 trillion and the population is nearly 330 million. This reveals an immediate fact. The US is producing more than 3 times the value of goods and services as Latin

Table 1.1: Population, GDP, and GDP per capita for Latin America, low-, middle-, and high-income countries, and the world.

	Population (millions)	GDP (billions of USD)	GDP per capita (USD)
Argentina	44.5	520	11,684
Bolivia	11.4	40	3,549
Brazil	209.5	1,885	9,001
Chile	18.7	298	15,925
Colombia	49.6	334	6,719
Costa Rica	5.0	61	12,112
Ecuador	17.1	108	6,296
El Salvador	6.4	26	4,068
Guatemala	16.3	73	4,473
Honduras	9.6	24	2,506
Mexico	126.2	1,221	9,673
Nicaragua	6.5	13	2,021
Panama	4.2	65	15,593
Paraguay	7.0	40	5,806
Peru	32.0	222	6,941
Uruguay	3.4	60	17,278
Venezuela, RB	28.9	202	6,997
Central America	47.8	257	6,656
Latin America	644.1	5,972	9,272
World	7,673.6	87,698	10,818
Low income	668.5	521	780
Middle income	5,769.2	32,165	5,575
High income	1,235.9	55,045	44,540

Source: World Bank, Economic Commission for Latin America and the Caribbean (ECLAC).

America with approximately half the population. GDP per capita in Latin America is less than $10,000 versus more than $60,000 in the US. Given the different histories of North, Central, and South America one should expect some differences. The purpose of the above is to give a reference point of where Latin America is relative to the richest country of the region. However, when using the world as a reference point Latin America is not that far. The average GDP per capita for the world is nearly $11,000. There are at least five countries in the region with GDP per capita above that level. Another sort of comparison is useful. The average GDP per capita for the middle-income countries of the world is a bit over $5,000. In this light, the Latin American data looks much more positive. There are only five countries that are below that average in the region and four are in Central America. By global standards, Latin America is not just middle class it is upper middle class. In reality, Latin America is only poor by the standards of high-income countries. This is what we meant from the statement above that Latin America is not an economic failure in absolute terms. Even the country with the lowest income in the region, Nicaragua, has a standard of living that most low-income countries would aspire to.

Unfortunately, the information above constitutes the good news. The economic underperformance of the region is in a relative sense. A good way to begin thinking about this is to go back 70 years to the end of World War II. In the preceding 100 years much of Latin America had experienced rapid economic growth. After the catastrophe of a global war, the region has escaped relatively unscathed and seemed poised to continue on a rapid growth path. In the 1950s, the conventional wisdom was that Latin America was a region with a bright future. Both Argentina and Venezuela were high-income countries at that point and there was the expectation that much of the rest of the region would be able to replicate that success. Alas, that was not to be the case. Growth was decent in the 1950s and 1960s but not that high in a relative sense. The world economy boomed from 1946 to 1973 and Latin America simply rode that wave. Some of the policy miscalculations that were made during this period began to be apparent in the 1970s and led to the Lost Decade of the 1980s. The growth record since then has been average at best. It is not that Latin America did not grow; it just never grew fast relative to the rest of the world.

If Latin America grew slowly, a fair question to ask is what would have constituted fast? In the postwar era, the standard of fast occurred in Asia. The economy of Japan recovered from the war faster than virtually anyone would have expected. However, Japan was already a developed country before the war so that success story is not completely relevant. The usual standard is the growth of the four "Asian tiger" economies: Hong Kong, Singapore, South Korea, and Taiwan. In the 1950s these countries all fell into the low- to barely middle-income categories. A good example of this is that at the end of the Korean War in 1953, when South Korea was barely more prosperous than India. Another example is that in the early 1960s, Taiwan's major export was rice. From this starting point, all of these countries made the leap from poor to rich in virtually one generation. However, this astonishing performance is perhaps not so easy to put into a Latin American context. Hong Kong and Singapore are city states. South Korea and Taiwan are more average countries, but they have a history that is quite different from that of Latin America.

To illustrate the problem of Latin America, we will compare the region to a large country in Asia that has much in common with the region: Indonesia. Like Latin America, Indonesia was a colony of various European powers for hundreds of years. Another similarity is that Indonesia is a major exporter of commodities. However, Indonesia is not considered one of the "star" economies of the world. It has grown at a rate that is good in comparison to the world, but below average compared to much of the rest of Asia. We can use Figure 1.1 to show how a small difference in economic growth rates can lead to substantial differences in absolute numbers such as GDP per capita over time.The figure is constructed to suggest what the region could have been with a simple counterfactual exercise. It is not easy to precisely answer this question (it would require a formal counterfactual analysis), but it helps us with basic intuition about possible outcomes. The bottom line in the graph shows the actual changes in the region that have occurred since 1960. The absolute gains are clear. Over the last 60 years, GDP per capita has tripled. The next line above contains a comparison with a relative strong economy of Latin America: Chile. This line shows what would have happened if the average growth in the region had matched the growth of Chile. The difference is dramatic. Average GDP per capita would have been more than 30 percent higher. Latin America has not only underperformed by global standards but by a local standard. The comparison with Indonesia is disheartening. If Latin America had grown at the rate of an "also ran" Asian economy, GDP per

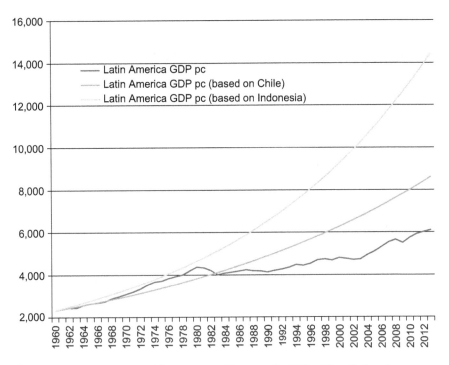

Figure 1.1: Actual versus potential changes in GDP per capita (GDP pc) in Latin America (constant 2005 US dollars).

capita in the region would have been more than twice as high. Look back at the data in Table 1.1 and think for a moment about what this means. Although an imperfect comparison, instead of GDP per capita being $10,000 it would now be $20,000. The region's wealthiest countries would now be high-income countries and the poorest would be at least lower middle class. Our task going forward is to try to explain how this happened. The resources necessary for success are there but are not being used effectively. As we will see next, history as usual is part of the explanation.

History Matters

> I come for gold, not to till the land like a peasant.
> Hernán Cortés

For our purposes, the history of Latin America begins with the pre-Colombian civilizations of Mexico and Peru. The Aztec and Inca empires are a part of the cultural heritage of the world. However, their wealth combined with the intrusion of Europeans in the late 15th century set the region on an unfortunate path. The quote above pretty much tells the story. The Spanish conquest of Mexico was fueled by the opportunity to obtain an enormous amount of gold and silver. The subsequent conquest of Peru was much the same story. The absolute sums are staggering. Between 1520 and 1660, approximately 200 tons of gold were moved from Latin America to Spain. The amount of silver shipped was approximately 18,000 tons. Essentially, the early modern history of Latin America amounts to the Spanish looting the continent of anything valuable that could be moved to Spain. This is not a situation that was conducive to economic development.

The relative depletion of gold and silver deposits led to a movement to utilize the abundant land resources of the region. A running series of agricultural commodity booms involving cochineal, indigo, tobacco, sugar, coffee, henequen, and rubber began in the middle of the 15th century and continue today. Unfortunately, the patterns of land ownership established a tendency towards income inequality that reverberates into modern times. In order to develop mineral wealth, Spain established *encomiendas*, which were large tracts of land granted to a Spanish citizen to develop. In theory, the person did not own the land but was holding it in trusteeship for the indigenous peoples. Abuses of the system inevitably occurred through the use of debt or the simple reality that workers could not easily find employment elsewhere. In any case, the workers were not facing what anyone would call a free labor market. This applies to the population that survived the initial contact with Europeans. In the 16th century, roughly half of the indigenous population of the region died from imported diseases. The subsequent labor short-age, particularly in Brazil, was filled by the importation of approximately 4.5 mil-lion African slaves. They toiled on *fazendas*, which were the Portuguese equivalent of the encomiendas. While the encomiendas were abolished in 1720, what followed was not an improvement. The Spanish introduced a Roman concept from antiquity, the *latifundia*. Titles to large tracts of land were given to develop agricultural prod-ucts for export. Earnings from this production were taxed, the *repartida*, and repa-triated to Spain. In any event the landowners had little incentive to pay taxes to provide for schooling or infrastructure other than what was necessary to move crops to the market. Given these patterns of landownership, it is not hard to imag-ine the resulting inequality in the distribution of income.

While the above description of colonial Latin America is discouraging enough, another policy of Spain made things even worse. Prior to the insights of Adam Smith concerning free trade it was normal for governments to attempt to manipu-late foreign trade. It was thought that promoting exports while suppressing im-ports would improve economic welfare. The usual term for this sort of trade policy is *mercantilism*. While completely discredited among economists, it is not difficult to hear its echoes in the 21st century. Unfortunately, combining mercantilism with colonialism creates a doubly pernicious situation for colonies. The colonies, in this case Latin America, were forced to do all of their foreign trade with the colonial power. This meant that all exports from Latin America had to pass through Spain or Portugal first. On the other hand, the colonies in Latin America could only im-port from the home countries. This meant that Latin America did not necessarily receive the best prices for their commodities and they paid inflated prices for im-ports. For Americans, the story should be familiar. The rupture between the US colonies and the British government partially was caused by the British version of mercantilism. More recently, the trade relationship between the former Soviet Union and Eastern Europe is somewhat similar. In all cases, a major power is pur-suing policies to manipulate the trade relationship with colonies or weaker coun-tries to the benefit of the former and the detriment of the latter. It is not a situation that bodes well if you are not the stronger partner in the relationship and can have lingering consequences. Logically, the possession of commodity wealth should lead to more rapid economic development. The potential tax windfall for the gov-ernment could be used to develop infrastructure and enhance social services such as education and health care. This could presumably lead to faster economic growth but that is usually not the case. All too often the extra revenue finds its way elsewhere and the effect on economic growth can be negative. This is such a common phenomenon that it has a name: the *resource curse*. In the 21st century, it is not hard to find. How many countries in the world that have commodity wealth have been able to use it effectively for economic development? Latin America is a case in point.

A key point to keep in mind is that Latin America's relationship with Spain spanned over three centuries. During this period, the economic development of the region was tied to exports of commodities. All that was being developed were areas with marketable commodities and any resources necessary to support that part of the economy. It was not a free market as we would now use the term. In a sense, it was more like state capitalism where earnings from commodities were being used to support a decaying monarchy in Spain. The decline of Spain eventually led to the independence of the Spanish colonies in Latin America. The colonial governments increasingly had become more local than Spanish. The same was true for the resources. While the Spanish government taxed these resources, their production predominantly was in local hands. At the dawn of the 19th century, the Spanish government was so enfeebled that it could not even effectively deter an invasion from France. The revolutions in Latin America quickly led to independence. The next 100 years were marked by two major periods that will be discussed in more detail in the next chapter. In the aftermath of independence, the region was marked by a large number of border disputes among the countries. To make matters worse, there was a large amount of internal turmoil that frequently was settled with guns rather than votes. In a modern context, some of the internal struggles that occurred in Africa after independence are an example of these sort of difficulties. In some cases, like overreliance on commodities, this propensity to settle disputes with violence has lingered into the modern era. The resulting effects on economic growth are not positive.

In the late 19th century and early 20th there was an economic boom in the region. It was not to last. Collectively, the governments of the region embarked on a development strategy known as *import substitution industrialization* (ISI). At that point the logic of ISI seemed compelling. Countries tend to follow a development pattern that starts with agriculture and then moves into light manufacturing followed by more heavy industrialization. Since agriculture is associated with relative poverty and industrialization with prosperity there is a natural tendency to try to move from the former to the latter as fast as possible. Skipping the details for the moment, ISI involves policies aimed at restricting imports and supporting domestic manufacturing. This is an old concept whose roots can be traced back to the mercantilists of the 16th century. In a modern context, Latin America was not alone. Similar policies were pursued in many of the developing countries of Africa and Asia. If there was a Latin American difference it was in the degree to which ISI was implemented. The policy was pursued at a higher level than in other areas to the degree that Latin America and ISI were as closely identified as Brazil and football (the real one). From the late 1930s to the late 1970s, Latin America tended to reduce its participation from world trade. Export earnings from commodities were used to subsidize heavy industry where the region had little comparative advantage and for consumption of foreign products. For those involved in these industries, all was well. On the surface ISI seemed to be working. The region developed a collection of urban areas that looked modern. For those involved in ISI industries or in government service, incomes were high by local standards. What was not so obvious was the untold millions being impoverished who migrated to large cities in search of work.

By the 1970s, the system was becoming unsustainable. Latin America is rich in resources but a lack of oil is a problem. The first oil shock forced many of the governments in the region to borrow from foreign banks to finance the increase in oil prices. The second oil shock led to a wave of defaults in the region as countries could no longer cover payments on the old debt and had lost access to new lending. The struggle to handle the accumulated debt led to the *Lost Decade* of the 1980s. During this period GDP per capita of the region was flat and high inflation became almost the norm. An intervention by the US government and international organizations in the late 1980s helped stabilize the situation both for the countries of the region and for US banks whose lending policies with respect to sovereign debt had been inconsistent. The economic cost of the Lost Decade was enormous. Fortunately, there were two unexpected benefits. The first was political. At the onset of the crisis, the nondemocratic governments of the region basically walked away from governing and handed the situation over to democratically elected governments. After 500 years of predominantly authoritarian rule (with a few exceptions) in Latin America, democracy suddenly became the norm. To anyone living in a country with a long tradition of political stability, the governments of the region often seemed chaotic, inefficient, and promoting corruption. Keep in mind that these democracies are historically new in a region with a long and unfortunate history of decidedly nondemocratic rule. In any case, the transformation was both unexpected and fast. Despite these problems, they are accomplishing one thing that eludes the governments of much more mature democracies over the last 30 years. For the most part, these governments are producing budgets that are balanced. Considering the history of the region, this is an accomplishment. After independence, a dreary cycle of macroeconomic instability descended on Latin America. Governments were chronically short of money and resorted to printing money to cover large budget deficits. The resulting cycles of inflation and attempts to reduce inflation were a serious impediment to economic growth. For many countries, the Lost Decade was a period of little to no growth coupled with crippling inflation. With the exception of Venezuela and to a lesser extent Argentina, Latin America has been enjoying unprecedented macroeconomic stability since 1990.

As the reader moves through the book, there is a key point to keep in mind. Macroeconomics and economic growth are related in the sense that both are concerned with overall economic output. However, they differ dramatically in the time frames under consideration. The former deals with how GDP and the price level are changing over short periods of time such as a year. For a macroeconomist, 18 months could be the long run. When studying economic growth, a decade is the short run. Economic growth is akin to examining a long-run trend and thinking about what causes that trend to be higher or lower. On the other hand, it is useful to think about macroeconomics as the study of what causes deviations from that trend. They are two ways of thinking about the same thing. As we move through the book, we primarily are concerned with economic growth both for the region and for individual countries. For much of its history, the region has experienced a complex mix of both macroeconomic policy miscalculations and other problems that led to low economic growth. It is with these latter set of problems that we will be concerned with. Macroeconomic problems are short run in nature and usually can be corrected over a few years. The problems of low economic growth are both less well understood and usually harder to correct.

The Continuation of Economic Underperformance

In the time since the Lost Decade, Latin America has experienced a revolution in macroeconomic stability. This is no small accomplishment but that success perhaps has masked the reality that economic growth in the region has been relatively slow for nearly a century. As we will see in the next chapter, the boom of the late 19th century was snuffed out by the Great Depression. To a large extent, it never returned. Chapter 3 is where this problem is discussed in more detail. A shorter version of that story is given here both as a preface to that chapter and to provide some background for the material in the next chapter. As mentioned before, when asked what are the two main causes for low growth in the region there seems to be a consistent answer: education and infrastructure. To one not familiar with the region, the former might be surprising. Almost all of the population of Latin America is literate. This is a dramatic change from the colonial past and is one of the greatest achievements of the region during the 20th century. At the dawn of that century, 64 percent of the adult population of the region was illiterate. The contrast with the present is stark. A typical person now has almost 9 years of schooling (at least a primary school education and usually more than that). From Table 1.1 we saw that by global standards the average resident of the region is comfortably middle class. More than 80 percent of the people of the region now reside in urban areas. The grinding rural poverty associated with the low-income economies of the world is quickly becoming part of the region's past. Although the contribution of education to this improvement in living standards is hard to quantify precisely, it can be done in general using a counterfactual. If literacy rates had not risen over the last century in Latin America, what would have happened to GDP per capita? One cannot precisely answer that question without a formal analysis, but a general answer is hardly in doubt. As we will see in Chapter 3, universal literacy is important but as countries grow their educational needs grow as well. Higher levels of income are associated with the production of goods and services that require ever higher amounts of human capital. In turn this requires secondary schools that are producing young people with the skills necessary to thrive in a 21st-century environment. It is at this point that the educational systems in the region are stumbling. Dropout rates for students in secondary schools are depressingly high. For those that stay the data on student achievement compared to other countries is not encouraging. Higher education in Latin America is plagued with other problems. Universities typically are underfunded and overcrowded. The deficiencies in the educational systems are creating problems for the private sector that inhibit growth. Employers struggle to find workers with the sufficient skills for a modern environment. At higher levels in the job market, finding workers with skill sets that include business or IT is a critical problem. In the 21st century, human capital has become like high-quality fuel. Without it, rapid growth in middle- or high-income economies is difficult.

Along with education, infrastructure limitations are a serious impediment to growth in the region. At the start, there is a definitional problem. It is composed of things like roads, bridges, and electricity. The basics are well understood. However, these basics are somewhat related to an earlier era. They are important, but no longer enough. The bar for what constitutes "good" infrastructure keeps going up over time. In that sense, Latin America still struggles to cover basic elements. Roads are a good example. According to the World Bank (2020), currently, in Latin America more than 60 percent of the roads are unpaved, and Pastor (2019) conclude that 21 percent of the paved ones need upgrading. Another example is access to clean water. Cavallo et al. (2020) conclude that about 25 percent of the population still struggles for access to drinking water. These two examples are not unusual. A similar situation appears in areas such as electricity, railroads, ports, and air transport. For more modern forms of infrastructure related to IT, the circumstances could be similar.

Unfortunately, the situation could be more complex than the official data indicates. As we have already mentioned, a substantial part of the population of Latin America lives and works in the informal sector. Many of the residents of urban areas live in housing that is unregistered with the government. Not surprisingly, informal housing also implies informal access to adequate infrastructure. Workers living in these communities often work in the informal sector as well. Informal communities lack the transportation infrastructure to get workers to better jobs in the formal sector. Workers in these communities tend to work in small, informal firms that may never grow. It creates a cycle of poverty that is reminiscent of the rural poverty of previous centuries. Inadequate infrastructure constrains growth in both the formal and informal sectors and traps resources in the latter.

The list of problems that are related to low growth are not confined to education and infrastructure. What is less obvious are the constraints on growth that result from a maze of taxes and regulations that would frustrate even the world's most accomplished managers. In the 1980s, a quiet revolution started in economic development. It had been known since the 1970s that the institutional quality of a country has an important impact on an economy's ability to grow. However, economists being economists dislike dealing with variables that are difficult or impossible to quantify. In the 1980s a start was made in quantifying these less tangible factors that influence growth. An easy target in this regard is corruption. It is easy to see corruption in developing countries. Based on surveys of business executives, Latin America had corruption levels that were, on average, above global averages. While this is true it is also a very incomplete story. When thinking about developing countries it is all too easy to get over-focused on corruption. It is visible, but just how important is it? A simple thought experiment may help. Pick a country in Latin America such as Mexico for a simplistic counterfactual example. If the level of corruption in Mexico suddenly was at US levels what would happen? The economy would probably grow a bit faster and life in the country would likely become less troublesome for the average Mexican. However, would a drastic reduction of corruption transform the rate of economic growth? The point is not that corruption does not matter. The point is to be aware that low growth in Latin America is not solely a function of one factor, like the level of corruption. There are other factors at work here.

By the late 1980s, researchers had begun to work on quantifying some of those other factors, particularly on the protection of property rights and the rule of law. Markets cannot function properly in an environment where property rights cannot be enforced. In a more general sense, there needs to be some basic framework to enforce the rule of law. However, these are not binary variables in the sense that a country either has them or does not. It is more like a continuum running from near anarchy to the standards prevalent in high-income countries. The main point is that we can now quantify the degrees of these variables observed in various countries. For instance, Chile has property rights protection and enforcement of the rule of law that is in line with high-income countries. For the low-income countries of Central America, the reverse is true. Sadly, the enforcement of property rights and the rule of law is a necessary but not sufficient condition for rapid economic growth. Costa Rica would provide a good example. Both of these factors are in place. However, the country has been facing barriers to grow faster, as there are other factors that matter. In his book, de Soto (1989) argued that the cost of complying with government regulations in Peru made it virtually impossible for small- and medium-sized businesses to operate. In Latin America and many other countries of the world, the level of business regulation is a strong impediment to growth. The point is a bit tricky but critically important. There is no implication that businesses should not be regulated. That is taken for granted. The problem is the complexity and cost of compliance. There is no social benefit in making the regulation of business so complicated that only a minority of large firms can deal with the complexity. This is not the same thing as eliminating business regulation. The point is to have regulations that are both necessary and can be complied with by smaller firms. This is not just a Latin American problem. Virtually any country could improve its business regulations in the sense described above. Excessive complexity and high compliance costs will slow growth in any country.

The problem for Latin America is that the level of business regulation seems excessive by global standards. The World Bank and others have devised systems to rank countries by the ease with which companies can do business and the data for Latin America is not particularly positive. Most of the countries in the region rank in the lower half of the global distribution. The common perceptions of Latin American growth problems such as education, infrastructure, and corruption are reflected. They are just a part of the story. Fighting through the maze of business regulations in a typical country is beyond the capabilities of most entrepreneurs. Taxes are a glaring problem. In some cases, the level of taxation can be considerable. A simple example from Argentina illustrates the point. The basic income tax on corporations is 30 percent. However, there is a basic value-add tax of 21 percent. In both cases, higher rates may apply and there are a plethora of other business taxes. Tax rates are not the only, or even most important, problem. Brazil consistently ranks among the top countries of the world in the complexity of their tax system. It is not an outlier. Argentina, Bolivia, Colombia, and Mexico are ranked in the top 20 in the world. Taxes are just a good example of the general principle. No one questions the necessity of collecting taxes from businesses. However, there is no social benefit in making this process difficult. For many countries in general and Latin America in particular, the problems are more subtle. The complexity of taxation and regulation creates a highly unlevel playing field. To operate in a legal fashion, companies need lawyers, accountants, and other highly trained business specialists. In such an environment, the larger and more profitable firms have a distinct advantage. These firms will have an advantage in any market economy. However, burdensome regulations and tax systems magnify this advantage to an extraordinary degree. This leaves many small and medium-sized enterprises (SMEs) in Latin America with a stark choice, either do not operate a business or operate but in the informal sector.

What this has led to is an informal sector in the region that is large in size and scope. There is going to be an informal sector in any economy at any stage of development. Many micro businesses are so small that any level of business regulation is not worth dealing with. There will always be illegal activity and tax evasion. In a typical developed country, the informal or underground economy may be about 10 percent of GDP. In Latin America, the average is 32 percent. Much of the material above was just setting the stage for this number. Many of the entrepreneurs and workers of the region are trapped in the informal sector, as the degree of regulation is so burdensome that in most cases it would be impossible to operate as a legal enterprise. As will be outlined later, the effects on the economies of the region are detrimental to growth. Firms in the informal sector have little access to credit and are unable to grow to their optimal size. What are normally the most dynamic firms in a healthy economy are thus trapped in a maze of regulation that prevents them from growing. For workers, this is a pseudo "free" labor market. Government labor regulations do not apply and wages and working conditions are set primarily by the strongest agent of the market. Virtually all of the participants in the informal sector work incredibly long hours. The survival of firms is a constant struggle with both the market and, in many cases, government officials. The result can be that regulatory complexity does not serve a social purpose but it may serve the purposes of some civil servants. The effects on economic growth are not unexpected. The governments of the region are constantly short of tax revenue needed for education and infrastructure expenditures necessary for economic growth. The existence of a large informal sector is a large part of that problem. In addition, SMEs in Latin America are probably not growing as they would in a less complex environment. With only these two factors feeding on themselves, it is little wonder that economic growth in the region is relatively slow.

Economic Geography

The term *economic geography* refers to the location of economic activity in physical space. In broad terms, the world has an economic geography. Most of the economic output of the world is not evenly distributed. It is concentrated in a few high- and middle-income countries in North America, Europe, and Asia. The same principle applies to regions. Economic activity is very concentrated in Latin America. Nearly two-thirds of the region's output is in just three countries: Argentina,

Brazil, and Mexico. Even within this group there is a striking degree of concentration. The Brazilian economy is more than twice the size of the Mexican economy. The difference between Mexico and Argentina is nearly the same. In the world economy, there is a clear distinction among countries that "matter" and those that are less important. The cut point tends to occur at a GDP of more than $1 trillion. By that standard, Brazil is clearly important and so is Mexico to a lesser extent. Below these large economies, there are a collection of five with GDPs in excess of $100 billion. These are Chile, Colombia, Ecuador, Peru, and Venezuela. This leaves us with a collection of small economies in South America consisting of Bolivia, Paraguay, and Uruguay. For the latter two countries land is a constraint. Central America is composed of six countries on divergent paths. While small, the economies of Costa Rica and Panama are fundamentally healthy, and the latter is one of the fastest growing economies in the region. Unfortunately, El Salvador, Guatemala, Honduras, and Nicaragua do not fare as well. A combination of institutional weakness, political instability, and natural disasters has made growth in all of these regions difficult.

There is another factor to consider that makes the economic activity of the region even more concentrated than it appears just by looking at the data on a country level. Within most of the countries of the region, economic output is strikingly concentrated. In Latin America, there are nearly 300 million people living in 200 large cities. In this case, a large city is defined by a population of 200,000. These urban areas collectively produce 60 percent of the region's GDP. In many countries, even this level of concentration is deceiving. The three largest cities in the region are Mexico City, São Paulo, and Buenos Aires. Each of these cities has GDP of more than $500 billion. In Mexico and Brazil, the two biggest cities contribute more than 20 percent of GDP. Buenos Aires dominates Argentina. A similar story can be found in nearly any country of the region. One or at most a few cities dominate the economic landscape of the country. These large cities are also strikingly wealthier than the rest of their home countries. Their GDP per capita normally is more than $15,000 and is more than $20,000 in a number of cities. What this means is that the economic output of the region is incredibly concentrated. The large urban areas utterly dominate the economic landscape of the region. This means that the data in Table 1.1 has to be interpreted with caution. What one is likely to encounter doing business in the region may be much more like doing business in Southern or Eastern Europe than in a developing country. However, the official data is partially masking the large amount of output and workers in the informal sector. Essentially, there are two parallel economies moving in the same direction but at very different levels. It is easy to see the one and forget the other. This is a common thing even for citizens of the countries involved. Like many errors, it may not be costly but it may lead to unexpected difficulties. The constraint on growth can be explained. How it effects the social and political development of the countries is more complex to measure.

Given the basic economic geography of Latin America the second half of the book will attempt to provide more country-specific detail. While the region is more homogeneous than most of the world's regions there is a substantial amount of variation. There is no easy template to follow so we have created one that perhaps is useful in an economic sense. The country-level information is contained in four groups. The first is Argentina and Brazil. These two large economies are linked by proximity and both are in the region's top tier of total GDP. The second group is composed of Chile, Colombia, Peru, and Uruguay. This is a collection of medium-size economies that are similar in terms of economic structure, economic policy, and relative success. The third group is composed of countries that to one extent or the other have been underperforming. These are Bolivia, Ecuador, Paraguay, and Venezuela. The first three have had either modern or historical problems that were sufficiently severe to inhibit growth. There is no complete way to adequately deal with the collapse that has engulfed Venezuela. It seems that the economy of the country has declined by almost 70 percent since 2014, what means that about 5 percent of the GDP of the region has evaporated. Additionally, about 6 million people have left the country, many for neighboring countries. These economic losses and displaced people are having economic effects on many other countries in the region. We know that there are losses, but the accurate amount still is unknown. The plight of Venezuela has not been forgotten here. It is just hidden in the background for lack of better information. A final grouping is Mexico and Central America. Mexico is the dominant economy of the northern part of Latin America and Central America is the bridge between the North and the South.

For each country we will attempt to provide a basic sense of the overall economic landscape, such as population, GDP, and GDP per capita. Each country has a distinct macroeconomic record that is important. The economic structure of each country also is covered. This structure accounts for the division of economic activity among agriculture, industry, and services. We also discuss some of the economic policies pursued in many countries that are important in any attempt at understanding the economy of each country. Finally, the economies of the region are dependent on foreign trade. In many cases there will be some historical or social background aspect that may be important for individual countries.

Chapter 2
A Brief Economic History

> The weight of the past has sometimes been more present than the present itself. And a repetition of the past has sometimes seemed to be the only foreseeable future.
>
> Enrique Krauze

In the previous chapter, we introduced some of the major themes that affect the economies of Latin America in the 21st century. One of these themes was the long economic history of the region. History always matters and that is especially true for the economies of Latin America. The region was one of the first in the world to experience the effects of large-scale colonization by European powers. From the start, it is useful to understand the concept of *path dependence*. We will apply it to Latin America, but it is a term with such general applicability that it is an exceptionally valuable thing to keep in mind. Path dependence is the dependence of economic outcomes on previous outcomes and not simply current conditions. In this sense, history does matter. We now know that economic outcomes that occurred far in the past can have significant impacts on current economic conditions. Military conflicts, political events, natural disasters, or just random chance often have effects that reverberate for centuries or longer. The extension of this idea to entities such as organizations, governments, or corporations should be obvious. To a greater or lesser extent, explaining the present cannot be adequately done without consideration of the past.

Armed with a little background information, the presence of this history in the 21st century is not hard to find. However, we will cut this long history up into pieces to make it easier to understand. The pieces are not equal in terms of length of time nor in terms of importance. Some of them are several centuries and others merely decades. Their influence may be easily seen or more nuanced today. All of them are important. They are equal only in the sense that one needs to have a grasp of all of them to understand the present. The start of the story is hundreds of years of colonial history. What followed was a brief but chaotic period as the countries of the region struggled for internal stability following colonial rule. In the late 19th century and early 20th, there was an economic boom in Latin America that coincided with rapid growth in the world economy. The end of this boom ushered in a dramatic change in economic policy. It also started an economic downturn that set the stage for the more recent economic performance of Latin America. All of these periods are important and shape the current economic structure of the region and its future.

https://doi.org/10.1515/9783110674934-002

The Dismal History

A part of the colonial history of Latin America can be easily traced back to Spain. Spain itself began its appearance in modern history as a colony of Rome. The term Latin America is more than just a phrase. The period before the 16th century in the Iberian Peninsula was important for two reasons. First, the area was divided into what became two distinct countries: Portugal and Spain. Second, the invasion of Spain by the Moors in 711 set off hundreds of years of warfare for control of the Iberian Peninsula. In one of those historical coincidences, the Moors were finally expelled in January of 1492 and Columbus discovered America in October. The southern part of Spain has traditionally been the poorest part of the country. Not surprisingly, the Spanish that came to the new world tended to hail from southern and southwestern Spain. The Spanish roots of Latin America were more from a part of the country rather than the country at large. An even larger cultural difference was transferred to Latin America in the form of the linguistic and cultural differences between Brazil and the rest of Latin America. This was formalized by the Treaty of Tordesillas that divided the Western hemisphere discovered by Columbus into regions controlled by Portugal and Spain. Columbus had discovered America as an accident while attempting to find a new route to Asia. His voyage had been financed by Spain, but there was a catch. More than a century before, the Pope had granted all lands south of the Canary Islands to Portugal. The potential dispute was settled by the treaty, but the situation was still complicated. The borders between colonial Portugal and Spain were not finalized until the signing of the Treaty of Madrid in 1750. This meant that colonial Latin America began as two distinct areas.

In the 16th century, Latin America was critically important to Spain as the country was simultaneously developing the region and continuously engaged in religious warfare in Northern Europe. This ultimately fruitless attempt to stop the Protestant Reformation led to a never-ending search by the Spanish monarchy for money. The rapacious extraction of gold and silver from Latin America was the result of heavy military spending for reasons that were related to both religious fervor and greed. From 1520 to 1660, about 200 tons of gold left Latin America for Spain. This is a conservative number as it includes only the amount included in official records. In the same period, the amount of silver shipped out of the region was approximately 18,000 tons. After the original plunder, it became necessary to begin mining gold and silver. It is from this period that the economic development of the region begins. To accomplish this, large tracts of land, known as encomiendas, were given to Spanish citizens to develop. In return, the Spanish government received a percentage, the *repartida*, of everything produced on the land. The production of gold was in decline by the middle of the 16th century. The focus then shifted to the production of silver. New technology made it possible to profitably produce silver with lower-grade ore. However, the new process required a much higher level of investment. The development of silver mining led to a larger presence of the Spanish in Latin America. The production was centered in Mexico and the Andes. The rest of the region was used to support the silver industry in these regions. The production of silver began to decline in the mid-17th century and coincided with the long decline of Spain as a world power.

The decline in the mining industry opened the way for the development of new agricultural production. The age of exploration provided Europeans with access to both old products that were never available to average consumers such as spices and new products such as tobacco. Some of the important commodities for Latin America were sugar, tobacco, cocoa, hides, cotton, and indigo. The production of agricultural commodities both diversified the economy and changed the economic geography of the region. For example, the production of cocoa, tobacco, sugar, and hides began in Venezuela, Cuba, Brazil, and Argentina. The production of these labor-intensive crops came with an unfortunate side effect. During the 16th century, the supply of labor in the region declined dramatically. Primarily due to the introduction of European diseases, the indigenous population declined by 50 percent. This catastrophe was equivalent to the Black Death in Europe in the 14th century. This drastic decline in population occurred just as the demand for labor was increasing. The tragic result was the importation of approximately 4.5 million slaves from Africa from 1500 to 1800. This is one part of what is known as *triangular trade*. Traders transported simple industrial goods to Africa and exchanged them for slaves. The slaves were then exchanged in Latin America for commodities that were then sent to Europe where the process started over. While the risks were high, so were the profits. As the economy moved from precious metals to agricultural commodities, the system used by the Spanish government to manage economic activity changed. Under the encomienda system, the land was technically still owned by the Spanish government. In 1720, the system was changed to private ownership of land. This created large landholdings known as *latifundia*. Rather than a reform of the previous system, this was more in the way of making what had occurred before official. As a result, much of the economic activity was concentrated in these areas. For the owners of the land, their incentives were not favorable for economic development. They had little interest in infrastructure investment unless it was related to the movement of production to the ports for transportation to world markets. Because they had a demand for unskilled labor, investment in education was not a priority. As the activities of the government were not important, the propensity of the local population to pay taxes was usually low. The system tended to trap resources into the production of commodities, and this set the region on a path that persisted into modern times.

The tendency for Latin America primarily to be a producer of agricultural products was reinforced by the application of *mercantilism* to the region. Basically, mercantilism is the idea that a country's welfare is related to its ability to create trade surpluses. This means that a country should try to maximize exports and reduce imports to a minimum. In a colonial system, this led to the creation of a strict system of trade between the colonial power and the colonies. Exports of Latin America could only be sent to Spain or Portugal for re-export to other countries. The system was symmetric in that the region could only import products from the colonial powers. In the case of Spain, the system had two further twists. Spain actively suppressed the development of manufacturing industries in Latin America. In addition, until 1778 Spain controlled the trade among the various parts of Latin America. Overall, the system tended to be very disadvantageous to the colonies. Latin America received less for its exports and paid more for imports than would have occurred in a free market. The system was subject to evasion especially after the United Kingdom (UK) obtained control of the slave trade in 1713. Any way that one views the colonial history, mercantilism greatly hindered the economic development of Latin America and contributed to the relative isolation of the region in the world economy. Unfortunately, in the 21st century, Latin America still struggles with being relevant in the world economy.

The story in Brazil was much the same although the timing was different. Gold was not discovered there until the 16th century and was not extensively mined until the 17th century. Initially, Brazil was a complement to earlier Portuguese settlements off the coast of Africa. The lack of mineral wealth led to the earlier development of an agricultural economy based on cotton, tobacco, and especially sugar. It also meant that the colony developed more slowly. The sugar boom powered the economy for nearly 200 years until the development of competitors in the Caribbean. The landholding patterns were similar. By just substituting fazenda for latifundia the other differences are details. Concerning the slave trade, Brazil was the dominant recipient of slaves in the region. This forced migration along with a different colonial power accounts for much of the difference between Brazil and the rest of Latin America. A note about Brazil is in order here. As seen in Table 1.1, Brazil is the dominant economic power in Latin America and is nearly 50 percent of the land area of the region. However, in most of the commentary on Latin America, the weight given to Brazil is far less. It would be nice to say that no such bias exists in this book. Sadly, that is not the case. This downward bias concerning Brazil is something that is quite difficult if not impossible to eradicate. The best we can do is to promise an honest effort to overcome this pernicious bias that seems to never go away in coverage of Latin America.

Since the bias is so pervasive, it is something to always keep in the background. The situation is slowly improving, but it is still quite pronounced.

Finally, there is a subtle but very important legacy of the colonial period. A question that has intrigued economists since Adam Smith is why are some countries wealthier than others? The Latin American case is especially interesting. In 1700, the per capita GDP in North America and Latin America were roughly equal. As we saw in the last chapter, the gap between the two is now enormous. How does one account for this? Modern research in economic development points to an interesting answer. The quality of a country's institutions is a critical factor in the success or failure of nations. Institutions in this sense is a hard thing to precisely define. In general terms, it means the set of laws and regulations that govern both life in general and economic activity in particular. A classic example is the legal system. A high-quality and impartial legal system both enhances personal freedom and promotes economic development. We use this example because one can distinguish "good" from "bad" primarily on one metric. Legal systems that are mostly independent of short-run political interference have the chance of being high quality. When the legal system is not well insulated from the political process, then the result is a debilitated system. The overall quality of a country's institutions usually is something that has developed over a long period of time. Sadly, institutions tend to form in a way that protects the interests of the elites. The problem with this is that elites normally are not very interested in change. Rather they are interested in the continuation of the status quo. What the status quo was in former colonies such as Latin America can become a critical determinant of later success or failure.

At the start, colonies differed in terms of initial conditions that fell into three broad types. Some colonies were based on tropical crops that required a lot of labor and not much capital. Colonies based on mineral wealth were different in that minerals require substantial capital investments along with labor. The third type of colony was one in which soil and climate conditions necessitated neither large amounts of labor nor capital. The first two types of colonies can lead to unfortunate results. In these cases, a small group of elites can extract most of the income obtained from the production of tropical crops or minerals. For Latin America, this meant the initial institutions were set up to protect the interest of a small group at the expense of the welfare of the population overall. Further, these initial conditions can be quite durable and adaptable to change. When Spain and Portugal withdrew from their colonies in the early 19th century, the aforementioned owners of land and resources remained unchanged. The subsequent almost 150 years of primarily authoritarian rule in the region should come as no surprise. North America developed with different institutions as the initial conditions were more favorable to those that protected the rights of a much larger percentage of the population. The spread of democracy in Latin America since 1980 has at least transferred de-jure power to the voters of the region. Whether this has also meant a transfer of de-facto power is an interesting question. While institutions are not the only factor that matters in economic development, they are quite important. In studying any country that was a former colony, the initial institutional conditions have usually left their mark and are crucial to understanding how the country has evolved.

The discussion above hinted at the fact that colonial power in Latin America was being slowly reduced. The defeat of the Spanish Armada in 1588 was a watershed moment in Spanish history and marked the beginning of its long decline as a world power. The money flowing to Spain from Latin America began to decline with the decreases in the production of gold and silver. The rising agricultural industries could never make up for these losses. Tensions between Spain and the colonies worsened over the years as a result of three main issues. The first was taxation. A substantial portion of tax revenues were being sent to Spain with no obvious benefit for the colonies. It should be noted in passing that the collection of tax revenues in the region is still a problem. This problem has deep historical roots and governments in the region struggle against an attitude that paying taxes is a waste of money. Second, the colonies were becoming increasingly autonomous, but the top leadership was always native Spaniards. In effect, the growing elites in the region were mostly treated as second-class citizens. Finally, there was the question of land. The distribution of land was highly unequal under Spanish rule. Independence at least held out the hope for positive changes. A similar set of circumstances was true of the relationship between Portugal and Brazil. The final dissolution of the colonial empire was a function of events in Europe. French control of the Iberian Peninsula exposed the true weakness of both Portugal and Spain. In a period of unrest from 1810 to 1825, the former provinces became independent countries. The independence movements promised to replace the colonial rule with liberal democracies reminiscent of the outcome of the American Revolution. Unfortunately, these new democracies were short-lived. The wars of independence left much of the region in need of post-war reconstruction. Instead, the period began with boundary disputes among the former colonies. The internal situation in many countries was no better. As the new democracies collapsed, groups began to seek power not with voting but frequently with violence. These internal struggles for power did not last for just a few years. In varying degrees, domestic violence in the region continued for decades. The struggles for power were largely over by 1860. However, a substantial amount of economic damage had been done. The independence movement started in 1810. This means that independence plus post-independence turmoil lasted for half a century. Now compare this with the experience of the United States. Except for two short wars, the country was at peace from 1783 to 1861. This period in Latin American economic history is known as the "lost decades." It does not fully explain why Latin America fell behind in economic development, but it is clearly part of the story. A country or a region cannot lose half a century of economic growth and expect to regain that lost ground quickly. Because of path dependence, such periods can create problems that last for generations.

The lost decades in Latin America are a perfect example of this. Economists rarely have anything positive to say about military conflicts. War and the associated violence lead to the destruction of both private and public property. As one can imagine, this does not enhance the ability of an economy to grow. In 19th-century Latin America, this was especially true. The region had a deficit of infrastructure to begin with and the various conflicts destroyed some of that. More importantly, there were decades of lost investment. In order for public sector investment such as infrastructure to occur, a country needs a stable form of government. Lacking this, improvements in transportation and other infrastructure stagnated in Latin America. The same was true of private sector investment. Private investors need a modicum of stability to make investments. Without this minimum, private sector investment can be below what is necessary to enhance economic growth. Investment can even be negative as the failure to utilize or maintain previous investments amounts to a decline in investment. The decades of problems interfered with the protection of property rights and the rule of law. Without these two basics, economic growth is negatively affected. For markets to function properly there has to be a system for determining who owns what. As economies develop, business activity will become more complex and involve agreements between businesses and/or individuals. Without a legal system to enforce these agreements, fewer transactions occur. In sum, economic activity becomes more difficult and growth slows. For all its faults, the Spanish government provided these conditions in Latin America for more than 300 years. The wars of independence and subsequent violence led to uncertain property rights and an inability in many areas to enforce the rule of law. The effects on economic growth were dire in absolute terms. Political stability following independence became a necessary condition for growth. Unstable governments can rarely perform their basic functions. As we will see in a later chapter, property rights and the rule of law are still challenging points for the region. These are not modern problems, but problems with deep historical roots.

By the 1850s, the worst of the wars and domestic conflicts had ended. The 1850s and 1860s were a period of transition from the post-independence conflicts to more stable forms of government. Unfortunately, stability is a relative term, and it can take many forms. The region had not developed strong democratic institutions. However, it did have a highly unequal distribution of land and income that was the legacy of Spanish colonialism. In a power vacuum, political power may accrue to whatever group or groups are strong enough to seize it. The result was that Latin America became home to governments of the economic elites frequently supported by the military. Under these circumstances, property rights and the rule of law become arbitrary. The law becomes a function of who is in power as opposed to laws that are the result of a democratic process. In this case, the function of the state is not to protect property rights and enforce the law. Rather, the state becomes an instrument for either personal gain or gains for a part of society. Political power can become a means to an end: wealth and income. Under these circumstances, political instability is understandable. The competition for political power in a nondemocratic country can lead to a monopoly of power that can then be used to rig the economic system for private gain. Further, if one gains power then there is a strong incentive to hold on to it. In Latin America, this sort of political leader has been so common there is a name for it: *caudillo*. Such political systems can provide enough stability for some economic growth. However, the leadership may not be primarily concerned with national economic welfare and economic growth. In fact, rapid growth seems to happen only when there is constant change in the status quo. Normally, the elites in these countries are interested in the maintenance of the status quo. The result is that change occurs but more slowly than would happen in a market that was freer from arbitrary applications of the law designed to protect specific groups from economic harm or enrich other groups. While the end of Spanish colonial rule was positive for the region, the resulting political equilibrium had unfortunate economic consequences. Political power frequently had an uncomfortable and unstable relation to economic power. The political instability that results was to plague the region until the late 20th century. Some countries of the region are still struggling to develop durable democratic institutions with impartial applications of property rights and the rule of law. Put another way, Latin America has a long history of "country risk." While that risk has fallen over time (significantly in some cases), once again it has deep historical roots.

What Could Have Happened: The Golden Age

The turmoil of the post-independence era slowly drifted into the "Golden Age" of Latin American economic history. From 1870 to 1914, the region began to fulfill its economic promise. A confluence of internal conditions and conditions in the world economy led to this favorable outcome. Internally, the postcolonial turmoil that had interfered with both property rights and the rule of law subsided. When unstable governments are unable to protect the property rights of the public, economic activity tends to slow to the bare minimum, and investment becomes rare. In the second part of the 19th century this basic problem slowly got fixed. As this occurred, economic activity picked up. Domestic residents began to invest in their own countries with some security that the government would protect those investments. Additionally, it never hurts to get lucky. As outlined below, the Golden Age coincided with a boom in the world economy. Any global boom is going to be accompanied by rising demand for commodities. The rise of China in the late 20th century and early 21st is just the most recent example. Latin America was poised to reap the benefits of this boom as a major exporter of commodities. In this case, domestic economic stability arrived at just the right time. Below, we will provide some further details about both the internal and external conditions that contributed to the Golden Age. Partially, this is just interesting background information about Latin America. However, there is something more practical here as well. The Golden Age slowly slid into a less favorable pattern that has become something like a regional norm. To understand the norm, it helps to know how it developed.

In the second half of the 20th century, political stabilization was occurring across the region. The story varies from country to country, but the example of the three largest countries is instructive. Argentina, Brazil, and Mexico dominate the economic landscape of Latin America. The other fourteen countries are hard-pressed to separate their economic outcomes from these three large economies. Argentina was the first country to be able to break away from Spanish colonial rule. Unfortunately, that was the easy part. From the 1820s to the late 19th century the country was wracked by political instability. There are two points about Argentina from this period that are worth keeping in mind. First, there is Buenos Aires and the rest of the country. This tension never completely goes away and makes the country difficult to govern. Second, Argentina experienced an enormous wave of immigration from Italy and Spain in the Golden Age. As a result, the population of the country is different from the rest of Latin America and it affects the relationship between the country and the rest of the region. The establishment of a relatively stable oligarchy gave the country the political stability necessary for early economic growth. The turmoil in post-independence Mexico was extreme. Civil unrest was compounded by a revolution in Texas, an unfortunate war with the US, and an intervention by France. The accession to power by José de la Cruz Porfirio Díaz in 1876 led to initial economic growth. A focus on the basics such as the rule of law, suppression of violence, and infrastructure contributed to producing some of this. While there was stability and prosperity, the inequalities in Mexico's political and economic systems ended up leading to a revolution. The ill-effects of insufficient infrastructure, growing inequality, and crime on economic growth in Mexico are modern reminders of what can still go wrong. For Brazil, the breakaway from Portugal created a local monarchy that lasted until late into the 19th century. The replacement of the monarchy by a stable oligarchy provided the necessary conditions for economic growth. These three short sketches of the largest countries in the region are indicative of what was happening on the whole. The defeat of the Spanish was followed by both disputes among countries and internal disputes over power. These internal disputes were occurring in countries without the established institutions necessary to accomplish political compromises. Decades of political instability resulted in more or less stable governments, that produced a positive effect for the countries. The necessary conditions for economic growth were established.

Fortunately, the return of internal stability in Latin America was matched by an unusually favorable period for the world economy. This favorable external environment had two components. The first was the end of the Napoleonic Wars. The decline of Spain allowed Latin America to escape colonialism more easily. The end of the war in Europe led to a century free of global military conflicts. Despite the internal conflicts in the region, the US made the Western hemisphere off-limits to any European power (the Monroe doctrine). The failed attempt by France to take over Mexico during the American Civil War was a demonstration of the necessity of that policy. During the 19th century, the UK was actively involved in Latin America. For strategic reasons, the UK had supported the independence movement. The end of colonialism meant the end of mercantilism. This environment of freer trade was in line with British interests. The other component was purely economic. In the second half of the 20th century, economic historians have been attempting to understand economic activity before World War II. Likewise, we are still trying to fully understand the causes of the Golden Age in Latin America. Although without abundant economic data, what is clear is that the world economy grew rapidly from 1850 to 1914. Rapid advances in transportation and communication helped fuel the growth of international trade. The value of the steamship for commodity exporters is hard to overstate. Wooden sailing ships were so expensive to operate that they could only profitably transport goods with a high value-to-weight ratio. This meant that they could only be used to transport luxury goods and, tragically, slaves. Steamships allowed for trade in cheap, bulky commodities like wheat. Later, ships with refrigeration could transport products such as meat. It is no accident that Latin America's Golden Age coincided almost exactly with this period. Of course, no boom lasts forever.

Wars and Depression

The boom in both the world and in Latin America was shattered by the beginning of World War I. After this point there were a number of fundamental changes both in the world and in the region. How Latin America responded to these changes has critical implications for the rest of the 20th century and continues to the present. In the first place, the war caused the usual decline in economic growth. However, the scope of the war and the globalization caused by the global economic boom of 1840 to 1914 meant that the repercussions were likewise global. Some commodities like oil skyrocketed in price to the benefit of countries like Mexico and Venezuela. Countries that were selling commodities for personal consumption, like Brazil with coffee, fared less well. In any case, the easy years of both rising prices and rising demand were over. After the end of the war, commodity prices became more unstable. They could rise for a time and then fall dramatically. The most dramatic fall came with the onset of the Great Depression. These periods set the tone for what is the "norm" for commodity producers: periods of high prices and prosperity followed by the reverse. These effects of commodity price swings are the other side of the opening up of the region to the world economy. Prior to the mid-19th century, Latin America was a colonial backwater and spent the first few decades of independence in growth stopping political turmoil. The Golden Age marked the entry of the region into the world economy. With that entry came enormous benefits. However, along with those benefits came increasing levels of risk tied to the performance of the world economy. The period running from World War I to World War II was a magnification and a compression of those risks.

These changes were accompanied by other structural changes in the world that Latin America had to adjust to. At the dawn of the 20th century, the US surpassed the UK as the world's dominant economic power. While the deep trade ties between the region and the UK were not severed, trade and other relationships turned from the East to increasingly North. The US became the dominant power in the Western hemisphere to a much greater extent than the past. For Latin America, this presented a large opportunity to increase trade and investment with a fast-rising power. As we will see, that moment passed. Rather, the economic difficulties of the region showed up in one old problem and one new one. Since the 1820s Latin America has gone through periods of heavy borrowing in international capital markets that did not end well. The difficulties associated with World War I and the Great Depression was a renewal of this old pattern. Financial strains led to currency devaluations, external debt defaults, and banking crises both in the early 1920s and early 1930s. This was nothing new for Latin America, but this time was different. In the 19th century, the problem normally manifested itself in the straightforward defaults on debt. The countries default, the creditors work out a new repayment schedule, and life goes on. What changed in the 20th century was devaluations of the currency. This was new in Latin America and deeply troubling. Periodic debt problems were now accompanied by depreciating exchange rates. If these depreciations are both large and sudden, they have the potential to create serious macroeconomic problems. Specifically, such events can simultaneously increase prices and reduce GDP. The result was that when this new and more open version of Latin America started experiencing the shocks that can go with more openness, they were startlingly large.

Import Substitution Industrialization

The response to these shocks was a radical turn in economic policy that still haunts the region in the 21st century. The story starts with manufacturing. Latin America had always had some small-scale industry along with the production of commodities. The exchange-rate turbulence of the interwar years gave a boost to that activity by making domestic production cheaper relative to imports. Then something else happened. It is a classic example of the remark by John M. Keynes concerning how much ideas matter. A Latin American economist, Raúl Prebisch had been studying the economic difficulties of the region in the interwar period. In fact, the Economic Commission for Latin America and the Caribbean (ECLAC), led by Prebisch, put together a theory of industrialization that had enormous impact on developing countries and on public policy debates. The central idea of this development strategy was that industrialization was the main channel to transfer technological progress, and that in that process the structure of production would shift from primary-based (agriculture) to industrial activities. The idea was that Latin America could never really advance just as an exporter of commodities. If commodity prices were continually falling relative to the price of manufactured goods, then trade would increasingly impoverish the region. Their policy recommendation was that Latin America should industrialize on its own to avoid having to pay ever-higher prices for manufactured imports. The proposers of these ideas argued that they were meant to redefine the international division of labor to obtain the benefits of technological progress through the process of industrialization. The impact of these ideas was such, that Hirschman (1968) referred to the "Latin American manifesto." In other terms, the argument was that the region could become better off by producing goods domestically (with government protection) rather than importing expensive foreign goods. The generic term for this set of policies was import substitution industrialization (ISI). The ideas of ECLAC rapidly spread throughout other developing countries, but they were also subject to criticism. In fact, the governments of the region took to these ideas hoping it would push their economies to the next level of development. However, the main argument of this development strategy was not proven and remained unnoticed until much later. The problem was twofold. First, there was not enough information at that time to analyze the cycle of commodity prices, and the fact that they do not go down forever. Interestingly, Ocampo and Parra (2003) show that there was no evidence of a decline in the terms of trade during ISI. Volatility and a never-ending downward trend are not the same things. The second problem was more fundamental. The policy required moving Latin America quickly into industries in which the region had little comparative advantage. Many other developing countries fell into the same idea and many are still struggling to exit from it. In fact, Webb (2000) explains that even the World Bank supported these ideas and invested in ISI projects until the late 1970s. Unfortunately, for Latin America, ISI meant a return to a pre-Golden Age past. The region would continue to export commodities. These exports were desirable to the extent that they earned the foreign exchange necessary to keep the ISI industries functioning. Domestic industries would produce manufactured goods for the domestic market. Latin America's interactions with the world economy were almost limited to commodity exports and imports of intermediate goods necessary for the ISI industries.

The Latin American version of ISI did have one distinguishing characteristic. It is hard to find anywhere in the world that the policy was adopted so quickly and so committed. First, let us think about the policy tools of ISI. Any push toward industrialization fostered by the government usually has two components: trade policy and industrial policy. The trade policy actions might consist of high tariffs to discourage imports and encourage domestic production. This can go further if high tariffs are insufficient. Quotas can be instituted to put a fixed limit on the number of imports. Exchange controls can be put in place that limit the ability of firms to obtain the foreign exchange necessary to buy imports that might compete with domestic production. Putting all of this together can drastically limit the amount of imports. The domestic industry can be encouraged through the use of aggressive industrial policy. Credit at subsidized interest rates can be channeled to favor industrialization. Taxes on the industry can be set at low rates to make domestic production more profitable. If that was not enough to obtain domestic production, then government policy was used to encourage foreign firms to produce locally via foreign direct investment (FDI). The final possibility was the establishment of state-owned enterprises (SOEs) to ensure local production. These large incentives to industrialize worked all too well. By the 1960s Latin America was well endowed with capital-intensive firms putting out a large volume of manufactured goods for local consumption. Unfortunately, these products could not be produced at a cost that would have allowed for their export.

The Collapse

To put it into the jargon of the 21st century, the development path of Latin America at the beginning of the second half of the 20th century was facing sustainability challenges. Ocampo and Parra (2003) show two deteriorations periods in the terms of trade in the 20th century, but despite commodity prices fluctuate they do not fall forever. Additionally, tying the future of the region to industries in which there was not a clear comparative advantage brought new problems. In simple international trade terms, Latin America has a comparative advantage in labor-intensive industries. This is because labor is abundant and relatively cheap. Unfortunately, the reverse is also true: capital is scarce and relatively expensive. However, ISI worked well in Latin America for some time. Growth in the 1950s and 1960s was relatively high (about 5 percent per year) and the urban areas of the region were becoming increasingly more developed. However, the system began to experience strain. The ISI industries required a considerable amount of protection that it was taking ever-larger amounts of subsidies to encourage the growth of these industries. Since they were producing for the domestic market, the industries could only grow roughly as fast as domestic GDP. With a few exceptions, there was an "export pessimism" associated with a disappointing performance of export growth, particularly in the 1950s. There was the potential to export to other countries in the region but that was rarely exploited. From the early conversations about free trade agreements in the Americas in the early 1960s it was clear the existence of an opposition to the liberalization of those exports. It was only in Argentina, Brazil, and Mexico that industries could obtain symptoms of economies of scale. This was condemning the region to a set of relatively small, fragmented markets with protected firms inefficiently serving those markets. Domestically produced goods were relatively expensive compared to foreign products. *Producto Nacional* was a popular slogan of the times. Interestingly, based on ECLAC data, Prados de la Escosura (2007) note that the poverty of the region was reduced from 1950 to 1980, but still represented about 40 percent of households. The distribution of income continued unequal during this period, but with the notable exception of Uruguay where inequality decreased significantly (Bertola, 2005).

By the late 1960s, the ISI was becoming more difficult to sustain. The heavy protectionism was a burden on any part of the economy not directly connected to ISI. The direct subsidies to industry were becoming an increasingly heavy burden on government finances. The governments of the region had limited capacity to borrow in domestic capital markets. Budget deficits were more frequently being covered by printing money. The resulting inflation (about 40 percent at the end of the 1960s) was applying economic pressure in two ways. Inflation is a burden for the public as the cost of living is rising. In the jargon of economists, the internal balance was becoming a problem. *Internal balance* refers to the maintenance of price stability, growth, and low unemployment. This balance was being upset by rising inflation. There also is an *external balance* that is the ability of the country to balance inflows and outflows with the rest of the world. Until the early 1970s, the world was operating on a system of fixed exchange rates. However, inflation and fixed exchange rates can be a difficult mix. High inflation makes the domestic currency worthless over time. But, if the amount of domestic currency needed to purchase a unit of foreign currency, like the dollar, is not changing then dollars are becoming progressively cheaper. This is making imports ever cheaper compared to domestic production. On the one hand, this makes ISI harder to sustain without more layers of protectionism. On the other hand, it is making it more profitable as imported intermediate goods are becoming cheaper. But there is a squeeze going on. The domestic inflation is making exports even more expensive. When these exports are mostly commodities, then this could be a serious problem. Commodities are sold in world markets mostly based on price. If Argentina's wheat is becoming more expensive, one can always buy Canadian wheat. With ever-rising imports and increasing difficulties exporting commodities, trade balances in the region were deteriorating.

The first oil shock of 1973 hit the world economy hard, but it was a crucial turning point for Latin America. For developing countries without oil, this created a serious external imbalance. Spending on imports rose rapidly with the price of oil and exports of commodities fell. With an inflexible exchange rate regime, the impact was magnified. The US and other developed countries had left fixed exchange rates before the oil shock. However, Latin America and most other developing countries had not. Given the development of ISI in the previous decades, a move to flexible exchange rates was hard to contemplate. Rapid currency devaluations would have sent shock waves through the industries as the price of intermediate goods rose. In effect, the countries were facing putting an exchange-rate shock on top of an oil shock. This was not a tenable solution. The logical solution in the short run was borrowing foreign exchange to cover the imbalances in trade. The lenders were predominantly US banks with excess reserves to lend. The result was that the decade of the 1970s was marked by increasing borrowing by Latin American countries and ever-rising ratios of debt to GDP. The countries were borrowing dollars and using them to support currencies that were increasingly becoming overvalued. Without exchange-rate adjustments, the payments imbalances persisted. Countries were experiencing ever-rising levels of debt just to continue the existing economic system. The debt was not being accumulated to enhance growth, but more to sustain the status quo.

The unsustainability was laid bare when oil prices rose again in 1979. The rising oil bill that came in the wake of this shock could no longer be supported by increased borrowing. Without the dollars to maintain the exchange rate, countries now had to face the aforementioned storm of an oil shock coupled with an exchange-rate shock. In addition, the countries were left with a crushing level of debt that was the legacy of the 1970s. As lending from the commercial banks dried up, the countries of the region were now forced to borrow from the lender of last resort, the International Monetary Fund (IMF). The IMF was set up in the late 1940s to oversee a global system of fixed exchange rates. Part of its mission has always been to loan money to countries with balance of payments problems. While the interest rates on its loans were low (relative to commercial banks), and at times the only available lender, the loans came with conditions. A country that has a balance of payments problem needs more foreign exchange than it is earning through exports. The conditions the IMF normally requested for its loans amounted to the engineering of both a decline in GDP and imports. As GDP slows down, imports fall and the need for foreign exchange falls. The usual term for this is an "austerity" program. If the imbalance is not large, then the resulting austerity program is likewise not large. The opposite is also true. Although austerity measures were popular during this time there are now a variety of theoretical considerations (including some coming from the IMF) against them, mainly arguing that without reforms they tend to exacerbate recessions.

The situation faced by Latin America in the early 1980s went beyond what the IMF was normally set up to do. To get a sense of the gravity of the situation, consider the raw data. The total external debt of the region at that time increased from about $75 billion in the mid-1970s to almost $350 billion by 1983, about 50 percent of the regional GDP. Just servicing such debts was creating enormous hardship. In the early 1980s, debt service payments amounted to 80 percent of export earnings. The result of this was there was very little resources to pay for necessary imports such as fuel. The debt payments were accounting for about 10 percent of GDP. Notice that these are regional averages and in some cases the situation was more challenging. In the short run, the IMF was providing foreign exchange to allow for the outflows of foreign exchange. However, as mentioned above some IMF's conditions were being imposed. In this case, the payments imbalances were large so the resulting austerity programs needed to eventually regain external balance were draconian. As the decade wore on two things became clear. First, the austerity programs alone were not going to provide an economic environment consistent with external balance or some reasonable level of economic growth. The GDP of most countries was either stagnant or falling. As populations were continuing to rise, GDP per capita was either flat or decreased. This is what produced the phrase "the Lost Decade." During the 1980s there was little or no economic growth in the region and GDP per capita flatlined. In the bottom half of the income distribution, there was real hardship. Poverty in the region climbed from about 40 percent to more than 48 percent, with some urban areas experiencing considerable jumps. The reduction in income and employment opportunities resulting from the contraction of the economies, plus the rampant inflation rates were the main contributors for this situation. The other factor was the creditors. The banks that were holding the debt were facing the uncomfortable possibility of a wave of defaults on these debts. This was hardly a remote possibility. All parties involved were aware that debt defaults in Latin America had been common since the end of the colonial period. Given the dire conditions being experienced by much of the population, this possibility was becoming increasingly likely.

The situation described above was grim and had no apparent solution aside from the countries eventually defaulting on their debts. At this point, the US government and international organizations became involved in finding a solution to the problem. A good part of this was self-interest. US banks had so many loans outstanding in Latin America that a large number of defaults in the region might have created uncomfortable problems in the US banking industry. From this self-interest, the Brady Plan emerged named after the US Secretary of the Treasury Nicholas Brady. The resolution of the problem involved the US government, the IMF, the World Bank, the governments of the region, and the private creditors. The solution was the swapping of the debts for 30-year bonds that were backed by the US government. In this process, the banks accepted an approximately 35 percent reduction on the face value of their previous loans or a reduction of their interest rates. For the countries of the region, the crushing burden of debt was both reduced and stretched out to the point where repayment was feasible in a macroeconomic sense. The IMF was able to reduce its role and remove the austerity programs. The stage was set for Latin America to escape the Lost Decade and return to something like normal economic growth.

The New Normal

What emerged from the Lost Decade was little short of miraculous. The Brady Plan was something like a silver bullet, but other pieces of the puzzle were coming into place. The Lost Decade was a period where the region was struggling with debt, austerity programs, recovery from the oil and debt shocks, and adjustments to exchange-rate shocks. It was also a period where new governments were learning to implement fiscal and monetary policies that were consistent with long-run growth. The Lost Decade also was a period where Latin America was becoming more integrated into the world economy. With the help of a stable world economy, the region was dramatically changed in the 1990s. This decade set the stage for Latin America that we see in the 21st century. As we will see, the accomplishments were large but what is left to be done is equally large.

As outlined above the repayment of all of this debt was not easy. Like in a domestic situation, the repayment of large debts means that other types of spending must be repressed. In the case of a country where the creditors are foreigners, the implications are particularly complex. To explain the problem, we can go back to the end of World War I. At the Treaty of Versailles, the winners forced Germany to pay reparations for the war. John Maynard Keynes forcefully argued that the amount was so high, the Germans could not be expected to pay it. He pointed out the *transfer problem*. The payment of external debts represents a transfer of real resources from the debtor country to the creditor country. The debtor country cannot be expected to bankrupt itself just to pay off foreign creditors. It took everyone involved in the Latin American debt most of the 1980s to come to grips with this, but a solution was eventually found. The transfer of resources involved suppressing the internal demand for goods and services to brutally low levels. This was necessary to free up enough resources to transfer to the creditors. Not surprisingly, this was having a detrimental effect on standards of living. Poverty levels increased in the region, while inequality deteriorated in most of the countries. The new democratic governments of Latin America were hardly oblivious to the welfare of the population. The typical reaction to this was a "looser" fiscal policy. For the most part, this meant increases in government spending to try to offset the effects of the debt repayments and austerity programs. In the process, this created large government budget deficits. These deficits could not be offset by further borrowing. In this case, the only feasible alternative was covering the deficits by printing money. If money creation is excessive, the result can be high to very high rates of inflation. While the intentions were responsible, the actual effects were detrimental. Inflation harms the welfare of almost all economic actors, but it can be devastating to the welfare of those with fixed incomes. An increasing amount of the population was being doubly hit by the loss of employment opportunities and the erosion of its living standards via inflation. Markets allocate resources via the signals being given through higher or lower prices. Inflation makes it very difficult to see the "real" prices. In this way, inflation causes misallocation of resources and slows down growth. In many ways, high inflation is something developing countries can ill afford. Unfortunately, persistent large government budget deficits mainly financed by printing money led to this dreaded high inflation.

The implementation of the Brady Plan gave the region the temporary breathing space it needed to escape these problems. The end of the austerity programs meant that governments could more easily get spending in line with tax revenue. It is one thing to say this but quite another to do it. This has been the miracle of Latin America for the last three decades. With the notable exceptions of Venezuela, and to a lesser extent Argentina, the countries of the region have pursued consistent fiscal policies. Budget deficits have been small, and surpluses have been mandated in some countries. For the last 30 years most of Latin America has had fiscal policies most OECD countries could not maintain. The other side of responsible fiscal policy has been the change in monetary policy. Freed from the necessity of financing government budget deficits, the central banks of the region have been able to focus on short-run economic management, bank regulation and supervision, and dealing with occasional external shocks. While the transition is not complete, there has been a consistent movement of countries whose central banks are more independent of the government. The result of the stabilization of fiscal and monetary policy has been an almost three-decade run of economic growth with low inflation. For a region that has been wracked by economic problems for nearly 200 years, this is quite an accomplishment. Additionally, the Lost Decade saw a transition from mostly authoritarian rule to true democracies across the region. This transition came at a time of severe economic crisis. With no long history of democratic rule, the new governments steered countries through the crisis and adopted prudent macroeconomic policies after the crisis had passed. It does not take much to conclude that the result of this transition could have gone in a far less favorable direction.

While the region recovered from the Lost Decade, other things did not change. In 1980, Latin America was still inequal and relatively closed with the rest of the world economy. To counterbalance some of this situation, governments made changes in international trade policy in the 1980s and 1990s when all countries joined what is now the World Trade Organization (WTO). The free-trade agreements that are now common in the region have produced more liberalization of trade. However, this liberalization has been mostly within the Western hemisphere than with the rest of the world. Only recently, this trend has started to change with the increasing importance of China in the world economy. The patterns of trade still seem familiar. Latin America produces commodities for export and imports food, fuel, and manufactured goods. This pattern of production and trade has been consistent with stability coupled with slow to moderate growth. However, for a variety of reasons, Latin America never became East Asia. In the following chapters, we will first deal with the sources of slow economic growth that has put Latin America on the opposite side of the comparison with Asia and other high-growth developing countries. Immediately after that, we will get into the details of the growth experience for last 25 to 30 years, country by country. As ambitious as that sounds, the main task will be to provide a brief summary of the most relevant topics concerning economic growth for Latin American countries after 1990.

Chapter 3
What is "Wrong": The Usual List of Suspects

It is a mistake to seek a single, overarching explanation for Latin America's relative failure.

Michael Reid

In the previous chapter, we quickly passed through nearly five centuries on the economic history of Latin America. The colonial era and the post-independence era both left deep marks on the past economic performance of the region. A legacy of this past is not hard to see in the 21st century. The end of the Golden Age marked a turn in the economic performance of Latin America that has not changed significantly in the last 100 years. The Golden Age represented several decades of very fast economic growth. Such periods in any country or region do not last forever. Inevitably, growth slows down. In the case of Latin America, the slowdown in growth has been both long and pronounced. In the first part of this chapter, we will document the modern economic history of Latin America and discuss what has happened. The second part of the chapter explains what economists know about this. In other words, we will be explaining why Latin America has become a relative growth laggard in the world economy. The final parts of the chapter deal with problems that are still constraining economic growth in the region.

Slow Growth

A good place to start the economic growth story for Latin America is at the end of the Golden Age in the early 20th century. From there we will be able to track Latin American growth through the decades and see clearly the associated challenges. This slow growth in GDP translates into slow growth in GDP per capita, which is a rough measure of economic welfare. Using this data, we will be able to see the conventional comparison between the underperformance of Latin America relative to the most successful countries of Asia in the 20th century. Finally, we will track how Latin America has compared over the past century using the United States (US) as a convenient benchmark. In an absolute sense, the region is much more prosperous than it was 100 years ago. In a relative sense, the region still lags behind the economic growth miracles of Asia. However, the region is now growing at about the same rate as the OECD countries. Unfortunately, this might not be enough. However, the good news is that it can be improved.

https://doi.org/10.1515/9783110674934-003

To get some sense of the data, consider Table 3.1. The table contains data on GDP growth for the largest economies in Latin America plus some other groups of countries that will be of interest for comparison purposes. From here, we can see why the Golden Age was special. At this point, it is useful to remember the rule of 70. This is a simple relationship between the rate of growth and the time it takes any variable to double. By simply dividing 70 by the growth rate we obtain the number of years to double the variable of interest. When looking at economic growth, the effects can be startling. At a growth rate of 7 percent, GDP doubles every ten years. This is the sort of growth that produces the occasional "growth miracle" such as the East Asian countries in the second half of the 20th century. Latin America has never been that fortunate. Economic growth was 4 percent for the first three decades of the 20th century. Growth slowed only slightly during the Great Depression and the 1940s. The period from 1950 to 1973 coincided with the rapid implementation of import substitution industrialization (ISI). Growth in this period jumped to more than 5 percent. It also coincided with a global boom in economic activity. Latin America performed well, but most of the rest of the world did better. For example, growth was 3 percentage points higher in Korea and Taiwan. The power of the rule of 70 is evident. With high growth rates, any country can become very well off in one generation. The rise of China is only the most recent example. During this period Latin America grew as fast as Portugal, but not as fast as Spain, and a collection of other de-veloped countries. Latin America mainly outperformed the UK and the US. Thus, ISI was already showing challenges as a development strategy even under a positive context. The first oil shock reduced growth in virtually every country of the world that was not an oil exporter. As outlined in the previous chapter, Latin America cushioned that blow via the accumulation of debts that were ultimately unsustainable. Moving to the next column in the table, the Lost Decade becomes obvious, with low growth rates. One can then see the turnaround in the 1990s and continuing into the 21st century. Growth has returned to the region, but it is nothing like the past. It is now more like the developed countries that include Korea and Taiwan. However, both Korea and Taiwan were low-income countries in the 1950s.

The growth rates of GDP have a large influence on the growth rate of GDP per capita. In this regard, the 20th century was critical for Latin America. The data for the growth rates of GDP per capita for Latin America and the rest of the world are shown in Table 3.2. Admittedly, GDP per capita is not a perfect mea-sure of economic welfare. However, it is a hard argument to make that it does not matter. The untold millions moving from low- and middle-income countries to high-income countries is a powerful illustration of the relevance of GDP per capita. One can see this even within Latin America. In the first half of the 20th

Table 3.1: Latin America: GDP, 1900–2019 (average annual compound growth rates).

	1900–13	1913–29	1929–50	1950–73	1973–80	1980–89	1990–2018
Argentina	6.4	3.5	2.5	4.0	3.0	-1.0	2.8
Brazil	4.5	4.7	5.0	6.9	7.2	2.3	2.3
Chile	3.7	2.9	2.2	3.6	2.8	2.9	4.7
Colombia	4.2	4.7	3.6	5.1	5.0	3.3	3.5
Mexico	2.6	0.8	4.0	6.5	6.4	1.4	2.7
Venezuela	3.3	8.2	5.9	6.4	4.1	-0.1	2.8
Arithmetic average	4.1	4.1	3.9	5.4	4.8	1.5	3.1
Korea	2.0	3.0	0.7	7.5	7.1	8.7	5.1
Taiwan	1.8	3.8	1.8	9.3	8.3	7.4	4.2
Arithmetic average	1.9	3.4	1.3	8.4	7.7	8.0	4.7
Portugal	1.7	0.6	2.6	5.5	3.2	2.5	1.5
Spain	2.3	2.4	0.1	6.1	2.1	2.8	2.1
Arithmetic average	2.0	1.5	1.4	5.8	2.7	2.7	1.8
France	1.7	1.9	0.6	5.1	2.8	2.2	1.6
Germany	3.0	1.2	1.4	5.9	2.2	1.9	1.7
Japan	2.5	3.7	1.1	9.6	2.9	4.0	1.1
Netherlands	2.3	3.6	1.5	4.7	2.4	1.8	2.2
UK	1.5	0.7	1.7	3.0	0.9	2.9	2.0
Arithmetic average	2.2	2.2	1.3	5.7	2.3	2.6	1.7
USA	4.0	3.1	2.6	3.7	2.1	3.0	2.5

Source: Hofman (2000), National Statistics Rep. China (Taiwan) (2020), and World Bank (2020).
Note: Data and calculations for Venezuela only available until 2014.

Table 3.2: GDP per capita, 1900–2019 (average annual compound growth rates).

	1900–13	1913–29	1929–50	1950–73	1973–80	1980–89	1990–2018
Argentina	2.5	0.9	0.6	2.3	1.4	-2.5	1.7
Brazil	2.3	2.5	2.6	3.9	4.7	0.2	1.0
Chile	2.4	1.6	0.6	1.4	1.2	1.3	3.4
Colombia	2.1	2.1	1.6	2.2	2.7	1.3	2.0
Mexico	1.9	0.1	1.6	3.3	3.5	-0.8	1.2
Venezuela	2.3	7.3	3.8	2.6	0.5	-2.5	1.0
Arithmetic average	2.2	2.4	1.8	2.6	2.3	-0.5	1.7
Korea	0.8	1.3	-1.3	5.2	5.3	7.4	4.4
Taiwan	0.4	2.1	-0.9	6.2	6.2	5.9	3.6
Arithmetic average	0.6	1.7	-1.1	5.7	5.7	6.6	4.0
Portugal	0.9	-0.1	1.5	5.4	1.3	2.6	1.4
Spain	1.6	1.5	-0.7	5.1	1.0	2.3	1.5
Arithmetic average	1.3	0.7	0.4	5.3	1.2	2.5	1.5
France	1.5	1.9	0.5	4.1	2.3	1.7	1.1
Germany	1.6	0.8	0.4	4.9	2.3	1.8	1.5
Japan	1.3	2.4	-0.2	8.3	1.8	3.4	1.0
Netherlands	0.9	2.1	0.3	3.4	1.7	1.3	1.6
UK	0.7	0.3	1.3	2.5	0.9	2.7	1.5
Arithmetic average	1.2	1.5	0.4	4.6	1.8	2.2	1.3
USA	2.0	1.7	1.5	2.2	1.0	2.0	1.5

Source: Hofman (2000), National Statistics Rep. China (Taiwan) (2020), and World Bank (2020).
Note: Data and calculations for Venezuela only available until 2014.

century, Latin American GDP per capita grew at a faster rate than almost any other country or region in the rest of the world. Using the rule of 70 again, peak rates of growth for Latin America yield a doubling of GDP per capita every 30 years. Sadly, those days are long gone. Since the 1980s, GDP per capita has risen at the slow rates, mostly comparable to developed countries. Furthermore, the roots of the Lost Decade are also in the table. Despite the buildup of debt, GDP per capita was barely growing. The eventual fall was stunning. In the 1980s, GDP per capita declined an average of 0.5 percent per year. This is a truly punishing reversal. The Lost Decade was not a period of stagnation but a period where the region was moving backwards. The subsequent decades have marked a recovery from this period, but growth still remains relatively slow.

As we suggested above, Latin America has grown at a slower rate than most of the rest of the world for nearly a century. Even rapid growth was slow in a relative sense. The faster growth rates during ISI collapsed in the 1980s. Growth since then has been relatively weak. For a region of developing economies, more rapid growth of GDP and GDP per capita are crucial. Without rapid growth, incomes and standards of living increase at a painfully slow rate. Clearly, Latin America is not East Asia and is unlikely to ever grow at those rates. However, are there clear reasons to understand the current rates of growth? For instance, Mexico is growing at 2 percent. The country is just a familiar mirror for the region. To blame this on the energy or the abilities of the workers and business owners in Latin America is fairly implausible. Market failures abound in the region but that is true in any market economy. One of the challenges seems to be the ineffective environment necessary to support good economic growth. In the following sections, we will outline the sources of economic growth. What the government does, or fails to do, is a crucial factor. Slow growth in Latin America might not be something inevitable.

Preconditions for Growth

The study of why some countries are wealthier than others is a subject that goes back to Adam Smith's *The Wealth of Nations* published in 1776. In the post-World War II period, tremendous strides have been made in our understanding of the causes of growth. In order to understand Latin American, we need to know the general principles of economic growth. In fact, before starting we need to think about the limitations of what we know. In economics there are three questions to answer: direction of change, magnitude of change, and timing. Economics is accurate in terms of direction of change. If we change something, we can be almost certain of the direction of change. The magnitude of these effects is less certain. A classic example is, if the price of a product falls by 10 percent it is very likely that sales will go up. How much they will go up is less certain. How quickly sales will rise is even less certain. In a sense, the study of economic growth is no different. We have a general understanding of what factors influence growth. How large the effects are and how quickly they work is much less certain. What is important for Latin America is that we also know what negatively affects growth. As in many areas of life, it is what is not done that can matter the most. In the process of discussing why Latin America grows slowly, we will also talk about what influences growth in any economy. This includes both regions of countries and even cities.

In order for an economy to grow there are some key preconditions. Thomas Hobbes pointed out in Leviathan (1651) that the main function of government was the prevention of anarchy. The four basic functions of government are the protection of property rights, the rule of law, the provision of public services and assistance, and the general safeguard of the nation. If the government cannot perform these functions, then countries grind to a halt. This might sound familiar. In the previous chapter we covered the economic collapse that befell the region in the decades following independence from Spain. In the 21st century one can still see countries that are struggling with this. The protection of property rights or the rule of law is not something that a country either has or does not have. They are not binary variables, but rather exist along a continuum. No country is totally lawless. On the other hand, countries are composed of a population of human beings. The protection of property rights and the rule of law always is imperfect. Like many things, the problem is one of ensuring the minimum and constantly trying to improve the performance. This has led economists to create systems to rank the countries of the world on their performance with regard to these preconditions. As expected, these measures are imperfect, however, they are useful "rough orders of magnitude." Understanding the limitations of the data, is important to use them to draw conclusions about the relative status of the countries of the world. The preconditions of property rights and the rule of law are good examples of economics at work. The presumption is that the better a country "scores" on these measures, the higher GDP growth is likely to be. The magnitude is uncertain. If a country improves the protection of property rights by 10 percent, how much higher will growth be? There would be no easy answer to that question other than the effect would likely be positive. For simplicity we are excluding nonlinearities that could come up at high levels of development. In any case, the enhancement of property rights and the rule of law goes beyond simple economics.

Property Rights

We start with the protection of property rights. Imperfections in the protection of property rights interferes with the ability of the public to engage in economic transactions. If the state struggles to protect the property, then there is little incentive to accumulate it. Even the production of a crop becomes risky if one cannot be sure that someone else might unlawfully expropriate it. Buyers become cautious for fear of buying property that actually belongs to someone other than the seller. In such an economy, there will be a propensity for fewer transactions and probably a lower GDP. These are extreme examples, but it is a matter of degree. The biggest property rights problem in Latin America is squatting. Squatting is the unlawful use of property that one does not own. The UNDP (2019) estimates that there are about 130 million squatters in the region. This is a quarter of the population of Latin America. One can see part of this problem in Table 3.3. The World Economic Forum publishes an enormous amount of detail on the economies of the world. For any given measure they use a scale of 1 to 7 with the former being the worst and the latter being the best. The table contains data for Latin America, Portugal, Spain, Canada, and the United States. Portugal and Spain are used not only as the former colonial powers but also because they tend to be rather average developed countries. Canada and the US are both in the Western hemisphere and typically are higher up in the rankings. The average property rights score for Latin America is 3.8. This is a relatively acceptable score, compared to the rest of the world, but of course it could be better. There is a lot of variation around this average, but the higher ranked countries have property rights scores matching developed countries. Also, a score of 3.9 for Guatemala is encouraging news, while a score of 3.6 for Argentina is the opposite case. Additionally, the abnormally low score for Venezuela is consistent with the collapse of its economy. Every country in the world can get better on all of the measures we will consider. This is an indication of the utility of this type of data. It is allowing countries to identify areas for improvement that they might not have recognized earlier.

The Rule of Law

In the conduct of economic activity, disputes between market participants are inevitable. All parties to economic transactions need to be reasonably certain that the economic "rules of the game" will be enforced. However, the rule of law is more complicated than property rights. The protection of property rights is reasonably simple. It is a determination of who owns what at a point in time. The rule of law is more complicated and subtle. In very general terms, it has four components.

Table 3.3: Property rights in Latin America.

	Ranking (1–7)
Argentina	3.6
Bolivia	3.4
Brazil	4.3
Chile	5.0
Colombia	3.9
Costa Rica	4.8
Ecuador	3.3
El Salvador	3.4
Guatemala	3.9
Honduras	3.8
Mexico	4.0
Nicaragua	3.4
Panama	4.8
Paraguay	3.6
Peru	3.6
Uruguay	4.8
Venezuela, RB	1.8
Latin America	3.8
Portugal	4.8
Spain	4.6
Canada	6.0
United States	5.8

Source: World Economic Forum (2019).

The first and most obvious is the enforcement of contracts. If this is a pervasive weakness in the legal system, it most likely will work as a barrier to economic growth. The second is the efficiency of the legal system. If the legal system is either slow and/or excessively difficult to access, then the rule of law is negatively affected. If the system is notoriously difficult to use, then the utility of the law as a means of controlling negative behavior is debilitated. Hence, this would tend to slow down growth. The third is favoritism in the decisions of government officials. This concerns not just the law but how it is administered. If the law is administered in an arbitrary or capricious way, this usually hinders economic activity. Favored participants in the market will produce more goods and services as opposed to less-favored participants. If the former are less productive than the latter, there is probably less potential GDP. This is where corruption raises its ugly head. In many cases, favoritism can be purchased. It is common knowledge that corruption is a problem in the region. What we have here is the source of the problem. A bribe is a payment to a government official to purchase treatment that is in violation of the law. If such purchases become common, then the rule of law is weakened. It is up to the governments of the region to reduce the scope of this problem. It is not easy and Latin America is not alone in this regard. The final aspect of the rule of law is judicial independence. If the judiciary is not well insulated from short-run politics, then the rule of law may be damaged by the jockeying for political advantage. While less well known, this is a serious problem. In too many countries, this insulation is rather weak and damages the rule of law. The countries of the region can be scored with a single index on their enforcement of the rule of law. These results are shown in Table 3.4. The data in the table is collected by the World Bank. Conveniently, the scores are given as percentile ranks in the world. Overall, the rank for Latin America is at the 36th percentile, while Portugal and Spain are around the 80th percentile, and the United States at almost 92nd. Again, the economic collapse of Venezuela is apparent. A serious problem here is the low scores for the majority of the countries relative to the rest of the world. At those levels, they can work debilitating economic growth.

Table 3.4: The rule of law in Latin America.

	Percentile rank (0–100)
Argentina	46.2
Bolivia	9.6
Brazil	43.8
Chile	81.7
Colombia	40.4
Costa Rica	67.8
Ecuador	25.5
El Salvador	20.2
Guatemala	13.0
Honduras	14.4
Mexico	31.7
Nicaragua	29.3
Panama	54.3
Paraguay	28.8
Peru	33.2
Uruguay	72.1
Venezuela, RB	0.5
Latin America	36.0
Portugal	84.1
Spain	81.3
Canada	95.7
United States	91.8

Source: World Bank (2018).

The Growth Model

If these preconditions are met, then we can begin to think about a simplified model of economic growth. The model is just a convenient way to think about this issue. Like all economic models, it considers many simplifying assumptions. To some, this makes the model look "unrealistic." But let us not miss the point. It is impossible to construct a model of almost anything where *every* factor is considered. Ponder for a moment all of the possible factors to consider when buying a car. There are just too many to deal with. Most likely, one would focus on a few important features and use those to make a decision. This process of abstraction is just part of life. In our growth model, we will focus on a few important variables. Let us start by considering the basic factor of economic growth: land. In order to produce, someplace to stand is needed. However, in economics land has a slightly different meaning than is commonly thought of. Land is not just dirt. It also includes all of the resources one can obtain from the land. In this sense, Latin America has a lot more land than just the square miles, or hectares. The region is blessed with a bonanza of natural resources ranging from precious (gold) to the plentiful (iron ore) and everything in between. As we pointed out in the previous chapter, this is both a blessing and a potential curse. The region was discovered and conquered as a result of the quest for resource riches. In the following 500 years, the region has had a troubling dependence on this abundance. For better or worse, land matters a lot in the context of economic growth in the region. A final note is that Latin America is relatively "empty." There are some major population centers and a lot of unoccupied space. This makes economic growth easier as land is not a constraint on growth.

In order to use the land, workers are needed. In Latin America, there is a plentiful supply of workers, as shown in Table 3.5. The labor force of the region is more than 300 million. This is nearly 10 percent of the workers on the planet, and it is also growing relatively fast. Latin America has added more than 140 million workers since 1990. They are very concentrated. Nearly two-thirds are Argentinian, Brazilian, or Mexican. Interestingly, there are more workers in Latin America than in all of the low-income countries of the world combined. The physically largest countries of the region also contain a substantial percentage of the workers. How these workers are being utilized is another matter. The problem of the informal sector of the economies of Latin America crops up again. A large number of firms in the region are not formally registered as such with their respective governments. The reasons for this are complex and will be covered below. However, a short answer here is that government taxes and regulations in Latin America tend to be complicated so it is difficult for small- and medium sized enterprises (SMEs) to operate in the formal sector. This also has consequences for the workers of the region. More than 60 percent of the region's workers are in the informal sector. They pay no taxes on their income, but they are also cut off from substantial amounts of government assistance. This has consequences for economic growth. The firms they work in tend to be small and have inherent limits to growth. Wages are usually low and employment uncertain. This can have negative implications for the productivity of those workers. In summary, the workers of Latin America are abundant but informality contributes to them being working suboptimally.

Table 3.5: The labor force in Latin America (millions of workers).

	1990	2019
Argentina	13.41	20.76
Bolivia	2.76	5.74
Brazil	59.94	106.5
Chile	5.1	9.56
Colombia	14.61	26.79
Costa Rica	1.17	2.47
Ecuador	4.07	8.55
El Salvador	1.92	2.79
Guatemala	3.11	7.25
Honduras	1.77	4.61
Mexico	30.43	57.14
Nicaragua	1.36	3.05
Panama	0.93	2.07
Paraguay	1.71	3.6
Peru	7.85	18.86
Uruguay	1.38	1.76
Venezuela, RB	7.82	12.36
Latin America	172.19	313.54
Low income	143.77	297.61
Middle income	1684.15	2546.75
High income	494.17	615.23
World	2322.09	3459.59

Source: World Bank (2020).

For an economy to grow normally, it needs capital to enhance the productivity of labor. Consider the example of digging a ditch. A shovel is a simple but essential piece of capital equipment to do this job. Now consider what can happen if a worker has a backhoe. With more capital to work with, a single worker can now do the work of many. The same principle applies to the whole economy. Everything else equal, the more capital a country has the more goods and services it can produce. A central feature of developing countries is that their stock of capital tends to be low. Thus, the accumulation of capital becomes a critical factor in economic growth. It is hard to change the rate of growth of the labor force. Changes in the stock of capital are much more flexible. In Latin America this has been a persistent challenge. The stock of capital in the region tends to grow relatively slow compared to other regions. This leads to the sources of growth of the capital stock. The primary source of capital is the ability of a country to generate savings. The savings are funneled into the financial system that doles it out in the form of loans to businesses. As a result, the amount of GDP that a country saves becomes an important component of economic growth. Latin America has a saving rate of approximately 20 percent. That may seem high for the US, but the developing country in the world saves about 28 percent of GDP. This is a large difference that compounded over decades, contributes to the low growth of the region. Domestic savings also can be augmented by foreign direct investment (FDI). In this regard, Latin America is relatively better in this front. FDI is about 3 percent of GDP, which is higher than the world average. This still leaves a substantial gap between the region and the more successful middle-income countries that hinders rapid economic growth. A critical variable in economic growth is the capital-to-labor ratio (K/L). This is simply the capital stock divided by the number of workers. The higher this ratio is, the more productive the workers of a country tend to be. It is a quantification of the ditch-digging example given above. Workers in an economy with higher levels of capital are more productive and the economy can produce more GDP. Also, the workers would benefit when there is a high correlation between wages and productivity. In general terms, the more a worker can produce in an hour, the more they could get paid. This means that increasing the capital stock of a country tends to have a double benefit. If the capital stock is growing rapidly, it is much easier for GDP to do likewise. As the capital stock grows, then the K/L ratio rises. If it is rising at a fast rate, then the productivity of labor will tend to increase too. The effect on wages is just the tail end of the process. The "growth miracle" stories in the world economy usually follow this pattern. High domestic savings augmented by FDI enhances rapid economic growth and increases wage growth. Unfortunately, growth in Latin America has tended to be relatively slow for the level of economic development.

The first theory of economic growth based on labor and capital was developed in the 1950s. The number of workers in an economy matters. However, the quality of the workers is hardly identical. In the 1970s and 1980s, an extension of the basic model of economic growth was formulated that partially accounts for these differences in workers. In more technical terms, the new growth model accounts for human capital. Human capital is the education, skills, and experience that workers possess. Everything else equal, the more human capital a worker has, the more productive she will be. In the aggregate, the stock of human capital adds to GDP in the same way as additions to the stock of physical capital. In terms of growth, the faster the stock of human capital is growing, the faster GDP will grow. Like physical capital, the effects on wages is the same. The raw material of human capital accumulation is education. More education enhances the amount of human capital directly and it equips workers to acquire even more in the future. As we will note below, deficiencies in education tend to have negative consequences in terms of economic growth. The new growth theory also focuses on the role of research and development (R&D). R&D is a form of investment in new technology that can enhance economic growth. In economics, technology has a specific meaning. It is anything that can improve the relationship between inputs and outputs. This is not just computer technology but involves anything that will make the production process more efficient. In high-income countries it is common for countries to invest anywhere from 2 to 5 percent of GDP in R&D. For the middle-income countries of Latin America, this percentage is closer to 1. One of the advantages of being a developing country is the ability to obtain technology for free. The simple impact of importing goods from high-income countries also involves the importation of technology. These transfers are even more pronounced in the case of FDI. The point is that Latin America is in the stage of development where low spending on R&D is not a significant problem. The final factor in economic growth theory is total factor productivity (TFP). TFP is defined as the ability of an economy to mix its resources to maximize GDP. In a statistical sense, it is a residual. It is commonly defined as the part of economic growth that is not explained by changes in labor, capital, human capital, and R&D. Past that, it is difficult to explain. For a variety of reasons, some countries utilize their available resources more effectively than others. We will return to TFP in the next section.

Growth Accounting

In the previous section, we outlined in general terms what causes economic growth. The theory of economic growth can be traced back to Adam Smith, but great strides were made in the post-war era. The pure theory of economic growth became much more refined. In addition, governments started publishing the sort of economic statistics that we now consider normal. Prior to World War II, such data did not really exist. Armed with better theory and new data, economists have been running countless studies on the sources of economic growth since the 1960s. What we know is not perfect, but we have very good information on the broad outlines of economic growth. As outlined above, the basic data tells us that there are some challenges affecting growth in Latin America. The problem did not seem severe prior to 1980. During that period, the region was underperforming, but the degree of underperformance was not high. The crisis during the Lost Decade and the subsequent slower growth has made growth in Latin America a much more important topic. In general, economists have been studying the overall economic growth process for many decades. However, the particular case of Latin America has been less researched.

While there are a number of studies with Latin American growth results, they all are telling a similar story. We will follow Cavallo and Powell (2019) since it is one of the most recent analysis and covers a longer time span. The time span is key for statistical reasons. The data points used in studies of economic growth are available only on an annual basis. Until the 1990s, the lack of data made it difficult to be confident about studies of economic growth with only 20 or 30 data points. We are now getting to the point where we have enough data that our confidence in what we are finding is rising. This study is a good example. The data is arranged to be able to compare Latin America with other parts of the world such as the US, other advanced economies, emerging Asia, and the rest of the world. In the first column of Table 3.6, one can see that the growth of per capita GDP in Latin America is only higher than that of the United States. It is less than half of the growth in emerging Asia. It is even lower than the advanced economies and the developing countries outside of Asia (rest of the world). This is also a good place to reflect on what these numbers mean. Think back to the rule of 70. For Latin America, 2.4 percent means that is takes nearly 30 years for GDP per capita to double. In emerging Asia, this doubling occurs in less than 15 years. Even with all of the drawbacks of using GDP per capita as a measure of welfare, this is a starling difference. It is in such numbers that the battle against poverty is fought. Our task now is to try to shed light about those differences.

The second column of the Table 3.6 is outlining the contribution of labor to economic growth. The number in the top row of the column is 0.20. This number

Table 3.6: Average economic growth in Latin America, 1960–2017.

	GDP growth (per capita)	Labor	Capital accumulation	Skills	TFP
Advanced Economies	2.71%	0.20%	0.92%	0.76%	0.84%
United States	2.04%	0.38%	0.28%	0.59%	0.79%
Emerging Asia	4.86%	0.77%	1.09%	1.28%	1.72%
Rest of the World	2.60%	0.20%	0.98%	0.98%	0.45%
Latin America and the Caribbean	2.40%	0.66%	1.01%	0.92%	−0.20%

Source: Cavallo and Powell (2018).

means that labor force growth accounted for 0.20 percent of the overall growth of advanced economies. The various numbers in the row add up to the overall growth of 2.71. It is a quantification of what we discussed earlier. If the labor force grows, then GDP and GDP per capita will grow as well. Notice that the number for Latin America is 0.66 and 0.76 for emerging Asia. Both are high by world standards because population growth in both regions has been higher than average. This is partially the reason why developing countries tend to grow faster. In any case, the accumulation of labor is not the only problem. The accumulation of capital in Latin America, or lack thereof, is the other challenging problem. Here we can see one of the sources of success in Asia. Latin America lags behind emerging Asia in its ability to accumulate capital. Less obvious is the fact that capital accumulation is not much higher than in the advanced economies. Notice that the effects of capital accumulation are powerful. GDP per capita in Latin America is growing at 2.4 percent and more than 1 percent of that is capital accumulation. This is not entirely surprising. Capital accumulation leads to increases in the K/L ratio that increases incomes and wages. A similar story emerges with respect to skills or human capital. In Latin America and other developing countries, increases in human capital are having a large effect on increases in GDP per capita. Workers with more human capital are more productive and this leads to more rapid increases in GDP. Incomes rise faster as this rising productivity leads to higher wages. In the final column of Table 3.6, one can see the primary challenge of growth in Latin America. The negative sign on TFP for Latin America is not a typo. Recall that TFP measures the ability of a country to mix resources together to produce GDP. Over time economies normally get better at this. For developed economies, it is crucial. In those economies there is naturally low growth of the labor force and rapid increases in capital are difficult once the capital stock is already large. In developing countries, TFP growth tends to be rapid as economies are importing and adapting new technology at a rapid rate. For TFP growth to be negative, something or multiple things have to be missing. It is the great puzzle of Latin American economic development. Flipping the sign on TFP coupled with something like a "normal" positive TFP would increase per capita GDP growth to more than 3 percent. In the next section, we consider how the information in Table 3.6 could be translated into changes that enhance growth.

Limits to Growth

The peculiar Latin American problem is the low numbers for TFP, identified from the standard drivers of economic growth The problem is that the determinants of

TFP are only dimly understood. From the initial intuition, let us start with the frequent answers to slow growth in the region: education and infrastructure. From there we will consider the taxation and regulation of business in Latin America. The raw data on these factors indicates that they may be reducing TFP and growth. The mechanism through which this is occurring is less straightforward, but informality may be playing a decisive role.

Education and Infrastructure

If we ask someone who is reasonably well informed about Latin America what are the main challenges of the region, there is a snap answer: education and infrastructure. Like almost any conventional wisdom there is a lot of truth in that answer. It is far from a complete answer, but it is part of the problem. We can start by thinking about the role of education in economic growth. A sound basic education allows for workers to not only have higher productivity now, but it allows them to acquire more in the future. Latin America is a good example of this process at work. In colonial Latin America there was little incentive for the Spanish government to invest in education. Workers were needed for manual labor in the mines or fields and illiteracy was not a handicap. In the early post-independence years, internal turmoil and public education were not exactly complementary. While the data is fragmentary, it is safe to say that in the until late 19th century illiteracy was more the norm than not in the region (with almost 70 percent of the adult population). It is also safe to say that the reduction of illiteracy in the 20th century is one of the great triumphs of the region. Today, this figure is between 6 and 2 percent of the adult population. Unfortunately, the educational requirements necessary for economic growth are constantly increasing. For a low-income country, a primary-school education may be sufficient. As Latin America has developed, it now needs a more educated workforce equipped with a solid secondary education. A common way to think about this is in terms of four different types of workers: unskilled, semiskilled, skilled, and highly skilled. A typical unskilled worker could be a rural farmer with little to no formal education. A semi-skilled worker has been to primary school and is capable of working in labor-intensive manufacturing or in the service sector. The textbook example of a skilled worker is a welder. The job requires an impressive command of a difficult technical skill. In general, these workers have some level of education past primary school. Such work requires skills that are usually associated with post-secondary education or beyond. As countries develop, their educational systems need to develop as well. They need to keep up with changes in job requirements in ever more sophisticated economies. Optimally, they will stay ahead of the curve and be producing graduates that match the needs of the economy. Literacy rates in most of Latin America are either at or approaching the levels in developed countries. It is beyond this basic level that the challenges begin to appear. Based on Fiszbein et al. (2016), in Latin America the percentage of workers with just a primary education is about 50 percent. A third of the workers have completed a secondary education, while a 20 percent of the workforce has completed a tertiary degree. Those figures in OECD countries are approximately 24 percent with primary education, 44 percent with a secondary degree, and 33 percent with a tertiary degree. In principle, the challenges for Latin America seem to be located between secondary and a higher degree of education. However, these numbers could be masking a grimmer reality. For convenience, economists and other social scientists have been using years of schooling as a proxy for human capital for decades. Until recently, it was difficult to determine to what extent a year of schooling in one country compares with another. The OECD is now running a testing project for many of the world's countries. Students are given a standardized test covering reading, mathematics, and science. Table 3.7 presents the results for the year 2018. Countries are grouped by level of proficiency such that scores from 480 to 550 are level 3; from 407 to 480 are level 2; and below 407 are level 1. The higher the level, the higher the proficiency in the subject. These thresholds apply to the reading tests but they are not far from the ones used for mathematics and science. Of the nine countries in Latin America for which there is data, the highest score for the reading test is 452 and the lowest score is 377. Most Latin American countries are in level 2, a few in level 1, and none in level 3. In fact, of the 79 countries for which data is available, 377 is seventh from the bottom. Additionally, most of the developed countries are in level 3, and some in level 2. Notice that, the countries from Latin America that participate in this project are mostly high-income ones, so there could be lower scores. The overall result is that students in Latin America are clearly falling behind and the quality of the education is far from the average. At a minimum, such numbers are not consistent with rapid growth in the 21st century.

The situation with respect to infrastructure is more challenging. It is not easy to have a perfect definition of infrastructure, but it could refer to a collection of public and private structures and services that enhance the ability to produce goods and services. Infrastructure can be missing entirely, such as the lack of railroads in some countries. In other cases, the infrastructure is there, but it is not properly maintained or it is not in usable conditions. In Table 3.8 we present data on infrastructure in Latin America published by the World Economic Forum. The ranking system goes from 0 to 7 on an ascending scale. The overall quality of

Table 3.7: Educational outcomes in Latin America, PISA scores for 2018.

	Reading	Mathematics	Science
Chile	452	417	444
Uruguay	427	418	426
Costa Rica	426	402	416
Mexico ·	420	409	419
Brazil	413	384	404
Colombia	412	391	413
Argentina	402	379	404
Peru	401	400	404
Panama	377	353	365
Latin America	414	395	411
Canada	520	512	518
United States	505	478	502
Spain	496	481	483
Portugal	492	492	492
OECD	487	489	489

Source: Schleicher (2019).

infrastructure is an average of scores for electricity, roads, railroads, ports, and air transport. Notice that the average for Latin America is below the world average, even when the average GDP per capita in Latin America is about the world average. The provision of electricity is the only area where the region is at the world average, but of course there is considerable variation across countries. The roads face an even more challenging situation given the average number of road fatalities per person (similar to the world average). Partly due to its geography, investment in railroads has been less than in other regions, which puts an even larger strain on a weakened road system. Likewise, ports and air transport are both below global averages. The data given in Table 3.8 is just a sample of infrastructure challenges in general. Unfortunately, the issues run the gamut from low technology (clean water) to high technology (information technology). Across the board, infrastructure is a persistent challenge in the region.

Business Regulations and Taxes

Once one moves out of these two obvious problems, the constraints on growth in Latin America become more difficult to define. The overall sentiment is that it still is a challenging place to do business. The tax laws and the complex business regulations present SMEs with a cruel choice. The laws can be so difficult to comply

Table 3.8: Infrastructure quality in Latin America (2017–2018).

	Overall quality	Electricity	Roads	Railroads	Ports	Air transport
Argentina	3.3	3.0	3.3	2.1	3.7	4.2
Bolivia	3.6	2.6	3.3	2.5	2.0	3.2
Brazil	3.1	4.5	3.1	2.0	3.1	3.9
Chile	4.7	6.1	5.2	2.5	4.9	4.5
Colombia	3.1	4.8	3.0	1.5	3.8	4.1
Costa Rica	3.1	5.9	2.6	1.9	3.4	4.5
Ecuador	4.5	4.9	5.1	–	4.6	5.1
El Salvador	–	–	–	–	–	–
Guatemala	3.4	5.7	3.1	–	3.6	3.4
Honduras	3.6	3.5	3.8	–	4.4	4.0
Mexico	4.1	4.9	4.4	2.8	4.3	4.4
Nicaragua	3.5	4.4	4.3	–	3.1	3.8
Panama	4.7	5.2	4.4	4.5	6.2	6.0
Paraguay	2.6	2.6	2.4	–	3.3	2.6
Peru	3.1	5.1	3.0	2.0	3.7	4.1
Uruguay	3.6	6.0	3.3	1.2	4.9	5.3
Venezuela, RB	2.5	2.1	2.8	1.5	2.7	2.7
Latin America	3.5	4.5	3.6	2.2	3.9	4.1
World	4.2	4.5	4.0	3.3	4.1	4.4

Source: World Economic Forum (2019).

with that usually large businesses are the ones that can afford the extra staff necessary for compliance. For smaller firms that cannot possibly comply with the laws, they can either not exist or move into the unregulated informal economy. A simple example, at least for US taxpayers, should allow an appreciation of the problem. Suppose that every spring one had to fill out income tax forms without the assistance of an accountant or a computer program. Are you sure you could accomplish this? Most SMEs in Latin America face a similar situation. Many times, they cannot even understand the complexities of the law and do not have the resources to deal with it. Quite rationally they just ignore the law and conduct their business as best they can. This has two immediate consequences that can deter economic growth. First, it can produce threshold effects. In developed countries, threshold effects occur when business taxes or regulations take effect at certain levels of income or employment. A common example is the progressive income tax. It is quite common for firms or individuals to defer income out of a current year into a future year to avoid being moved into a higher tax bracket. For a small firm in Latin America, it means remaining small to avoid the notice of government officials. Second, firms in the informal sector are usually deprived of the usual access to capital. A firm that does not officially exist cannot easily obtain funds to expand the business. Because firms are trapped in the informal sector, this produces a constraint on the overall growth of the economy. Unfortunately, this complexity creates two additional negative externalities. First, overly complex regulations can become an obvious source of corruption. Government officials could take payments to allow firms to unofficially continue in business. In other words, they are being "taxed." It just is not an official tax. As an aside, this should make one wary of cultural explanations for corruption. If a system is set up that invites corrupt behavior, one should not be too surprised when it occurs. Second, the labor market in the informal sector is devoid of all of the usual regulations on wages, hours, conditions of employment, but also of government assistance.

To illustrate these problems, we will look at three common types of data. The first measure is the difficulty of officially starting a business. Similar to developed countries, developing economies are full of very small businesses. These types of firms exist in Latin America, but they are informal. To understand the challenges at hand, there are three measurable parts of the process of starting a business, as shown in Table 3.9. First, there is the number of procedures one has to go through to obtain permission to start a business. In Latin America, the average number is more than 8. Second, how many days does the process take? The average for the region is nearly a month. The third part is the cost of getting this done as a percentage of per capita income. The result is nearly 37 percent. In order to start a business, it is going to take a month of time and about 4 months of income. Since the World Bank calculates this data for most of the world's countries one can rank the countries of Latin America relative to the rest of the world (fourth column of the table). The relative rankings are quite clear. The regional average is more than 100 (not shown in the table). The high-income countries are barely in the top third, and eight are ranked more than 100. Other ranking systems using slightly different methodologies produce very similar results. Firms in Latin America tend to start out in the informal sector for perfectly clear reasons. Since the system creates a disincentive for small firms to grow, the economy tends to become overpopulated with small and less productive firms. The effect on GDP growth is unlikely to be positive.

For SMEs in Latin America the tax systems exacerbate the problems involved in starting or maintaining a formal business. The data given below is based on surveys by the World Bank of average sized firms. Here we can look at the problems of taxation that firms face in three parts. Normally, we think of tax problems in terms of the highest tax rate, but this might be incomplete. A more complete measure is to total all of the business taxes and mandatory

Table 3.9: Starting a business in Latin America (2018).

	Procedures (number)	Time (days)	Cost (% of per capita income)	Rank
Argentina	11	11	5.3	119
Bolivia	14	43.5	46	156
Brazil	11	20.5	5	109
Chile	7	6	5.7	56
Colombia	8	11	14	65
Costa Rica	10	23	9.5	67
Ecuador	11	48.5	21.2	123
El Salvador	9	16.5	45.1	85
Guatemala	6	15	18.1	98
Honduras	11	13	40.7	121
Mexico	8	8.4	16.2	54
Nicaragua	7	14	63.6	132
Panama	5	6	5.4	79
Paraguay	7	35	40.3	113
Peru	8	24.5	9.9	68
Uruguay	5	6.5	22.6	95
Venezuela, RB	20	230	391.3	188
Latin America	8.2	27.8	36.8	..

Source: World Bank (2019).

contributions payable by business as a percentage of profits. Results are presented in Table 3.10. The number for Argentina is correct. If an average firm pays all of its taxes, it will go broke. To be fair, the regional average is 6 percentage points higher than the global average. However, the range is extreme. In many countries, the attractiveness of operating informally is understandable. The second problem is the frequency of tax payments. The more often that firms have to go pay a tax, the less time they have to actually conduct their business. The average firm in Latin America is making more than 26 payments a year or about one every two weeks. This is higher than the global average, but again the differences within countries are extreme. The data for many countries in the region looks like the situation in developed countries, i.e., only a few payments per year. However, in the more extreme cases the payments are almost weekly. This amount of trouble is not really conducive to the operation of SMEs. When both tax rates and the frequency of payments are high, it should come as no surprise that the taxes are complex. A measure of this complexity is the number of hours it takes the average firm to comply. The global average is 237 hours. The average for Latin America is 329. The notorious complexity of taxes in the region implies that the average firm in Latin America will have to assign 40 percent more time to comply with taxes than the global average. Large firms are probably well positioned to deal with both the total amount of taxes and the complexity. They have the resources to both pay the taxes and hire the necessary tax specialists. Unfortunately, for small firms, informality is almost a foregone conclusion.

Table 3.10: Business taxes in Latin America (2018).

	Total tax (percentage)	Number of payments	Time to comply (hours)
Argentina	106	9	311.5
Bolivia	83.7	42	1025
Brazil	65.1	9.6	1958
Chile	34	7	296
Colombia	71.9	11	255.5
Costa Rica	58.3	10	151
Ecuador	32.3	8	664
El Salvador	35.6	7	180
Guatemala	35.2	8	248
Honduras	44.4	48	224
Mexico	53	6	240.5
Nicaragua	60.6	43	201
Panama	37.2	36	408
Paraguay	35	20	378
Peru	36.8	9	260
Uruguay	41.8	20	163
Venezuela, RB	64.6	70	792
Latin America	46.3	26.4	329
World	40.4	23.8	236.8

Source: World Bank (2019).

A final, but crucial, business regulation in Latin America is the labor law. For many, this is unfamiliar territory, so a bit of explanation is in order. Virtually every government in the world has laws that regulate the labor market. Laws are put in place to regulate hiring, firing, wages, hours, conditions of employment, and rules concerning unionization. To begin, we stress that labor unions are not the heart of the problem. Only 14 percent of the labor force in Latin America is unionized and while unions wield considerable political power in some countries, their economic influence is not the problem. The major challenge seems to be the existence of employment protection legislation (EPL). Most countries have some system to protect workers from random economic shocks such as recessions. In doing so, the major choice is between EPL and a social insurance fund that provides workers without jobs with temporary payments. Both systems protect workers, but their effects are quite different. In the typical EPL system, employers are discouraged from dismissing workers as there is a large mandated payment that the worker would receive. The result is that it turns labor into something like a fixed cost. Once a worker is hired, she becomes increasingly expensive to dismiss as her seniority grows. Given this situation, firms become reluctant to hire workers unless they are absolutely necessary. The labor market becomes less flexible as there are few dismissals but very few new hires. Social insurance funds provide for much more labor market flexibility. Firms feel free to hire new workers as they will not be that costly to dismiss. The costs to firms of dismissal are paid into an insurance fund over time. Having flexible labor markets can also help getting better matches between firms and workers with increased labor mobility. Most of Latin American countries use some sort of EPL system. While this may be a trivial decision in a developed country, it could have deeper implications in a developing country. When an SME faces a serious downturn, it may not be able to stay in business because the cost of downsizing is too high, but it may not be able to continue to pay the workers. Just how flexible labor markets in the region are can be seen in Table 3.11. In a global ranking scheme of labor-market flexibility, the Latin American average is more than 100. No country is in the top 50. Portugal, Spain, Canada, and the United States were inserted for perspective. The US is clearly the most flexible labor market. What is less obvious is that Spain has considerably inflexible labor markets by the standards of developed countries. Only one country in Latin America (Costa Rica) has more flexible labor markets than Spain. EPL tends to benefit established workers in the formal sector. For other workers, the results have been discouraging. In fact, David et al. (2020), among other authors, recently presented new evidence that informality seems to be associated with stringent labor market regulations. Furthermore, aside from encouraging informality, it can hinder economic growth in another way. EPL and labor-intensive production for export tend to be incompatible. Firms producing these products do not just look for "cheap" labor. They also need the flexibility to scale up or down as demand changes. If this flexibility is not possible due to local labor laws, then the production could probably be moved to another country with different labor laws.

Finally, there are a number of annual indexes about the ease of conducting business around the world. The most widely used is *Doing Business* published by the World Bank. The data covers 10 different topics that capture the institutional quality aspects of conducting a business. A few of the more important to Latin America were discussed above. Within these 10 topics, there are 41 different subcategories. The scores on all of these indicators flow into the topics that then yield global rankings. The ranking is presented in Table 3.12. The Latin American average is nearly 102. There is no country in the region that is in the top 50. The bottom

Table 3.11: Labor market flexibility in Latin America.

	World rank
Argentina	133
Bolivia	138
Brazil	131
Chile	78
Colombia	85
Costa Rica	54
Ecuador	121
El Salvador	96
Guatemala	124
Honduras	97
Mexico	91
Nicaragua	75
Panama	88
Paraguay	71
Peru	90
Uruguay	112
Venezuela, RB	139
Latin America	101.4
Portugal	38
Spain	67
Canada	9
United States	1

Source: Fraser Institute based on Gwartney, et al. (2018).

country, Venezuela, is ranked 188 out of 190. What was conveyed from the material above is consistent with this aggregate measure. As indicated, the data from the World Bank is not the only source. The World Economic Forum and other groups also publish annual reports that contain a wealth of data on economic and social factors that influence not only the ease of doing business but also the quality of life. This data is further supplemented by organizations that are concerned with specific issues. One of the most well-known is the ranking on the perception of corruption published by Transparency International. In all of these ranking systems, Latin America does not fare particularly different from what we discussed above.

What this is leading to is that Latin America is one of the most challenging areas of the world to do business in. With a few exceptions, in most countries of the region the complex business environment contributes to creating a persistent

Table 3.12: Measures of institutional quality in Latin America.

	Doing business (world rank)
Argentina	119
Bolivia	156
Brazil	109
Chile	56
Colombia	65
Costa Rica	67
Ecuador	123
El Salvador	85
Guatemala	98
Honduras	121
Mexico	54
Nicaragua	132
Panama	79
Paraguay	113
Peru	68
Uruguay	95
Venezuela, RB	188
Latin America	101.6
Portugal	34
Spain	30
Canada	22
United States	8

Source: World Bank (2019).

informal sector. When SMEs are not able to function legally, they tend to become part of the underground economy. More than 32 percent of the GDP of Latin America originates in the informal sector. As we noted above, the firms in the informal sector lack access to capital and tend to be labor intensive. The overall result is that more than half of the workers in Latin America are in the informal sector. This means that the majority of the workers in the region are in a virtually unregulated labor market. Aside from the social cost, the effects on economic growth can be significant. In the world economy, negative growth in TFP is not a common phenomenon. Normally, workers and firms get better at what they do over time. Collectively, this translates into a normal positive rate of growth of TFP that enhances overall growth. However, in Latin America, SMEs face a daily struggle of infrastructure problems that sometimes prevent workers from getting to work, getting the lights turned on, making sure they have drinkable water, fending off the next government bureaucrat, and trying to pay their workers. The current business environment seems to be holding virtually all of the countries of the region back. Informality is like a debilitating condition. It may not kill you, but it will slow you down. Only by understanding the problem, a solution can be proposed.

Chapter 4
Argentina and Brazil

The Basics

With a GDP of almost $1.9 trillion, Brazil is Latin America's largest economy (and the ninth largest in the world) while Argentina, with about $520 billion, is the second largest. In terms of GDP per capita, Brazil is slightly below the average for Latin America with $9,000, while Argentina is at more than $11,500 per capita (see Table 4.1). Both countries are endowed with abundant natural resources and cover an extensive area of the east coast of South America. With a territory of 2,780,400 square kilometers, Argentina has abundant fertile lands, with reserves of natural gas and lithium, and promising prospects for renewable energy. Furthermore, it is a leading food producer with large-scale agricultural and livestock industries. Brazil has a land area of 8,515,767 square kilometers, which makes it the fifth largest country in the world. It is also home to the massive Amazon River basin with its unparalleled biodiversity and natural resources such as gold, iron ore, tin, and platinum. Similar to Argentina, Brazil is a leading producer of food with highly integrated agricultural and livestock industries. Combined, both countries cover 57 percent of Latin America's land and represent 40 percent and 50 percent of the region's population and GDP, respectively.

For the last two decades, Argentina and Brazil have been growing at 1.9 and 2.3 percent, respectively, a below average rate compared to the 3.1 for Latin America. During that same period, the GDP per capita (measured in 2005 PPP dollars) increased by 20 percent and 30 percent, respectively, for Argentina and Brazil, while the average for the region was at almost 47 percent.[1] Figure 4.1 shows the evolution of the growth rate for Argentina and Brazil, and the average of Latin America. From this figure, we can distinguish at least two marked V-shapes for

---

1 Purchasing power parity (PPP) refers to the rate at which one country's currency is converted into that of another country to eliminate the differences in price levels (that is, to buy the same amount of goods and services). For example, suppose that inflation in the US is zero and 100 percent in Mexico. Then, a beer in Mexico that cost 100 pesos last year would cost 200 pesos this year. In that case, the exchange rate would have to change to keep prices in the US and Mexico equivalent. If the exchange rate changed from 100 pesos per dollar to 200 pesos per dollar, then the purchasing power of the two currencies has remained the same. This is the essence of PPP. Using a PPP exchange rate is just factoring out these national differences in exchange rates.

https://doi.org/10.1515/9783110674934-004

Table 4.1: Population, GDP, GDP per capita, poverty, and inequality in Argentina, Brazil, and Latin America.

	Population (millions)	GDP (billions of USD)	GDP per capita (USD)	Poverty ($5.5 per day)	Poverty percentage (year)	Income inequality (Gini coefficient)	Inequality-adjusted education index
Argentina	44.5	520	11,684	9.6	35.5	0.41	0.79
Brazil	209.5	1,885	9,001	19.9	25.0	0.54	0.53
Central America	47.8	257	6,656	30.5	36.7	0.47	0.46
Latin America	644.1	5,972	9,272	23.3	33.8	0.46	0.56

Source: World Bank (2020), Economic Commission for Latin America and the Caribbean (ECLAC) (2019), United Nations Development Programme (UNDP) (2019).
Notes: Population, GDP, GDP per capita from 2018. Poverty from 2018, excepting Guatemala, Nicaragua, and Venezuela from 2014. Poverty percentage from 2018, excepting Bolivia, Chile, and Panama from 2017, Guatemala from 2014, Nicaragua from 2015, and Venezuela from 2019. Income inequality from 2018, excepting Guatemala, Nicaragua, and Venezuela 2014. Inequality-adjusted education index from 2018.

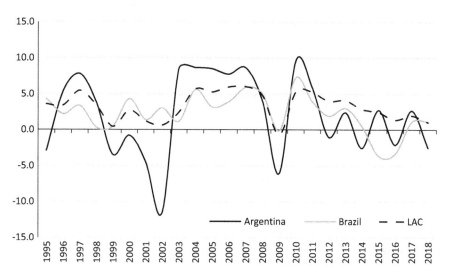

Figure 4.1: Economic growth (real GDP annual growth, percentage).
Source: World Bank (2020).
Note: LAC is the simple average of 17 countries in Latin America, excluding the Caribbean.

Argentina and an erratic performance of the Brazilian economy. For the last two decades, Argentina has been amplifying the Latin American business cycle (during a period of boom, the Argentine economy would grow more than the average of Latin America, while during a bust the economy would contract more) while Brazil follows the average quite closely. This helps explain, to some extent, why we tend to observe stronger crises and booms in Argentina and more mild performances in Brazil.

Let us divide in three periods (2000 to 2002, 2003 to 2008, and 2010 until today) the analysis of economic growth for these countries. Following the Russian crisis of August 1998, both Argentina and Brazil experienced financial crises. For Argentina, a severe recession started at the beginning of the 2000, contributing to a financial crisis that included a default on its sovereign debt in December of 2001, forcing the collapse of the *Convertibility Plan* (we will explain this below) in January 2002. For Brazil, it was even before, in January 1999, with the devaluation of the local currency (the real), spurring the first signals that a slowdown was coming to the Southern Cone. During this period of crisis and stagnation (from 1998 to 2002), Argentina's economy contracted 20 percent while Brazil grew at an average of 1.8 percent, compared to the average of 1.7 percent for Latin America. Immediately after this, from 2003 to 2008, the region experienced a revival of capital inflows, a boom in commodity prices, a strengthening of the domestic currencies, and a strong growth pattern. During these years, the Argentine economy experienced an average growth rate of 7.7 percent. Just at the end of this period new inflationary pressures started blooming again whilst the government was running expansionary fiscal policies. At about this time was when Argentina introduced a new consumer price index, casting doubts about the credibility of its statistics. For Brazil, 2003 to 2008 was also a period of rapid economic growth, with an average rate of 4.1 percent per year. During this time, Brazil was able to reinvigorate aggregate consumption putting in place the Growth Acceleration Program (Programa de Aceleracao do Crescimiento) to increase public and private investment. More importantly, the Brazilian government was able to stabilize the public debt, fiscal deficit, and domestic prices.

Both Argentina and Brazil were affected by the global financial crisis (GFC) of 2008. Argentina was affected by the reduction of international demand for its exports, a *sudden stop* of capital inflows, and the very limited fiscal space to perform counter-cyclical policies. GDP grew by 4.0 percent in 2008 and contracted by 6.1 percent in 2009. Brazil was also affected by the GFC, but mostly felt the slowdown in 2009 when the economy contracted by 0.13 percent. To mitigate the negative impacts of the crisis, both Argentina and Brazil were able to implement counter-cyclical policies, such as income tax reductions, taxes on external trade, increases in infrastructure investments, temporary assistance to households, and support for small and medium enterprises.[2] Finally, the post-crisis period (2010 until today) is characterized by a fast recovery, followed by a generalized slowdown and a series of contractions. Argentina grew at 9.6 percent in 2010 and then slowed down to an average of 0.4 percent after 2011. In the case of Brazil, the GDP grew at 7.2 percent in 2010, and then slowed down to an average of 0.6 percent. Both countries, were affected by the end of the supercycle of commodities in 2014. This was particularly serious in the case of Brazil, which entered a recession in 2015 and 2016, when its GDP contracted approximately 3.5 percent each year, only to later stabilize at about 1 percent annual growth rate. The plunge of commodity and oil prices, the contraction of the demand for exports, and a rising inflation, forced the private sector to reduce spending and cut jobs. All this was happening amid a domestic political crisis that had President Dilma Rousseff impeached from December 2015 to August 2016, and eventually removed from office.

From a long-run perspective, although Argentina and Brazil experienced periods of strong growth in GDP, higher than the region in some cases, growth in income per capita has not been sufficient to reduce their income gaps relative to the rest of the world. Following Birdsall et al.'s (2008), Panel A in Table 4.2 traces the evolution of the income gap relative to the world's most advanced economies (in terms of health, education, and income).[3] After advancing in the 1990s, both Argentina and Brazil seem to be at the same level after almost two decades. In fact, there was a slight move backwards from 2010 to 2018. Panel B in Table 4.2 traces the evolution of this gap relative to countries with a similar level of development. Since 2000, there is a closing of this gap for both Argentina and Brazil. Nevertheless, we also observe a small retrenchment for Brazil in the last decade. Finally, Panel C in Table 4.2 traces the evolution of this gap relative to the average of Latin America. At the beginning of the 1990s, both Argentina and Brazil were approximately at the same level of the average for Latin America. Since then, they now represent more than the average of Latin America in terms of GDP per capita.

---

2 Kacef and Jiménez (2009) estimate that the cost of these measures for Argentina and Brazil were approximately 6 percent and 3.6 percent of GDP, respectively.

3 Based on the Human Development Index (HDI), we first construct an equally weighted subindex of health, education, and income. The most developed countries are those in the top decile of this subindex. Countries are classified as having similar level of development if they are ranked in the same decile of this subindex. Finally, Latin American countries is the average of the seventeen countries within Latin America. A greater figure implies a better performance with one being the threshold when the comparison renders the same.

Table 4.2: Income gap based on relative GDP per capita.

	1990	2000	2010	2018
Panel A: Most developed countries				
Argentina	0.19	0.35	0.39	0.35
Brazil	0.20	0.23	0.33	0.29
Panel B: Similar level of development				
Argentina	0.55	0.51	0.47	0.74
Brazil	0.91	0.58	1.13	0.85
Panel C: Latin American countries				
Argentina	0.97	1.79	1.49	1.33
Brazil	1.03	1.18	1.26	1.12

Source: World Bank (2020), United Nations Development Programme (UNDP) (2019) based on Birdsall et al. (2008).
Note: A value of 1 represents absence of income gap, while a value smaller (greater) than 1 implies a negative (positive) gap. Individual GDP per capita in 2011 dollars at purchasing power parity relative to the average of each comparison group of countries. *Most developed countries* refers to the group of countries in the top decile of a subindex of health, education, and income of the Human Development Index. *Similar level of development* refers to the group of countries in the same decile of a subindex of health, education, and income of the Human Development Index. *Latin American countries* refers to the group of countries from Latin America in a subindex of health, education, and income of the Human Development Index.

In the last 20 years, poverty and inequality have relatively fallen in Argentina and Brazil. In the case of Argentina, there was a considerable increase during the crisis of 2002, with a downward trend the following years, and a recent increase in 2018. Interestingly, in both countries, the decline in poverty indicators was not affected by the GFC of 2008. Cruces et al. (2017) argue that this downward trend in poverty is consistent with an increase in labor earnings during this period due to increases in the minimum and nominal wage and the use of anti-poverty programs. Cash transfer programs have played an important role in the fight against poverty in both Brazil and Argentina.[4] For instance, Ferreira et al. (2010) estimated that, in Brazil, the Bolsa Familia (a conditional cash transfer program) and the Beneficio de Prestacao Continuada (an unconditional cash transfer program) helped to reduce poverty and inequality. In Argentina, Gasparini and Cruces (2010) also argue

---

4 The basics benefit of this type of programs is a cash transfer to families living in extreme poverty, with or without conditions for receiving the money. Conditions can include, among other things, children school attendance and/or getting the appropriate vaccinations.

that social public spending, like Asignación Universal por Hijo (a conditional cash transfer program) helped alleviate poverty and inequality. In Table 4.1, using the absolute measure of 5.5 dollars per day, a global standard of poverty, Argentina and Brazil have almost 10 percent and 20 percent, respectively, of their population living in poverty conditions.[5] These figures compare with 23.3 percent for Latin America, and almost 31 percent for the average country in Central America. When using the official poverty line, the figure for Argentina currently reaches 36 percent while in Brazil represents 25 percent of the population, while the average for Latin America is almost 34 percent. The trend of poverty usually follows the evolution of the economy, particularly that of GDP. However, as Cruces et al. (2017) explain, the differences between these poverty lines could also be due to extreme fluctuations in food prices, key elements in official poverty lines. Furthermore, income inequality, measured by the Gini coefficient, also experienced a relative decline but still remains high.[6] In particular, Argentina is at 0.41 while Brazil is at 0.54 (the highest score for Latin America) and the whole region is at 0.46. Brazil's high coefficient can be capturing, to some extent, the consequences of the recession of 2015 and 2016, which impacted the level of employment and income of most Brazilians, leading to a deterioration of the distribution of income, and hence, the Gini coefficient. The distribution of income can be influenced by the distribution of human capital. Thus, the distribution of human capital is influenced by the distribution of educational opportunities. Using the inequality-adjusted education index, Brazil shows a score of 0.53, similar to the average for Latin America, but lower than Argentina's 0.79.[7] In fact, Argentina shows a less unequal distribution of education relative to Brazil. However, it is worth noting that this

---

5 The World Bank has an international poverty line for upper middle-income countries (most of Latin American countries) that captures the concept of absolute poverty by setting a threshold of 5.5 dollars per day (in 2011 PPP terms). Absolute poverty is defined as the lack of monetary resources to meet certain basic needs of human existence. Official poverty lines are based on household surveys with population weighted averages and include more comprehensive structures of basic needs. Despite considerable improvement and harmonization of household surveys in Latin America, comparison across countries might not be perfect.

6 Income inequality is usually measured using the Gini coefficient. The Gini coefficient is a measure of the deviation of the actual income distribution from perfect equality. It ranges from 0 to 1, 0 being perfect equality and 1 implying perfect inequality. No country in the world conforms to either extreme. There are at least two caveats regarding the use of the Gini coefficient. The Gini coefficient does not capture subgroup (region, ethnic group, etc.) changes and puts equal weight to the entire distribution. That means that the lower end of the distribution has a similar weight in the index than the upper end. This feature could be masking important changes in the dynamics of the distribution.

7 The inequality-adjusted education index is the HDI education index value adjusted for inequality in the distribution of years of schooling of the adult population, drawn from household surveys

information is based on the number of years of education obtained, but might be less informative about the quality of education. That is, one issue is the amount of time spent at school and another issue is how successful the learning process is in providing students with the basic tools to thrive in a modern economy.

The Macroeconomic Record

When discussing the macroeconomic performance of countries like Argentina and Brazil, inflation is inevitably one of the first issues. Both countries ended the 1980s witnessing massive hyperinflations, with Argentina experiencing a 3,080-percentage rate while Brazil suffered a 1,431-percentage rate. These hyperinflations can be traced to the fact that both countries relied on printing money to finance their fiscal deficits.[8] In other words, facing a shortfall of credit inflows, a fall in commodity prices, with no clear access to sovereign debt or foreign exchange reserves to finance expenditures, both Argentina and Brazil mainly opted to print money to cover their deficits. By doing so, they ended up creating an inflation tax, which eroded the real value of money and of people who relied on salaries, social security transfers, and pensions.

In the 1990s, both countries implemented stabilization plans that reduced their inflation rates: In 1991, Domingo Cavallo introduced in Argentina the Convertibility Plan, a currency board regime that pegged the peso to the US dollar, while in 1994 Brazil introduced a new currency (the real) that was linked (not pegged) to the US dollar. A decade later, Argentina was experiencing a deflation of 1.2 percent and Brazil an inflation rate of 4.9 percent. Interestingly, during this decade both countries were able to finance their deficits using (short-term) debt instead of printing money. However, the inflation inertia and its consequences were not over yet.

The 2000s started with considerable crises for Argentina and Brazil, but with the exception of a couple of years, they both managed to keep inflation at lower rates, similar to the average of Latin America (see Panel A in Table 4.3). Argentina abandoned the Convertibility Plan in January 2002, shifting to a floating exchange rate regime, with a considerable devaluation of the peso but a smaller impact on inflation. In fact, the inflation rate in 2002 reached 26 percent and declined to 10.6 percent by 2013. Interestingly, at the end of 2013, Argentina entered a period of non-compliance

(UNDP, 2019). The inequality dimension is estimated by the Atkinson measure, capturing subgroup (region, ethnic group, etc.) changes and putting more weight to the lower end of the distribution. This index is constructed by the United Nations Development Programme (UNDP) and ranges from 0 (most inequal) to 1 (most equal) in terms of education equality.

8 *Structuralism* would argue that inflation is not necessarily a monetary phenomenon but the result of institutional rigidities that prevented competition in sectors such as agriculture and trade.

with respect to the accuracy provision of its measure of inflation. In other words, the reported measure of inflation was casting doubts (domestically and internationally) about its validity. This was particularly troublesome for macroeconomic management, but also in terms of consumers' and investors' expectations. Argentina returned to complying with inflation statistics in 2016, and by 2019 the inflation rate hit a record of 54.4 percent, the highest since 1991. Unfortunately, the struggles of Argentina with inflation have been a distinctive factor for the last 30 years.[9]

Brazil, on the other hand, adopted an inflation-targeting regime in 1999 with a flexible exchange rate regime. The main objective of this framework is to mitigate price fluctuations and its costs on society. Adopting inflation targeting typically implies that a central bank has an announced numerical target for inflation and a commitment to transparency and accountability. As Mishkin (2004) explains, fully implementing an inflation-targeting framework may take several years, but the evidence also suggests that inflation-targeting countries have lower inflation rates. Brazil is certainly an example of such behavior. Since adopting an inflation-targeting framework, Brazil has been able to keep its inflation rate considerably

Table 4.3: Inflation rate and central bank independence.

	1990–1999	2000–2009	2010–2018*	2019
Panel A: Inflation rate, percentage				
Argentina	252.9	8.6	16.8	54.4
Brazil	843.2	6.9	6.1	3.8
Central America	15.4	6.6	3.6	3.0
Latin America	140.1	8.2	483.9	11,116.8
Latin America**	145.5	7.5	4.7	6.1
Panel B: Central bank independence index (Garriga, 2016)				
Argentina	0.72	0.79	0.77	
Brazil	0.25	0.25	0.25	
Central America	0.51	0.64	0.64	
Latin America	0.57	0.59	0.62	
Latin America**	0.56	0.59	0.61	

* = 2010–2014 in Panel B; ** = without Venezuela
Source: World Bank (2020) and Garriga (2016).
Note: The Garriga (2016) index goes from 0 to 1, with 0 being completely dependent and 1 being independent.

---

9 In March 2016, the central bank of Argentina announced a transition towards an inflation-targeting framework. However, after two years of dealing with inflationary pressures authorities decided to abandon the framework, for a monetary base target.

below 10 percent with the exception of 2003, after the Argentinian crisis. The other noticeable exception happened in 2015 and 2016, when inflation climbed to 9 percent, in the middle of an economic and political crisis. Nevertheless, for the last two decades, the average inflation rate in Brazil has been about 6.3 percent per year, consistent with the upper bound of the targets.

A reasonable question at this point is the role of the central bank. A key element of a sound macroeconomic policy is the capacity of the central bank to freely pursue monetary policy. Several authors, including Garriga and Rodriguez (2020), have discussed the negative relationship between the degree of independence of the central bank and the inflation rate in developing countries. Panel B in Table 4.3 shows that, in general, the region has increased its central bank independence (using the Garriga (2016) index that goes from 0 to 1, with 0 being completely dependent and 1 being independent). Argentina stayed constant in its monetary independence, since the 1990s, and formally is at a higher degree compared to the average country of Latin America. Brazil, on the other hand, has had a relatively low degree of independence and did not show improvements throughout our period of analysis.

The other side of this discussion is the exchange rate. The financial crises of the early 2000s forced an end to the exchange rate systems in Argentina and Brazil. Argentina abandoned the Convertibility Plan accumulating a 250 percent devaluation in 2002, while the devaluation of the real in Brazil represented more than 50 percent from 2001 to 2002. These crises created a considerable impact in both countries and the fear of debasing for holders of domestic currency turned out to be a reality. Immediately after these abandonments, both countries started a period of flexible exchange rate regimes, joining other developing countries during that period. The yearly average currency depreciation for Argentina and Brazil from 2004 to 2017 was about 14.4 percent and 1.2 percent, respectively. In fact, during this period, both countries experienced events that contributed to the depreciation of domestic currencies, as seen in Figure 4.2. For instance, Argentina suffered a depreciation of almost 40 percent from 2015 to 2016, following the removal of foreign exchange restrictions. After the depreciation of the 2002 election campaign in Brazil (when President Luiz Inácio Lula da Silva was leading the polls), during 2015 social unrest erupted against President Rousseff, ending with her impeachment and removal from office. However, there have been more recent events of currency depreciations associated with rampant inflation and financing conditions in Argentina, and political uncertainty ahead of the presidential election and concerning economic performance in Brazil. After a severe depreciation in 2018, by 2019 Argentina accumulated a depreciation of the peso of almost 240 percent since 2017. In the case of Brazil, the real depreciated almost 30 percent during that period.

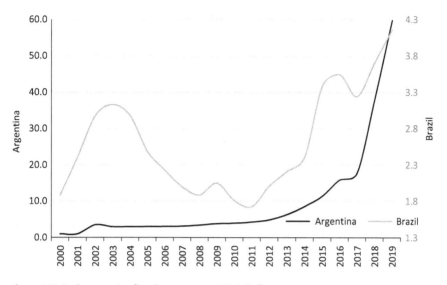

Figure 4.2: Exchange rates (local currency per US dollar).
Source: World Bank (2020).

Other components of the macroeconomic record, closely related to what we just discussed above, are the fiscal and debt dynamics. The collapse of the Argentine economy in 2002, after the default on its sovereign debt, was followed by a fast recovery with fiscal surpluses until 2008. After being excluded from international credit markets following the 2001 default, Argentina was mainly relying on its central bank to finance its deficits. This assistance to the Treasury included profits, advances, and use of reserves. Benefitted by the boom in commodities, initially, these transfers were not very significant, but after the arrival of the GFC things started to change. The combination of a weak global economy, the cost of the counter-cyclical measures of 2009, and energy subsidies brought the fiscal deficit to 3.3 percent of GDP by 2013 (see Panel A in Figure 4.3). Buera and Nicolini (2018) estimate that at this point almost two-thirds of the overall fiscal deficit was covered with loans from the central bank. With markets (still) closed for foreign borrowing, the government decided to print money, with the subsequent impact on inflation (and casting doubts about the accuracy of the reported statistic). The administration that took office at the end of 2015 embarked on a series of fiscal policy measures to control the increasing deficit and to manage what was left of the 2001 default. By 2016, Argentina reached an agreement that included all bondholders, allowing the government to access foreign borrowing for the first time since 2002. As Buera and Nicolini (2018) argue, this might be the main reason why the deficits of 2016 and 2017 were not financed by printing money but rather through foreign debt.

Panel A in Figure 4.3 presents the debt dynamic. Buera and Nicolini (2018) present a detailed analysis of the debt crisis of 2002. They argue that a combination of factors explains the considerable increase of the debt in 2002: the debt default, a bailout to the financial sector, debt from subnational governments that required assistance from the national government, and social protection programs designed to alleviate the impacts of the crisis. During these days, Argentina's debt was far from being sustainable at almost 155 percent of GDP. After two renegotiations with bondholders in 2005 and 2010, the public debt dropped to almost 43 percent of GDP. Additionally, between this period and 2015, the central bank of Argentina also provided foreign currency loans to the Treasury (in the form of reserves) to finance the repayment of public debt. By 2016, Argentina was able to access foreign borrowing again, and negotiated a loan with the IMF of approximately $57 billion, the biggest in the IMF's history. At the time of writing this chapter, Argentina's debt to GDP ratio was about 94 percent of GDP, which raises questions about its sustainability in the context of low growth and high fiscal deficit.

Following the switch to a floating exchange rate regime in 1999, Brazil immediately adopted an inflation-targeting framework with fiscal policy targets. The Fiscal Responsibility Law from 2000 was a key component of these targets. However, a considerable energy crisis affected the entire country in 2001, boosting Lula's presidential run of 2002. With a favorable and strong external demand and a boom in commodities, the first half of the 2000s was very stable in terms of fiscal result, with positive primary results hovering at 3.2 percent of GDP (see Panel B in Figure 4.3).[10] Things changed after 2006. The reelected government of President Lula moved to a more interventionist policy, playing a central role in the development process of the country. In 2007, the government started the Growth Acceleration Program to promote investment projects and boost the economy. At the same time, through the Brazilian Development Bank (Banco Nacional do Desenvolvimento Economico e Social -BNDES), the government encouraged investment in national companies to increase competitiveness. Additionally, Petrobras (Petróleo Brasileiro S.A.), the semi-public Brazilian petroleum corporation, was promoting large investments in the search for oil. With BNDES and Petrobras not included in the public sector statistics, these policies were not necessarily affecting the fiscal budget targets.[11] The GFC brought challenges to this strategy and counter-cyclical policies were implemented. Furthermore, the end of the supercycle of commodity prices in 2012 was an important milestone of fiscal deterioration. Facing a

---

10 The primary (fiscal) result is the fiscal result without the accrual of interests to be paid.

11 Ayres et al. (2018) refer to this as *contabilidade criativa* (creative accounting).

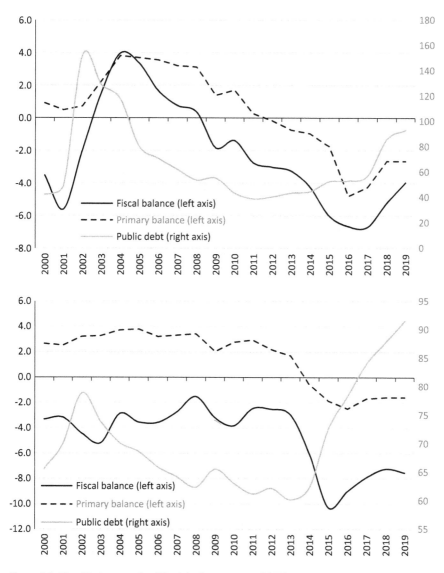

Figure 4.3: Fiscal balance and public debt (percentage of GDP).
Source: World Bank (2020) and International Monetary Fund (2020b).

shortfall of funds, the government used resources from public banks to cover social security pensions, but never paid them back. This created a loss for public banks without directly affecting the fiscal result. Ayres et al. (2018) explain that this strategy ended up with the impeachment of President Rousseff. In fact, between the end of 2015 and mid-2016, President Rousseff was impeached by

Congress, removed from office, and replaced by Michel Temer. With GDP contracting about 7 percent from 2014 to 2016, the fiscal deficit reached about 9 percent of GDP in 2016, with a primary result of about 2.5 percent of GDP.[12] There have been some improvements in the fiscal performance after these years, with a current fiscal deficit of almost 7.5 percent of GDP, but the fiscal situation still seems delicate.

The debt dynamic in Brazil follows closely the fiscal performance. From a broader perspective, Ayres et al. (2018) argue that during the 2000s, the focus was on the structure of the debt. That is, improving the maturity profiles, focusing on short-term debt, replacing external debt with domestic debt, and the gradual increase in fixed interest rate debt or debt indexed to inflation. This strategy successfully decreased the debt to GDP ratio from almost 80 percent of GDP in 2002 to 62 percent of GDP in 2008. When the GFC arrived, Brazil implemented counter-cyclical fiscal policies that demanded almost 3.6 percent of GDP, according to Kacef and Jimenez (2009). By this time, the government started borrowing more amid weakened economic conditions. With an increasing cost of borrowing, the economic and political crisis of 2015 and 2016 that brought higher inflation, a depreciation of the local currency, and a contraction of activity, the dynamic of public debt (particularly that denominated in dollars) became even more challenging. The debt trajectory, depicted in Panel B in Figure 4.3, transitioned from a high level to a potentially unsustainable one. By 2017, the public debt reached 84 percent of GDP, leading some credit agencies to downgrade Brazil's sovereign debt rating to BB.[13] At the time of producing this chapter, the debt to GDP ratio reached almost 92 percent, raising further concerns about its sustainability.

Economic Structure

Argentina is endowed with abundant natural resources and an export-oriented agricultural sector with dynamic industries. Although the share of the agriculture in GDP declined since the 1970s to about 11 percent (and about one-fifth of all exports), it still employs 10 percent of the active population. Furthermore, Argentina ranks among the top producers in many agricultural products for export with soy production accounting for 50 percent of the nation's crop production. The industrial sector employs almost 22 percent of the labor force, and used to

---

[12] The primary result is the fiscal result without the accrual of interest to be paid.

[13] This rating placed the Brazilian sovereign debt in the non-investment grade speculative category.

represent a higher share of the economy, but today accounts for about 28 percent (see Table 4.4). Most of this reduction is associated with the increasing share of services in the economy. Manufacturing is the largest single sector of the economy (about 15 percent of GDP) and is integrated with the agricultural sector, particularly for export purposes. The leading sectors in industry are food processing (including beverages), production of vehicles and auto parts, and oil/minerals such as natural gas and lithium. Argentina, along with Bolivia and Chile, shares a region known as "lithium triangle" with a large proportion of the world's lithium reserves. In fact, Argentina produces about 12 percent of the world's lithium. Finally, Table 4.4 also shows that the service sector is the largest contributor to the value added of the economy, accounting for approximately 60 percent and employing almost 80 percent of the active population. Within services, Argentina has a myriad of subsectors, such as tourism, financial services, corporate services, real estate, transport, and communication services. Similar to other countries of the region, Argentina has moved to a service-driven economy in detriment of the manufacturing sector.

Table 4.4: Economic structure (percentage of GDP).

	Agriculture	Industry	Services
Argentina	10.8	28.1	61.1
Brazil	6.6	20.7	72.7
Central America	*10.5*	*23.4*	*66.1*
Latin America	*9.0*	*28.3*	*62.8*

Source: World Bank (2020) and United Nations Development Programme (UNDP) (2018).

Brazil also has considerable natural resources along the Amazon rainforest, including reserves of minerals such as gold, iron, uranium, and timber. The share of the agricultural sector in GDP declined since the 1970s to about 6.6 percent (see Table 4.4) and employs approximately 9 percent of the active population. Brazil is the main producer of coffee in the world, also producing soybeans, wheat, rice, and sugarcane. Interestingly, the agricultural production in Brazil has been operating as enclaves for many years: in the northeastern region the sugarcane is predominant while coffee is the main production of the southern region (where more income is concentrated).[14] Similar to Argentina, Brazil has developed a business model integrating agriculture with the manufacturing

---

14 Brazil has three main regions: a central-western region (savannah), the northern region, and parts of the northeastern region (considered semi-arid).

sector. In fact, Brazil has one of the largest manufacturing sectors in Latin America that shrunk since in the 1970s to about 21 percent, employing 20 percent of the labor force. Current industries include a diverse range of textiles, chemicals, production of cars, steel, aircrafts, cement, and consumer durables. The most important company is Petrobras, valued at approximately $61 billion. Finally, the service sector accounts for the largest component of the GDP, with more than 63 percent. This sector includes financial services, insurance, telecommunications, and tourism, and employs about 70 percent of all workers.

In both cases there are common patterns: the agricultural sector shrunk in the last 40 years but still is considerably relevant; the industrial sector also contracted to about 21 percent of GDP in Brazil and 28 percent of GDP in Argentina; and the service sector increased considerably to above 60 percent of GDP. There is something distinctive about all these sectors in Latin America: informality. Although most of the informal employment can be found in the agricultural sector, the service industry also seems to have a growing informal component.[15] This link could be a red flag for the transformation of Argentina and Brazil as service economies. Overall, Bonnet et al. (2019) report that Argentina and Brazil have about 47 percent of informal employment. Informality has been shown to be an important determinant of low productivity in Latin America. Powell (2013) and Busso et al. (2013) present evidence that a major source of low productivity in Latin America is the high degree of informality in the private sector. This is something that can be particularly relevant for a country like Brazil. We will extend this argument at the end of this chapter.

Foreign Trade

In the background for a discussion on foreign trade is the ability of countries to move financial flows. That is, the integration of countries to international financial flows and their ability to engage in financial transactions is a key element for foreign trade. Argentina and Brazil have had an interesting experience in this sense, in a region characterized by strong financial openness. According to the Chinn and Ito (2006) index, in Table 4.5, during the 1990s both countries were at a low level of financial integration, only comparable to South Asia.[16]

---

15 Bonnet et al. (2019) highlight that, for the Americas, informal employment represents 77.5 percent in the agricultural sector and 35.5 percent in the service industries. Kedir et al. (2018) may be one of the first articles that connects the service sector with the informal economy.
16 The Chinn and Ito (2006) index takes higher values the more open a country is to cross-border capital transactions. In particular, the normalized version ranges from 0 to 1.

During the mid-1990s, the whole region embarked on a process of capital account liberalization, reducing the restrictions on capital transactions across countries. Argentina followed this path until the early 2000s, when the financial crisis of 2002 brought back many restrictions. Only recently, some restrictions on capital transactions were lifted again. Brazil, on the other hand, shifted from capital controls in the 1990s to lifting much of the restrictions by 2010. However, the GFC brought back some of those restrictions on capital inflows to reduce the risks associated with the fluctuations of the exchange rate. Currently, Argentina stands as relatively more open than the rest of Latin America and other developing regions, while Brazil still is one of the less open in the world.

Table 4.5: Capital account openness.

	1990	2000	2010	2018
Argentina	0.17	0.76	0.25	0.76
Brazil	0.00	0.17	0.48	0.17
Latin America	0.26	0.53	0.56	0.53
East Asia and Pacific	0.55	0.49	0.68	0.61
Europe and Central Asia	0.52	0.62	1.00	1.00
Sub-Saharan Africa	0.23	0.29	0.30	0.23
South Asia	0.19	0.27	0.29	0.32

Source: Chinn and Ito (2006) index, where higher values indicate a country is more open to cross-border capital transactions.

In terms of trade flows, Argentina and Brazil remain relatively closed. That was the situation at the beginning of the 1990s, and still is the situation after three decades (Figure 4.4). During the 1990s, Argentina and Brazil had a ratio of exports plus imports to GDP (a usual measure of trade openness) of about 15 percent, and currently hovers at about 30 percent. In both cases the ratios doubled relative to 1990, but still are only half way to the average of Latin America (approximately 60 percent of GDP). This implies that export flows might have limited scope to mitigate the lack of financing resulting from an external shock to their current accounts. To some extent, this is associated with exports remaining concentrated in commodities.

Unfortunately, commodity prices regularly experience booms and busts that can affect the revenues from exports.

A fairly common pattern, consistent across countries in Latin America, is the relatively high ratio of exports that are commodities. For Argentina and Brazil those numbers are 66.7 and 61.8 percent, respectively, compared to 61.3 percent for

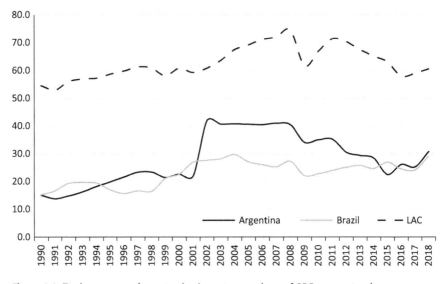

Figure 4.4: Trade openness (exports plus imports as a share of GDP, percentage).
Source: World Bank (2020).
Note: LAC is the simple average of 17 countries in Latin America, excluding the Caribbean.

the average of Latin America (see Table 4.6). In other words, similar to the average country in the region, most of the exports of Argentina and Brazil are in the form of commodities. About 55 percent of Argentinian exports are associated with soybeans, corn, wheat, and other vegetable and food products. The main destinations for these exports are Brazil, the United States, China, Chile, Vietnam, the Netherlands, and Germany, accounting for almost 50 percent of total exports. Brazil has a similar concentration of exports on commodities, with minerals like oil and iron, soybeans and other vegetable products, and other food products accounting for more than 50 percent of total exports. Brazil's main trade partners are China, the United States, Argentina, and the Netherlands, representing about 50 percent of total exports. Given the high volatility in commodity prices, the concentration of exports on these types of products reveals the vulnerability of these countries to the commodities cycle. The challenges arising from this concentration can be more pronounced the higher the dependency on these commodities exports for GDP. Interestingly, the commodities exports as a share of GDP for Argentina and Brazil only represent 6.1 and 6.6 percent, respectively. Thus, although important drivers of exports, commodities do not seem to represent a significant share of their GDP.

Table 4.6: Commodities' share of exports and GDP in Latin America (2019).

	Commodity exports (mill of USD)	Exports (merchandise) (mill of USD)	Commodity/ Exports	Commodity Exports/ GDP
Venezuela	72,277	74,714	96.7	15.0
Ecuador	17,772	19,122	92.9	17.0
Paraguay	7,702	8,680	88.7	19.4
Chile	59,621	69,230	86.1	21.5
Bolivia	6,423	7,846	81.9	17.1
Uruguay	6,305	7,888	79.9	11.2
Colombia	28,168	37,881	74.3	9.0
Peru	33,007	45,275	72.9	15.6
Argentina	39,072	58,622	66.7	6.1
Brazil	134,706	217,826	61.8	6.6
Guatemala	6,358	11,001	57.8	8.4
Nicaragua	2,493	5,170	48.2	18.0
Costa Rica	4,298	9,556	45.0	7.5
Honduras	3,351	8,675	38.6	14.6
El Salvador	1,374	5,760	23.9	5.5
Mexico	67,085	409,401	16.4	5.8
Panama	1,050	11,093	9.5	1.7
Central America			37.2	9.3
Latin America			61.3	11.8

Source: World Trade Organization (2020).

Country Specific Details

Argentina: Crises and Defaults

Unfortunately, the terms "debt" and "Argentina" have been closely connected, at least for the last century. As with most such connections, this is not accidental. According to a 2015 update of the Reinhart and Rogoff (2009) article, Argentina defaulted eight times on its sovereign debt between its inception in 1827 and 2014. As these authors notice, almost all of these episodes are preceded by a period of strong growth of the economy, with fiscal spending, debt expansion, and strong procyclicality in public policies.[17] Interestingly, there are different approaches regarding Argentina and its history of defaults. For instance, scholars like Reinhart et al. (2003) and Reinhart and Rogoff (2004), argue that Argentina falls in the category of serial

---

17 In this context, procyclicality implies an expansionary monetary or fiscal policy during "good times" of the economy, or a contractionary monetary or fiscal policy during "bad times."

defaulters and is subject to debt intolerance, mostly as a result from its reliance on external debt above the limit of tolerance. Some others, like Mussa (2002), argue that Argentina's pace of public spending is to blame for the crises and defaults. Alternatively, scholars like Damill et al. (2003, 2005), argue against the previous hypotheses, claiming that the market structure and the international financial architecture (particularly that of the IMF) are to blame for those defaults.

Here, we discuss a simplified version of the events regarding debt management in Argentina during the crisis of 2001–2002. When President Carlos Menem took office in July 1989, inflation was reaching 150 percent per month, real GDP was lower than in 1980, GDP per capita contracted by 20 percent, the fiscal deficit was about 6.6 percent of GDP, and there were approximately $4 billion in arrears in payments on the external debt. In this context, with a banking crisis in place, the government decided on a sequence of privatizations and centered its program on the Convertibility Plan. With this law, Argentina established a currency board, fixing the peso at parity with the dollar. This way, the government managed to control the hyperinflation fears by "anchoring" the exchange rate to gain confidence. As a result, inflation declined from almost 4,900 percent in 1989 to 4 percent in 1994. For some time, this currency board was effective in controlling inflation and promoting growth.

Unfortunately, this recovery was short lived. After the experiences of the Mexican crisis of 1994, the Asian and Russian crises of 1997 and 1998, and the devaluation of the Brazilian real in 1999, there was a growing concern within private lenders and the IMF, that Argentina was accumulating a considerable amount of dollar denominated debt. With an economy that was already reliant on the dollar, this contributed to more uncertainty about the solvency of the banking system. In effect, the currency board was working, but the reserves necessary to sustain it were being borrowed and shrinking. In 2000, the IMF loaned Argentina approximately $14 billion (an operation known as *blindaje*), supplemented by almost $6 billion from private lenders. Not long after that, a bank run on deposits broke out at the beginning of 2001. Moreover, the currency board was not requiring the monetary authority to be *lender of last resort* for foreign currency deposits. The situation worsened as the government tried to gain some time by extending existing debt for new debt with longer maturities.[18]

By November 2001, private deposits accumulated a decline of about 27 percent in a year. This spiral led to some banks being unable to honor their deposits, rising further concerns about a devaluation of the peso. In early December, the IMF stopped providing new loans and Argentina officially lost access to

---

[18] Later that year, the IMF provided further funding for almost $8 billion.

financial markets. At that point, in order to stop the bank run, the government restricted bank withdrawals in dollars, creating almost a freeze on deposits known as *corralito*. This was the end of this government (but not the end of the *corralito*) and the beginning of a period when Argentina had five presidents in less than two weeks.[19] In the midst of this crisis, on December 26, 2001, Argentina defaulted on a total of almost $95 billion of its external debt, most of which was issued from 1998 to 2001. Soon after this, the currency board ended in January 2002, the exchange rate was allowed to float (devaluating the peso by almost four times), inflation spiked to almost 40 percent, and GDP fell about 11.5 percent in 2002.[20] As Kehoe (2007) puts it, this was Argentina's "great depression."[21] After defaulting, Argentina slowly walked a long process of debt restructuring that started in 2005. The first round of debt swaps in 2005 moved 76 percent of bonds (with interest due by December 31, 2001) out of default. Additionally, by the end of 2005, Argentina repaid the entire stock of debt borrowed from the IMF (about $10 billion) since it was considered a "preferred creditor" (and had priority in being repaid). The second round of debt swaps in 2010 brought the total participation of bonds out of default to almost 92.3 percent. From that percentage, typically bondholders ended up receiving about 30 percent of the face value of bonds. The remainder 7.6 percent were the so-called "holdout" bondholders. These were bondholders that did not accept any of the two swaps and claimed in courts for full repayment of their bonds.

The details of this dispute can be intricate. Table 4.7 summarizes all the components of the holdouts. The so-called *pari passu* group comprises the group of holdouts represented by hedge funds that obtained a favorable ruling from Judge Thomas Griesa, from the US District Court for the Southern District of New York.[22]

---

19 This sequence can be summarized like this: (i) President Fernando de la Rúa resigned on December 20, 2001 after restricting withdrawals from banks; (ii) Ramón Puerta, president of the senate took office as interim president on December 21, 2001 while the Congress decided on the new president; (iii) Adolfo Rodríguez Saá was designated president on December 23, 2001; (iv) on December 30, 2001, President Rodríguez Saá resigned and Eduardo Camaño was designated interim president; (v) at midnight of January 1, 2002, Congress designed Eduardo Duhalde as the new president.

20 The necessary funds that were supporting the currency board, were coming from borrowing in dollars from private lenders or the IMF. In fact, according to Blustein (2006) and Tanzi (2007), without such borrowing, the system would have probably collapsed much sooner.

21 Kehoe (2007) analyzes the determinants of this collapse in Argentina and compares this episode with other depressions of the twentieth century.

22 Weidemaier and Gulati (2014) explain that they are called *pari passu* because they refer to a clause in sovereign bonds that is supposed to ensure equal treatment among equal creditors.

Table 4.7: Distribution of holdouts after the 2002 default of Argentina.

	Percentage
Pari passu group	0.6
"Me too" group	2.8
Litigants in other US courts	1.0
Litigants in ICSID	1.3
Litigants in other courts in Europe	0.3
Unknown identity (no litigants)	1.6
Total	7.6

Source: Porzecanski (2016) and Guzman (2020) based on Argentina's Ministry of Finance.
Note: ICSID is the International Centre for Settlement of Investment Disputes.

The so-called "me too" group are another group that got a favorable ruling from Judge Griesa. The ICSID group comprises bondholders that filed under the International Centre for Settlement of Investment Disputes. There were different solutions for each group, but all were eventually resolved. Interestingly, in July 2014, during the legal drama with the *pari passu* and the "me too" groups, Argentina, ended up missing payments of its debt, although on a lesser scale. Basically, Argentina sent the interest payments to the banks managing the cases in New York for them to pay the bondholders that accepted the restructure. However, Judge Griesa ruled that Argentina could not distribute funds unless the *pari passu* and the "me too" groups were paid on the defaulted debt. This put Argentina in *selective* default according to international risk agencies such as Standard & Poor's and Fitch.[23] Unfortunately, this was not the end of the dispute, and Argentina stayed in courts until 2016. The urgency of Argentina to return to international debt markets and Judge Griesa's ruling of February 2016, lifting the requirements to pay the holdouts, ended this saga. By the end of February 2016, Argentina finally announced settlements with all remaining holdout bondholders. Thus, in April 2016, Argentina was able to pay to the bondholders of 2005, 2010, and those that were still in default, putting an end to a 15-year standoff that had haunted Argentina since 2001.[24]

---

23 The categorization of selective refers to the fact that some bondholders were receiving payments while others were not.
24 Technically, after May 2016, there was still $1 billion defaulted bonds that remained unpaid. However, by November 2016 Argentina reached an agreement to pay the outstanding defaulted debt in January 2017.

Brazil: Cost of Doing Business

Informality is common in low- and middle-income countries. The distinctiveness of Latin America is that informality is unusually high. Loayza (2016) defines informality as a "set of firms, workers, and activities that operate outside the legal and regulatory framework or outside the modern economy." One way to capture this underground economy is to measure economic activities that should be measured but are not captured by national accounts as a percentage of GDP. Medina and Schneider (2018) present estimates of the "shadow" economy, defined as all economic activities that are hidden from official authorities for monetary, regulatory, and institutional reasons. Using their approach, in Argentina and Brazil about 25 percent and 36 percent of GDP, respectively, account for the production that is generated informally. With an average of 32 percent of GDP (and a median of 40 percent of GDP), Latin America is one of the regions with the highest share, only behind Sub-Saharan Africa. There are usually many methodological discussions regarding how to estimate these figures, but what is clear is that the informal sector in Latin America is large on both absolute and relative terms. Within Latin America, Brazil is of particular interest given the size of its economy.

The causes of informality are complex. They are usually associated with low productivity, lack of physical and human capital (La Porta and Shleifer, 2014), or can be the result of erratic and unsustainable governance (De Soto, 1989). At least part of the problem can be traced to the difficulty adhering to regulations. This is compounded by tax rates that are higher than the regional and global average and a cost of complying with the tax regulations that is considerably higher than the average. In a sense, this is encouraging informality. La Porta and Shleifer (2014) also suggest that, among other things, tax evasion and regulations are key elements for informality. In a similar way, Vuletin (2008) concludes that an inefficient tax system, rigid labor markets, large dependence on the agricultural sector, and inflation are key determinants of informality in Latin America. The essence of informality is that small businesses tend to be informal. An entrepreneur starts a small business and for some reason never registers it with the State. The World Bank, through the works of Simeon Djankov, has been developing an index measuring the ease of doing business by focusing on the regulatory environment and public services.[25]

Table 4.8 gives a sense of the difficulties of starting a business in Brazil and the region. The first column shows the number of procedures necessary to start a

---

25 See for instance, World Bank (2019).

Table 4.8: Starting a business in Latin America (2018).

	Procedures (number)	Time (days)	Cost (% of per capita income)	Rank
Argentina	11	11	5.3	119
Bolivia	14	43.5	46	156
Brazil	11	20.5	5	109
Chile	7	6	5.7	56
Colombia	8	11	14	65
Costa Rica	10	23	9.5	67
Ecuador	11	48.5	21.2	123
El Salvador	9	16.5	45.1	85
Guatemala	6	15	18.1	98
Honduras	11	13	40.7	121
Mexico	8	8.4	16.2	54
Nicaragua	7	14	63.6	132
Panama	5	6	5.4	79
Paraguay	7	35	40.3	113
Peru	8	24.5	9.9	68
Uruguay	5	6.5	22.6	95
Venezuela	20	230	391.3	188
Latin America	8.2	27.8	36.8	102

Source: World Bank (2019).

business. The regional average for Latin America is below 9, however Brazil shows 14 procedures. Of course, there is time associated with these procedures. While the regional average is 28 days, in Brazil it takes 21 days. That is still almost a month to fill out the necessary paperwork to start a business. Clearly, all that time has a monetary cost. While the regional average cost of starting a business is 37 percent of per capita income, interestingly, in Brazil that figure is 5, the lowest of Latin America. The World Bank also ranks all countries in the world for ease of starting a business. The average rank for a country in Latin America is 102, with Brazil ranked at 109. Even given the limitation of the data, the number of procedures and regulations puts a heavy burden on Brazilian firms that contributes to informality. However, this is not the end of the connection with informality since businesses also need to pay taxes. Table 4.9 uses data from the World Bank's annual *Paying Taxes* report. The regional average tax rate is about 46 percent. Interestingly, Argentina and Brazil (and Bolivia) are at the top, with the highest rates, all above 65 percent. Additionally, there is the time associated with complying with the tax law (in the second column). In Brazil, it takes an astonishing amount of 1,958 hours to comply with the tax law, that is, six times more than the average for Latin America and more than eight times the average for the world. Put another way, small

Table 4.9: Business taxes in Latin America (2018).

	Total tax (percentage)	Time to Comply (hours)	Number of payments
Argentina	106	312	9
Bolivia	83.7	1,025	42
Brazil	65.1	1,958	10
Chile	34	296	7
Colombia	71.9	256	11
Costa Rica	58.3	151	10
Ecuador	32.3	664	8
El Salvador	35.6	180	7
Guatemala	35.2	248	8
Honduras	44.4	224	48
Mexico	53	241	6
Nicaragua	60.6	201	43
Panama	37.2	408	36
Paraguay	35	378	20
Peru	36.8	260	9
Uruguay	41.8	163	20
Venezuela	64.6	792	70
Latin America	46.3	329	26
World	40.4	237	24

Source: World Bank (2019).

businesses in Brazil would need to have almost three months (of full-time work) and the resources to comply with the tax laws. It is difficult to imagine that businesses in Brazil would be able to afford such cost.

Another potential contributor to informality and low productivity can be the difficulty of complying with labor laws. In fact, recent studies by Busso et al. (2013), Loayza et al. (2005), Loayza (2018), and Ohanian et al. (2018) all conclude that labor market regulation can be a serious impediment to growth. In other words, a labor market that can rapidly adjust to a shock confers a number of benefits: faster recovery from recession, faster and less costly adjustment costs of technological change, and more productive matches between workers and jobs. Argentina and Brazil are no exception to this complex phenomenon of labor markets. To analyze this angle, we use a measure constructed by Gwartney et al. (2018) that ranks the countries of the world according to a variety of conditions in the labor market. This index combines six different variables including hiring regulations and the minimum wage; hiring and firing regulations; centralized collective bargaining; hours regulations; mandated cost of worker dismissal; and conscription. The combined index allows one to rank the countries based on the relative regulation of their labor markets. The results are shown in Table 4.10.

Table 4.10: Labor market regulation in Latin America.

	World Rank (2018)
Argentina	136
Bolivia	157
Brazil	153
Chile	142
Colombia	110
Costa Rica	102
Ecuador	141
El Salvador	152
Guatemala	156
Honduras	135
Mexico	117
Nicaragua	107
Panama	140
Paraguay	151
Peru	65
Uruguay	104
Venezuela	162
Latin America	131

Source: Fraser Institute based on Gwartney et al. (2018).

The average country in Latin America is ranked at number 131 out of 162 countries in the sample. In particular, Brazil is ranked 153 out of 162 countries, only behind Bolivia and Venezuela. There are three things that are quite striking. First, Latin America has relatively more regulated labor markets with respect to the world. Second, Brazil, appears significantly high in terms of labor market regulations. Third, this degree of regulation is consistent with the level of informality previously discussed for Brazil and Latin America. When employment in the formal labor market comprises a large number of rules and regulations, there seems to be a tendency of businesses to evade these regulations by operating in the shadow economy.[26] Although labor market regulations cannot be the sole explanation for the existence of the informal labor market, they might contribute to its existence.

---

26 Mondragón-Velez et al. (2010) argues how labor market rigidities increase the probability of transition into informality in Colombia.

Chapter 5
Chile, Colombia, Peru, and Uruguay

The Basics

With an area of 756,096 square kilometers and a population of approximately 18.7 million, Chile is ranked in fifth place in Latin America in terms of GDP with almost $300 billion.[1] Along its 4,270 kilometers of territory from north to south (but only 350 kilometers from west to east) between the Andes Mountains and the Pacific Ocean, Chile is endowed with a remarkable variety of climates and natural resources, particularly copper and nitrates. Furthermore, it is a leading food producer with large-scale agricultural. The Central Zone is the main metropolitan center that concentrates most of its population, fertile lands, and agricultural production. Chile has had border disputes with Peru, Bolivia, and Argentina. Maybe the one with Peru and Bolivia, in the context of the War of the Pacific in 1879, is the most significant one.[2] Additionally, in the northern area of the country, bordering with Argentina and Bolivia, the "lithium triangle" has one of the largest concentrations of reserves of lithium in the world. Chile is considered a high-income economy (with a GDP per capita of almost $16,000) with high levels of human development (see Table 5.1). Furthermore, it is one of the most stable countries in Latin America when ranked by a wide variety of indicators. Additionally, Chile was the second country from Latin America to join the OECD, in 2010.

Colombia has a total area of 1,141,748 square kilometers, a population of about 50 million, and is ranked in fourth place in Latin America in terms of GDP with approximately $334 billion.[3] Along its territory, which includes access to the Pacific Ocean and the Caribbean Sea, Colombia is one of the countries with the highest biodiversity in the world and harbors the majority of Earth's species. It comprises the Amazon rainforest, highlands, grassland, deserts, and islands and coastlines. The Andes are the prevailing geographical feature that defines the regions of the country, with most of the population in cities in the highlands. Colombia is endowed with a diverse stock of natural resources, such as fuel, oils, and agricultural products, and most of its electricity production comes from

---

1 Chile also controls Easter Island, Juan Fernández Islands, and Sala y Gómez Island, all of which are in the Pacific Ocean to the east of the French Polynesia.

2 We will address this historical event when discussing Bolivia in the next chapter.

3 The Archipelago of San Andres – two island groups in the Caribbean Sea – is also under control of Colombia.

https://doi.org/10.1515/9783110674934-005

renewable energy sources (about 70 percent is obtained from hydroelectric generation). With a GDP per capita of $6,700, Colombia is regarded as one of the most stable economies in the region, having recently been admitted to the OECD group of countries in 2020.

Peru covers an area of 1,285,216 square kilometers and is the 19th largest country in the world. With a population of almost 32 million it is ranked in 6th place in Latin America in terms of GDP with approximately $222 billion. The history of the territory of Peru is a vast one, which would require a self-study of the topic: it hosted the oldest civilization in the Americas at about 3,000 BC and the largest state in pre-Columbian America. Most of the population lives in urban areas, with Lima, the capital city, capturing almost one-third of the entire population. Peru has a large diversity of climates with tropical areas, the arid plains of the coast, the Andes mountains, deserts, two ocean currents, and the tropical Amazon rainforest to the east of the Amazon river. Peru's stock of reserves of copper, gold, and zinc are one of the most distinctive features of the economy since its inception. Peru is considered an upper middle-income level country (with a GDP per capita of almost $7,000) and one of the world's fastest growing economies since 2002 with an average rate of 5 percent per year.

Uruguay is the second smallest country in South America and the eleventh smallest in Latin America, with an area of 176,215 square kilometers. Its population is about 3.5 million of whom half live in the metropolitan area of its capital city, Montevideo. In terms of its size, the Uruguayan economy is ranked 13th with a GDP of just over $60 billion, among the smallest in Latin America. Uruguay has a uniform climate, mostly humid subtropical, with some sections considered oceanic. This feature makes for very pronounced seasonal variations. Uruguay's landscape includes low hills and rolling plains with a coastal line of about 660 kilometers. Although it is one of the world's main producers of soybeans, wool, horse meat, and beeswax, beef is the main single export commodity of the country. As an interesting fact, in 2007 the USDA estimated that the Uruguayan cattle heard was approximately 12 million head, which implied the highest number of cattle per capita in the world with a ratio of 3.5. Uruguay is regarded as a high-income country (with a GDP per capita of $17,300) with one of the most stable democracies, low levels of inequality and poverty, low perception of corruption, and most socially advanced countries in Latin America (see Table 5.1).

Figure 5.1 shows that for the last two decades, Chile, Colombia, Peru, and Uruguay have been growing at 3.7, 3.8, 4.6, and 2.6 percent, respectively, compared to a rate of 3.1 for Latin America. Interestingly, from 1999 to 2019, GDP per capita (measured in 2005 PPP dollars) increased for the region about 47 percent, while Chile, Colombia, Peru, and Uruguay increased 70, 67, 106, and 61 percent,

Table 5.1: Population, GDP, GDP per capita, poverty, and inequality in Chile, Colombia, Peru, Uruguay, and Latin America.

	Population (millions)	GDP (millions of USD)	GDP per capita (USD)	Poverty ($5.5 per day)	Poverty percentage (year)	Income inequality (Gini coefficient)	Inequality-adjusted education index
Chile	18.7	298	15,925	3.7	8.6	0.44	0.71
Colombia	49.6	334	6,719	27.8	27.0	0.50	0.55
Peru	32.0	222	6,941	22.1	20.5	0.43	0.57
Uruguay	3.4	60	17,278	2.9	8.1	0.40	0.68
Central America	*47.8*	*257*	*6,656*	*30.5*	*36.7*	*0.47*	*0.46*
Latin America	*644.1*	*5,972*	*9,272*	*23.3*	*33.8*	*0.46*	*0.56*

Source: World Bank (2020), Economic Commission for Latin America and the Caribbean (ECLAC) (2019), United Nations Development Programme (UNDP) (2019).

Notes: Population, GDP, GDP per capita from 2018. Poverty from 2018, excepting Guatemala, Nicaragua, and Venezuela from 2014. Poverty percentage from 2018, excepting Bolivia, Chile, and Panama from 2017, Guatemala from 2014, Nicaragua from 2015, and Venezuela from 2019. Income inequality from 2018, excepting Guatemala, Nicaragua, and Venezuela 2014. Inequality-adjusted education index from 2018.

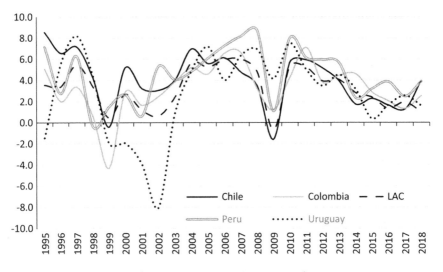

Figure 5.1: Economic growth (real GDP annual growth, percentage).
Source: World Bank (2020).
Note: LAC is the simple average of 17 countries in Latin America, excluding the Caribbean.

respectively. Hence, all of the countries in this group grew more than the average for Latin America. Figure 5.1 shows the evolution of the growth rate for Chile, Colombia, Peru, Uruguay, and the average of Latin America. Let us try to understand the details of these interesting performances.

Since the early 1990s, Chile has been following a set of policies and reforms that promote trade openness, financial integration, control of inflation, an exchange rate regime with bands, and fiscal discipline. After the Asian and the Russian crises of 1997 and 1998, the Chilean economy suffered a sudden stop of capital inflows and a deterioration of the terms of trade. Faced this pressure, in September 1999, the central bank adopted a floating exchange rate regime, ultimately only targeting the inflation rate. Additionally, during 1999, after a drop in private expenditures that were affecting aggregate demand, Chile implemented counter-cyclical fiscal policies, such as government-sponsored temporary employment programs, which were possible due to savings from the previous expansionary period.

Fiscal arrangements in Chile are a key element of the landscape of policies. In fact, in 2000, Chile introduced a fiscal rule to show commitment to fiscal responsibility. The basic idea was to smooth fiscal expenditures and the price of copper to prevent excessive fluctuations during periods of crises and booms. In order to work against the cycle, this rule planned to generate savings during good times so the government could increase spending during bad times. As Caputo and

Saravia (2018) argue, the introduction of this rule also improved the credibility of the government that would operate with a transparent framework that reduces policy uncertainty. This development strategy was successful at fostering growth and macroeconomic stability despite some vulnerabilities associated with external shocks. It was not until the global financial crisis (GFC) that Chile experienced a new episode of instability. The GFC of 2008 affected Chilean export prices and volumes, and thus, aggregate demand. Similar to 1999, Chile was able to implement counter-cyclical policies again, such as temporary income tax reductions, temporary housing projects, increases of public spending, support for small and medium enterprises, and support to strategic sectors.[4] After one year of contraction in 2009, the Chilean economy was able to quickly recover the growth path based on a combination of policies: a fiscal rule, an inflation targeting framework, a sound financial system, and the implementation of a stimulus plan. Since then, Chile has been growing at an average 3.3 percent per year, compared to a 2.9 percent for Latin America.

From a long run perspective, Colombia has had a stable growth pattern. In the first half of the 1990s Colombia experienced a credit boom associated with an expansion of the financial system (in terms of loans and number of intermediaries). Unfortunately, this quick expansion was followed by an imperfect financial liberalization that affected the quality of bank loans and elevated the financial fragility of the economy. At the end of the 1990s, it experienced a significant slowdown as a result of the Asian and the Russian crises of 1997 and 1998, its first recession in more than 60 years. By 1999, a sudden stop of capital inflows affected the exchange rate, contracting the aggregate demand. The combination of a higher cost of credit, with the expectations of a devaluation of the peso ended up increasing the domestic interest rates. This was the start of a financial crisis: according to Gomez-Gonzalez and Kiefer (2009), the ratio of non-performing loans to total loans (a proxy of loan quality) deteriorated from 7.9 percent in mid-1998 to 16 percent by the end of 1999. The government capitalized some financial institutions, and others were closed. In the midst of this financial crisis, the central bank switched to a floating exchange rate regime. It was a *twin* crisis: financial and currency. Furthermore, in July 1999, in an effort to prevent more exchange rate volatility and to increase confidence, Colombia signed, for the first time, an extended facility arrangement with the International Monetary Fund (IMF). Interestingly enough, this was a relatively short-lived economic crisis. By 2000, an economic recovery started, benefiting

---

4 According to Kacef and Jiménez (2009), the cost of these measures was approximately 3 percent of GDP, of which 46 percent was channeled into tax cuts and benefits.

from external factors such as the price of petroleum (and coffee, to a lesser degree). The expansion observed during the period 2000 to 2008 represented an average of 4.2 percent per year achieved by a combination of prudential fiscal management, an inflation-targeting framework with a flexible exchange rate regime, and the supercycle of commodities. The GFC was the end of this expansionary cycle for Colombia, creating a slowdown without a full crisis. Following the policy response of many countries at that time, Colombia pursued a variety of counter-cyclical measures to contain the crisis. Argüello (2011) lists, among other measures, policies regarding interest rates, government spending on infrastructure, and public debt financing. This was another relatively short episode for Colombia, which by 2010 recovered pre-GFC growth levels. The last ten years have seen Colombia growing at an average 3.6 percent per year, compared to a 2.9 percent for Latin America.

When aggregating the period 1999 to 2019, the Peruvian economy shows possibly one of the strongest growth rates in Latin America. Its GDP per capita (measured in 2005 PPP dollars) doubled during that period. Despite the fact that most of the growth is concentrated from 2002 to 2012, there is some justification to denote this decade as a "Peruvian miracle." Let us get into the details.

Similar to most countries in Latin America, Peru experienced the consequences of the Asian and Russian crises of 1997 and 1998. Capital inflows fell sharply from 1997 to 2001 with a significant deterioration of the terms of trade. This slowed down Peruvian GDP in 1998, but by 2002 it was at similar levels of 1997. From 2002 to 2012, the Peruvian economy enjoyed its strongest growth in decades. During this period a combination of factors can be noted. For instance, a strong domestic investment and private consumption, and fast return of capital inflows. Additionally, a strong demand for Peruvian exports (higher volumes and prices) and favorable terms of trade (probably the highest in the last two decades). In fact, this strong export sector significantly contributed to tax revenues through income taxes, allowing the government to improve its fiscal performance and achieve a reduction of its fiscal deficit and public debt.

The GFC was responsible for a slowdown in 2009 (from a growth rate of 8.7 in 2008 to 1.0 percent in 2009), but the Peruvian economy was able to rapidly bounce back to a strong path of growth in 2010.[5] The ability of the Peruvian economy to navigate and rapidly overcome the GFC is rooted in the fiscal savings and foreign exchange reserves buffers accumulated over almost a decade,

---

5 Morón et al. (2009) argue that most of this recession or slowdown can be explained by a fall in demand for Peruvian exports, a drop in remittances from abroad, and shortage of investment and external credit.

with the timely counter-cyclical policies that the government implemented. In particular, the government allowed for corporate income tax reductions, increases in public spending for infrastructure and housing, and support for small and medium enterprises and strategic sectors. The costs of these interventions were estimated by the IMF (2013) at about 4.0 percent of GDP. Additionally, the central bank increased the liquidity in the system, and implemented a reduction of the interest rate. All these policies proved successful and by 2010 Peru was back on its growth path. During the period 1999 to 2012, the Peruvian economy had a strong performance, with a real GDP that expanded 95 percent, significantly above the average of the region (61 percent), and a GDP per capita that grew 76 percent. In the last period, 2013 to 2019, Peru has expanded about 26 percent, comparable to 15 percent for the average of Latin America.

After the Asian and Russian crises of 1997 and 1998, Uruguay entered a period of slowdown, mostly associated with a sudden stop of capital inflows and a gradual depreciation of its currency. However, the cornerstone of the analysis for Uruguay is associated with the devaluation of the Brazilian real in 1999 (that created a deterioration of the terms of trade) and the collapse of the Argentine economy at the end of 2001. During these years, Uruguay was vulnerable to external shocks from Argentina and Brazil due to the strong commercial and financial linkages between these countries (Sosa, 2010). The financial crisis and default in Argentina, ignited a massive bank run in Uruguay, that eventually led to a floating exchange rate regime, creating a temporary but steep devaluation of the currency. During this period, from 1999 to 2002, the Uruguayan economy contracted about 13 percent and unemployment climbed to 20 percent. In the context of these financial, debt, and currency crises, the Uruguayan government designed an operation that included an IMF program (to regain credibility and support) and a debt exchange program (that lengthened the maturities of bonds while avoiding reductions to the amount of the principal or coupons).

Since 2003, Uruguay rapidly began its longest growth period in many years. As Marandino and Oddone (2018) explain, the combination of a strong external demand for Uruguayan products, the boom of commodities prices, and favorable financial conditions were largely responsible for this period of growth. Interestingly enough, the GFC did not have a significant effect on the Uruguayan economy: there was a slowdown in the growth rate in 2009, which was rapidly reverted in 2010. As Ocampo (2017) argues, Uruguay was among the leading Latin American countries in terms of public expenditures during the crisis, a factor that could explain the relatively stable performance of the economy during this period. Similar to other countries in the region, Uruguay implemented counter-cyclical fiscal policies, such as increases in public spending for infrastructure and housing, and support to small and medium enterprises and agricultural producers. From

2002 to 2012, the Uruguayan GDP grew 63 percent, above the average of the region (53 percent), while its GDP per capita grew 63 percent.

The last period of analysis from 2012 to 2019 exhibits a similar pattern across countries, characterized by a gradual slowdown that has not materialized into a recession, but speaks of a marked deceleration of Latin American economies. The main characteristics of this period are the reduction of the demand for Latin American products and a generalized drop of international commodities prices.

From all this information, an interesting picture emerges. First, while Chile, Peru, and, to a lesser degree, Colombia, were above the average growth rate in Latin America, Uruguay performed below that average. This was mostly the result of Uruguay facing a severe crisis in 2002 but a relatively minor slowdown during the GFC (see Figure 5.1). Second, in the last two decades all four countries were able to increase their income per capita, considerably more than the average of the region. The best example is Peru, which was able to double its GDP per capita since 1999.

To analyze how this group of countries performed in terms of their income gap relative to the rest of the world, we follow Birdsall et al.'s (2008) methodology. Panel A in Table 5.2 traces the evolution of this gap relative to the world's most advanced economies (in terms of health, education, and income).[6] Relative to most developed countries, Chile, Peru, and Uruguay were able to increase their level of development since 1990. Colombia, on the other hand, seems to be at the same level after almost three decades. Panel B in Table 5.2 traces the evolution of this gap relative to countries with a similar level of development. Since 2000, Chile, Colombia, and Peru have not been able to close the gap. Uruguay might be seen as an exception. However, when analyzed since 1990 this picture speaks of an extensive period when these four Latin American countries have not progressed as much relative to other countries of a similar level of development. Finally, Panel C in Table 5.2 traces the evolution of this gap relative to the average of Latin America. In this case, we observe some interesting patterns. First, Chile, Colombia, and Uruguay were above the average for Latin America in 1990 and still were in 2018. Second, Chile and Peru, to a lesser extent, are the two countries that improved their performance, relative to where they were three decades ago. Third, although it remains above the average performance

---

6 Based on the Human Development Index, we first construct an equally weighted subindex of health, education, and income. The most developed countries are those in the top decile of this subindex. Countries are classified as having a similar level of development if they are ranked in the same decile of this subindex. Finally, Latin American countries is the average of the 17 countries within Latin America. A greater figure implies a better performance with one being the threshold when the comparison renders the same.

Table 5.2: Income gap based on relative GDP per capita.

	1990	2000	2010	2018
Panel A: Most developed countries				
Chile	0.27	0.30	0.46	0.48
Colombia	0.26	0.20	0.26	0.27
Peru	0.12	0.13	0.23	0.25
Uruguay	0.32	0.30	0.40	0.42
Panel B: Similar level of development				
Chile	0.79	0.59	1.25	0.60
Colombia	1.15	0.49	0.78	0.52
Peru	0.55	0.42	0.71	0.49
Uruguay	0.92	0.59	1.08	0.90
Panel C: Latin American countries				
Chile	1.38	1.53	1.75	1.83
Colombia	1.29	0.99	0.98	1.02
Peru	0.62	0.68	0.89	0.95
Uruguay	1.62	1.54	1.52	1.62

Source: World Bank (2020), United Nations Development Programme (UNDP) (2019) based on Birdsall et al. (2008).
Note: A value of 1 represents absence of income gap, while a value smaller (greater) than 1 implies a negative (positive) gap. Individual GDP per capita in 2011 dollars at purchasing power parity relative to the average of each comparison group of countries. *Most developed countries* refers to the group of countries in the top decile of a subindex of health, education, and income of the Human Development Index. *Similar level of development* refers to the group of countries in the same decile of a subindex of health, education, and income of the Human Development Index. *Latin American countries* refers to the group of countries from Latin America in a subindex of health, education, and income of the Human Development Index.

of Latin America, Colombia decreased its gap relative to 1990. Finally, Uruguay remained practically at the same levels, relative to the average country in Latin America, for the past three decades.

Poverty and inequality have followed a declining trend in Chile, Colombia, Peru, and Uruguay in the last 20 years. However, there is some heterogeneity in this behavior. Chile and Colombia show a consistent improvement in their levels of poverty and income inequality since 2000, with some exceptions during the GFC. In the case of Chile, an increase in the inflation rate during the GFC, as a consequence of international food price surges, prevented further decreases of poverty. In the case of Colombia, the GFC slowed the flow of remittances received by the country, leading to lower levels of household income. The aftermath of the Asian and Russian crises in Peru led to increases in the number of people living in poverty at the beginning of the 2000s, but later to a consistent decrease until 2018. This pattern of poverty reduction was not affected by the GFC. Finally, in Uruguay, the combination of the contraction of the economy at the beginning of the 2000s with the subsequent financial crisis in 2002 led to increases in poverty indicators. Only after the economy returned to positive growth rates did poverty levels start a downward trend until recent years. In fact, it took an entire decade to return to the poverty levels of 2000, with almost no effect of the GFC. This downward trend in poverty observed in all countries is consistent with an increase in labor earnings, as argued by Cruces et al. (2017), and with the use of government programs to support the vulnerable population. Cash transfer programs, in particular, have played an important role in the fight against poverty in Chile, Colombia, Peru, and Uruguay. For instance, conditional cash transfers programs like Chile Solidario in Chile, Mas Familias en Acción in Colombia, Juntos in Peru, the Plan de Asistencia Nacional a la Emergencia Social (Panes) and Asignaciones Familiares – Plan de Equidad in Uruguay, contributed to explaining the reduction in poverty and income inequality. In Table 5.1, using the absolute measure of 5.5 dollars per day, a global standard of poverty, Chile and Uruguay have 3.7 and 2.9 percent, respectively, of their population living in poverty conditions, while Colombia and Peru have 27.8 and 22.1 percent, respectively.[7] These figures compare with 23.3 percent for Latin America, and almost 31 percent for the average country in Central America. When using the official poverty line, the figures for Chile and Uruguay look similar at about 8.6 and 8.1 percent of the population, while Colombia and Peru still have 27 and 20.5 percent, respectively. These poverty trends usually follow the evolution of the economy, particularly that of GDP. However, as Cruces et al. (2017) explain, the differences between these poverty lines could also be due to fluctuations in food prices, key elements in official poverty lines. Furthermore,

---

7 The World Bank has an international poverty line for upper middle-income countries (most of Latin American countries) that captures the concept of absolute poverty by setting a threshold of 5.5 dollar-a-day (in 2011 PPP terms). Absolute poverty is defined as the lack of monetary resources to meet certain basic needs of human existence. Official poverty lines are based on household surveys with population weighted averages and include more comprehensive structures of basic needs. Despite considerable improvement and harmonization of household surveys in Latin America, comparison across countries might not be perfect.

income inequality, measured by the Gini coefficient, also experienced a relative decline but still remains high.[8] In particular, Chile and Peru have similar coefficients at 0.44 and 0.43, respectively, with Colombia at 0.50 and Uruguay at 0.40 (one of the lowest scores for Latin America), while the whole region is at 0.46. The distribution of income can be influenced by the distribution of human capital. Thus, the distribution of human capital is influenced by the distribution of educational opportunities. Using the inequality-adjusted education index, Chile shows the highest score of the group with 0.71, followed by Uruguay at 0.68, while Colombia and Peru have similar scores to the average of Latin America at 0.56.[9] That is, Chile and Uruguay show a less unequal distribution of education compared to Colombia and Peru. However, it is worth noting that this information is based on the number of years (*quantity*) of education obtained, but might be less informative about the quality of education.

The Macroeconomic Record

The macroeconomic discussion in these countries is inevitably linked to the inflation dynamic, at least since 1990. Let us get into the details since not all countries in this group went through similar experiences. On the one hand, there are Chile and Colombia, and on the other hand Peru and Uruguay. After inflation reached a high of 26 percent, Chile adopted an inflation-targeting framework with controls to reduce the inflow of capitals. It was one of the first developing countries to adopt this monetary policy, setting the first de facto target in 1991. Among other things, this policy increased the independence of the monetary authority and required the preservation of the value of the currency. The strategy proved

---

8 Income inequality is usually measured using the Gini coefficient. The Gini coefficient is a measure of the deviation of the actual income distribution from perfect equality. It ranges from 0 to 1, 0 being perfect equality and 1 implying perfect inequality. No country in the world conforms to either extreme. There are at least two caveats regarding the use of the Gini coefficient. The Gini coefficient does not capture subgroup (region, ethnic group, etc.) changes and puts equal weight to the entire distribution. That means that the lower end of the distribution has a similar weight in the index than the upper end. This feature could be masking important changes in the dynamics of the distribution.

9 The inequality-adjusted education index is the HDI education index value adjusted for inequality in the distribution of years of schooling of the adult population, drawn from household surveys (UNDP, 2019). The inequality dimension is estimated by the Atkinson measure, capturing subgroup (region, ethnic group, etc.) changes and putting more weight to the lower end of the distribution. This index is constructed by the UNDP and ranges from 0 (most unequal) to 1 (most equal) in terms of education equality.

successful, and reduced inflation from 26 percent in 1990 to 3.3 percent in 1999. In fact, both inflation and the target were reduced. After 1999, the central bank decided to keep inflation at about 3 percent by using a target but also a lower and an upper bound of 2 and 4 percent, respectively. This mechanism was more consistent with traditional schemes of inflation targeting. Although it could be argued that the reduction of inflation was a common feature in the 1990s, there is vast evidence that suggests inflation-targeting countries were able to reduce inflation more than non-targeting countries. Additionally, capital controls, such as reserve requirements for foreign loans and taxes on foreign currency loans, helped the Chilean economy when the Asian and Russian crises arrived.

By the 2000s, the central bank of Chile was operating under an inflation-targeting framework with a floating exchange rate and relying on the interest rate as the only instrument for monetary policy. Since then, until the end of the period of analysis, the inflation rate for Chile has been averaging 3.2 percent, which is slightly above the official target of 3 percent, but significantly lower than the average for Latin America. Despite the GFC created a period of high volatility for inflation, the overall performance reflects a low and controlled rate. During 1990 and 1992, Colombia navigated a period of structural reforms that reshaped institutions. Among other things, these reforms included trade liberalization, labor reform, and capital account openness with an increase of the independence of the central bank. Furthermore, from 1991 to 1998, the central bank and the government of Colombia also implemented policies to expand the degree of financial development. During this period, the inflation rate decreased from a high of 31 percent in 1991 to 18 percent in 1998. When Colombia suffered a sudden stop in capital inflows during the Asian and Russian crises, the exchange rate came under pressure and the central bank decided to focus on inflation letting the exchange rate float. In 1999, after abandoning the exchange rate regime (a crawling peg) in place since the late 1960s, Colombia started the process to adopt a *full-fledged* inflation-targeting framework, establishing a long-term goal of 3 percent.[10] This policy was successful enough to keep inflation under control since then, with a minor increase during the GFC. Inflation went down from 9 percent in 1999 to 3.6 in 2019, slightly above the long-term target (see Panel A in Table 5.3).

---

10 During this process, the monetary policy was based on interest rates as the sole instrument, considering the inflation targeting, with minimal exchange rate intervention just to accrue international reserves as needed. The formal definition of *full-fledged* inflation targeting assumes that authorities committed to a specific inflation rate or range within a time frame, they regularly announce their targets, and have institutional arrangements to make sure they meet their targets.

On the other hand, Peru and Uruguay have gone through periods of substantial inflation for many years. At the end of the 1980s, Peru was going through a considerable hyperinflation, with an annual rate of about 3,400 in 1989. This unsustainable situation was dragging the economic and political conflicts of the last years of the first presidency of President Alan Garcia. By 1990, Alberto Fujimori took office and implemented a plan to stabilize the economy ("the Fuji shock"). It was a combination of an exchange rate stabilization policy with monetary, fiscal, and wages policies (known as a monetary-based stabilization program.)[11] This program ran in parallel with an agenda of structural reforms, which included, among other things, market deregulation, removal of price controls, and subsidies to interest rates, capital market liberalization, and unification of the exchange market. Eventually, this program brought inflation down, from almost 7,500 percent in 1990 to 400 percent in 1991 to 73 in 1992, but at a slow pace. There are many arguments that could help understand the slow pace, but one that resonates with scholars studying these processes is the one associated with the degree of dollarization of the economy. Kiguel and Liviatan (1995) argue that the high degree of dollarization (about 82 percent of loans denominated in US dollars) might have discouraged the government from using inflationary taxation, because of the potential cost of a relapse. In any case, Martinelli and Vega (2018) show that although slower and harder to manage than an exchange rate-based stabilization program, Peru's monetary-based programs proved more resilience to external financial crises.

As a result of the Asian and Russian crises of 1997 and 1998, Peru also experienced a sudden stop of capital inflows and a *credit crunch* (shortage of funds). Martinelli and Vega (2018) explain that as a result of these factors, inflation dropped to 1.9 percent by 2001, with some signs of deflation. In this context, the central bank adopted an inflation-targeting framework in 2002 before pursuing an expansionary monetary policy. It was a very particular case, since the adoption of this framework aimed to *increase* inflation (to the desired target of 2.5 percent). Similar to the case of Colombia, the effect on inflation of the GFC was temporary, and only felt in 2008 when the target was missed. The average inflation since adopting the inflation-targeting framework in 2002 has been 2.7 percent, less than half of the average for the region.

The case of Uruguay has many similarities to what happened in Argentina. By 1990, the annual inflation rate topped 113 percent when the government started the implementation of a stabilization plan introducing a crawling peg

---

11 A distinctive feature from this stabilization program was the use of money as the *anchor* in combination with an administered exchange rate.

with a fiscal adjustment. Overall, this exchange rate-based stabilization was successful to reduce inflation, which was brought down from 134 percent at the beginning of 1991 to less than 10 percent in October 1998. This was the first time since 1956 that Uruguay experienced a single-digit inflation rate.

Nevertheless, the impact of the Asian and Russian crises, was particularly disruptive for Uruguay. However, the first signs that a slowdown was coming to the Southern Cone arrived after the devaluation of the real in Brazil. These crises produced a stall in capital inflows, tightening the external financial needs, and pressuring the exchange rate regime. When Argentina defaulted on its debt in December 2001, this led to a bank run on deposits in Uruguay (from residents and non-residents). This put a lot of pressure on the central bank that tried to defend the system using international reserves. To make things worse, De Brun and Licandro (2006) argue that although there was no formal deposit insurance in place, there was a perception that the government would follow previous episodes bailing the financial system out in case of a bank run. The continued reduction of international reserves further challenged the commitment to the exchange rate regime and the sustainability of the policies. By July of 2002, this process ended up with a banking crisis that forced the abandonment of the regime for a floating alternative, with a temporary but steep initial devaluation of the peso.[12] Interestingly enough, although inflation immediately increased, reaching almost 20 percent in 2003, it rapidly went down to less than 10 percent and stayed at an average of 8 percent until 2019. Even though there is some discussion about when it was officially introduced, in 2004 the central bank announced the intention to follow a target for the inflation within a range of 6 to 8 percent. Later, in 2007, the framework got the traditional shape of a full-fledged inflation targeting regime with the policy rate as the main monetary instrument, increasing the credibility and transparency of the monetary authority. The GFC of 2008–2009 did not have a significant effect on inflation for Uruguay; it was mostly concentrated on the reduction of the demand for some exports, and the sudden stop of capital inflows. Even during the period 2011 to 2017, when the inflation rate was above the target of 8 percent, inflation never reached double digits.

At this point, an interesting feature to highlight is the extent of the independence of the monetary authority. Let us recall that a key element of a sound macroeconomic policy is the capacity of the central bank to freely pursue monetary policy. Several authors have analyzed how even for developing countries, there is a negative relationship between the degree of independence of the central bank

---

12 This was the end of the use of the exchange rate as a nominal anchor and started a period where the monetary base would be the nominal anchor for the economy.

Table 5.3: Inflation rate and Central Bank independence.

	1990–1999	2000–2009	2010–2019*
Panel A: Inflation rate, percentage			
Chile	11.8	3.5	2.8
Colombia	22.1	6.3	3.8
Peru	807.9	2.6	2.8
Uruguay	48.9	8.6	8.0
Central America	*15.4*	*6.6*	*3.6*
Latin America	*140.1*	*8.2*	*483.9*
*Latin America****	*145.5*	*7.5*	*4.7*
Panel B: Central Bank independence index (Garriga, 2016)			
Chile	0.82	0.82	0.82
Colombia	0.61	0.69	0.69
Peru	0.72	0.80	0.80
Uruguay	0.41	0.59	0.63
Central America	*0.51*	*0.64*	*0.64*
Latin America	*0.57*	*0.59*	*0.62*
*Latin America****	*0.56*	*0.59*	*0.61*

* = 2010–2014 in Panel B; ** = without Venezuela
Source: World Bank (2020) and Garriga (2016).
Note: The Garriga (2016) index goes from 0 to 1, with 0 being completely dependent and 1 being independent.

and the inflation rate. Panel B in Table 5.3 presents the Garriga (2016) index that goes from 0 to 1, with 0 being completely dependent and 1 being independent. Until the mid-1990s, Uruguay was the country with the lowest degree of independence from this group, about 0.18. Marandino and Oddone (2018) describe that, in 1995, Congress approved a law limiting the capacity of the central bank to lend to the Treasury to avoid inflationary financing. These modifications implied an increase of the Garriga index to 0.71 in 1995. However, not all of these measures were kept throughout this period, and after removing some of them in 1997, the index dropped to 0.58, and remained unchanged until 2008. Panel B in Table 5.3 shows that the average index for Uruguay during the 1990s and 2000s were 0.41 and 0.59, compared to 0.57 and 0.59 for Latin America, respectively. Only during the last decade from 2010 to 2019, Uruguay was able to move above the average of the region.[13]

Other components of the macroeconomic record, closely related to what we just discussed, are the fiscal and debt dynamics. Let us start with Chile. Maybe the most central aspect of the Chilean fiscal policy is its counter-cyclicality. In 2000, the Chilean government introduced a fiscal rule setting the target of the structural surplus at 1 percent of GDP.[14] This target was later adjusted to 0.5 percent in 2008 and to 0 percent in 2009 in the midst of the GFC. The basic idea was to avert procyclicality in fiscal policy and encourage the accumulation of resources for "bad times."[15] Although it was not a formal rule until 2005 (when a fiscal responsibility law was approved), this mechanism increased the credibility of the policymakers by reducing uncertainty and stabilizing public expenditure. As Caputo and Saravia (2018) explain, until the GFC of 2008, when the price of copper was high, the government generated fiscal savings. In 2009, Chile embarked on a series of counter-cyclical policies to counteract the GFC, switching the positive result to a negative fiscal balance. Until 2009, Chile was also able to keep its public debt at relatively low levels (6 percent of GDP), even for OECD standards. What happened after 2010 is mainly linked to a prolonged period of economic weakness and lower copper prices.

Panel A in Figure 5.2 shows that the fiscal balance recovered in 2010 and 2011 but since then has been running a deficit, with an average of –1.1 percent of GDP from 2011 to 2019. Additionally, there has been a sustained increase of the central government's gross debt: since 2007 it rose from 4 percent to 28 percent of GDP in 2019. The IMF (2018) estimates that since 2011, Chile has suffered a 3 percent GDP loss in copper revenues as a result of declining prices that has contributed to this situation.

At the end of the 1990s, the fiscal situation of Colombia was delicate, with a fiscal deficit of almost 5.5 percent of GDP largely financed with (non-investment grade) public debt. After the 1999 crisis, Colombia was starting a new era with a floating exchange rate, and a monetary policy focused on controlling inflation.

---

13 During this period, there were a sequence of reforms to the charter of the central bank, including the creation of the monetary policy committee, which granted greater technical independence to the central bank, also increasing the Garriga index from 0.58 to 0.63.

14 A structural fiscal deficit is the fiscal deficit that would exist should the economy grow at its potential output.

15 *Procyclicality* implies pursuing an expansionary monetary or fiscal policy during "good times" of the economy, or a contractionary monetary or fiscal policy during "bad times." Counter-cyclicality, on the other hand, refers to a contractionary monetary or fiscal policy during "good times", in order to save for expansionary policies during "bad times."

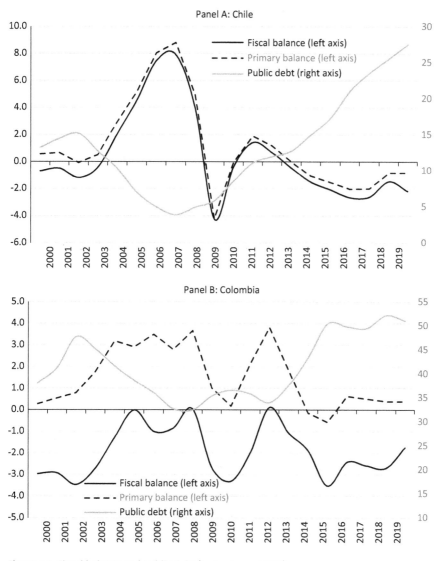

Figure 5.2: Fiscal balance and public debt (percentage of GDP).
Source: World Bank (2020) and International Monetary Fund (2020b).

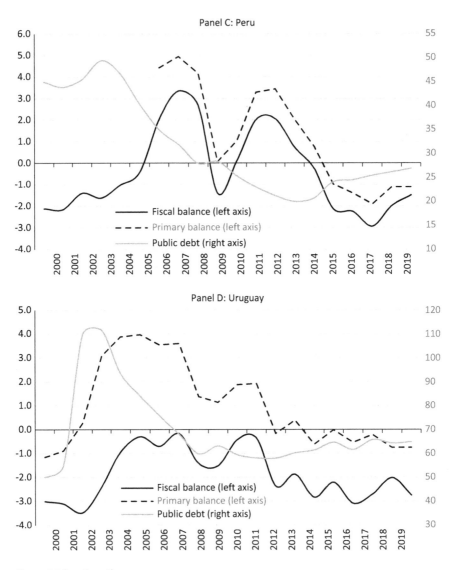

Figure 5.2 (continued)

By 2001, the central bank started the implementation of a full-fledged inflation-targeting framework that would coincide with the start of the longest expansionary period. After the public debt reached almost 40 percent of GDP (see Panel B in Figure 5.2), exposing the country to external shocks and exchange rate volatility, Colombia passed a fiscal responsibility law to define a medium-term fiscal framework. As Perez-Reyna and Osorio (2018) explain, this implied a commitment to a rule that constrained fiscal policy with a 10-year horizon and with public debt ceilings. There is broad agreement that this institutional arrangement was successful in containing the fiscal deficit and public debt during the 2004 to 2008 period. In fact, during the GFC, Colombia was able to pursue counter-cyclical measures to contain the crisis, in contrast to the crisis of 1999, mainly because the fiscal result was balanced by 2008 and public debt was at 32 percent of GDP (its lowest point in 10 years). During 2008 and 2009, there were programs towards infrastructure, social protection, financial credit lines, and housing that expanded the deficit back to 3.3 percent of GDP. It was in 2011 that Colombia adopted a more formal fiscal rule for the distribution of oil royalties and with specific targets for the structural fiscal deficit of 2.3 percent of GDP by 2014, and below 1 percent after 2022. Although Colombia's tax system has gone through a variety of reforms in 2012, 2014, 2016, and 2018, they all tried to improve revenues while meeting key spending needs under the fiscal rule. Unfortunately, the significant reduction in commodity prices, particularly that of oil revenues after 2014, has led to an adverse dynamic of public debt that reached 52 percent of GDP in 2019.

After going through a sequence of structural reforms in the 1990s, the Peruvian economy was able to attain consistent foreign direct investment (FDI), stable economic growth, and low inflation. At the beginning of 2002, the central bank adopted an inflation-targeting framework in a financially dollarized setting. It was an unusual move at that time, for an economy with a high degree of liabilities in dollars to adopt an inflation-targeting scheme.[16] However, to deal with the risks associated with this high degree of dollarization, the central bank promoted a series of policies to reduce the volatility of the dollar while keeping inflation under control. Additionally, the period between 2000 until the arrival of the GFC in 2008 was characterized by strong demand for Peruvian products for exports, mostly associated with natural resources.[17] During this period, Peru was able to adjust its fiscal accounts by almost 4 percentage points of GDP; that is, from a fiscal deficit of 1.4 percentage of GDP in 2002 to a surplus of 3.4 in 2007 (see Panel C in Figure 5.2). Moreover, the Peruvian economy started developing a debt market in domestic currency (the sol) while pre-paying external debt. According to the IMF (2016), Peru was able to lengthen the maturity of the government debt to 20 years, hence public debt decreased from almost 50 percent

---

16 More than 80 percent of private credit and 90 percent of its public debt was denominated in dollars at that time.

17 Income from these types of exports are usually more volatile than revenue from other sources. Hence, during an expansionary cycle, income might increase more than the trend while during a contraction might fall more than the trend.

of GDP in 2003 to 28 percent in 2008. The arrival of the GFC came with a sudden stop of capital inflows and a sharp deceleration of the growth rate. However, the ability of the Peruvian economy to navigate and rapidly overcome the GFC was rooted in its fiscal savings. By mid-2009, the government implemented a package of anti-crisis fiscal measures equivalent to nearly 4 percent of GDP. Those measures included support for affordable housing, access to drinking water, support for small and medium enterprises, public investment, and social programs to workers. There was a relatively fast recovery and by 2010 the counter-cyclical measures were discontinued. Unfortunately, no long after this, the fiscal budget started a period of slow but consistent deterioration: after a balanced 2014, external and domestic conditions alerted the government for a new fiscal stimulus to boost aggregate demand (through public investment). This time the size of the stimulus was about 3 percent of GDP, according to the IMF (2016). Interestingly, the IMF (2020) reports that Peru has been able to meet its fiscal targets (until 2019) mainly because of high revenues and low execution of public investment. Furthermore, between the GFC and the end of our period of analysis, Peru was able to stabilize its public debt below the ceiling of 30 percent of GDP as a result of favorable debt dynamics and a lower degree of dollarization.

At the end of the 1990s and the beginning of the 2000s, Uruguay was subject to many external shocks: the Asian and Russian crises of 1997 and 1998, the Brazilian devaluation in 1999, Argentina's default at the end of 2001, and finally the end of the Argentinian Convertibility Plan in January 2002. Times like these were not easy. After the inevitable switch to a floating exchange rate regime in June 2002, Uruguay was facing a considerable problem with three components: (i) the debt level was high (it was even before the crisis), and by mid-2002 reached 100 percent of GDP; (ii) almost all of that debt was denominated in foreign currency; and (iii) the fiscal deficit was almost 4 percent of GDP. All three components contributed to a complex debt dynamic. Under this troubled scenario, the Uruguayan government requested an operation with the IMF to regain credibility, and a debt exchange program that was well-regarded internationally. The IMF operation included the participation of the World Bank and the Inter-American Development Bank for two tranches of about 1.7 percent of GDP each to contain the bank run and reestablish the weakened financial system. The debt exchange program, implemented in May 2003 consisted of postponing half of the debt with private creditors by about five years, with some reduction on the present value.[18] This deal was widely viewed as positive since the government avoided a default, involved investors from the early stages of the negotiations,

---

[18] According to the IMF (2005), the net present value reduction was about 10 to 20 percent.

and most of them accepted the proposal.[19] In fact, the Uruguayan solution to the debt crisis brought some innovation to the technical features of these deals.[20]

After the debt-exchange program of 2003, Uruguay started a strong period of growth with low debt services and access to international credit markets. As Marandino and Oddone (2018) explain, the growth observed from 2003 to 2014 was mostly due to the strong cycle of commodity prices, a strong external demand for Uruguayan products, and a stable business environment. During this period, Uruguay was able to replenish the stock of international reserves, granted more independence to its central bank, strengthened bank regulation and supervision, and a low inflation rate enabled a reduction of the share of dollars in public debt from almost 100 percent in 2002 to about 42 percent in 2014.

The impact of the GFC on the Uruguayan economy was mainly concentrated in its exports with a decrease in capital inflows. Similar to other countries in the region, Uruguay implemented counter-cyclical fiscal policies in 2008 and 2009 by an amount of 1.7 percent of GDP, increasing its fiscal deficit. The post-GFC period, from 2010 to 2019, is characterized by an expansionary phase of growth with procyclical fiscal policy. As a result, this period shows a gradual but consistent widening of the fiscal deficit and inflation rates above the target.[21] Public debt, which was about 58 percent of GDP in 2011, was the main source of financing of the government during this period, ending at 65 percent in 2019 (see Panel D in Figure 5.2).

Economic Structure

Chile is endowed with abundant mineral resources such as copper and lithium. Copper is an important part of the Chilean economy and is almost regarded as a national sentiment. Chile has the largest mine of copper in the world, producing almost 30 percent of the world supply. All mining associated with copper represents 20 percent of Chilean GDP and almost 60 percent of its exports. The production of lithium, the other abundant metal in Chile, represents about 23 percent of the global production and contributes about 1.3 percent to exports. Although it

---

19 De Brun and Della Mea (2003) explain that 93 percent accepted the proposal while the remaining 7 percent got their payments under the initial conditions.

20 The inclusion of exit consents, collective action clauses, and aggregation clauses were later used in other debt-restructuring contexts.

21 Marandino and Oddone (2018) argue that the persistence of inflation was, to a great extent, a result of the collective bargaining agreement in place that established automatic wage increases across sectors once the inflation rate rises above 10 percent.

currently provides only a relatively small contribution to the Chilean economy, the production of lithium could be a strategic element of the development agenda.[22] This is particularly relevant in the context of an increasing demand for lithium batteries for electric vehicles and power grids. When considering those mineral resources with the processing of food for exports, beverage production, sugar refineries, cotton and woolen, and the production of cement, the Chilean industrial sector represents about 33 percent of the GDP and employs 22 percent of the labor force. In fact, currently Chile ranks among the most industrialized countries in Latin America. This sector used to be larger in the 1970s, mostly concentrated on import substitution, but since then has gradually shifted toward export-oriented production. Table 5.4 presents the economic structure of the economy. Similar to Argentina and Brazil, Chile has developed a business model integrating the agriculture with the manufacturing sector.

Chile has a wide range of climates and geology that determine the role of agriculture. Although this sector's share has steadily declined since the 1970s and today represents about 4 percent of GDP, employing 10 percent of the country's labor force, Chile is one of the top producers of wine, fresh fruit, dairy, meat, forestry, and fishery products. The geographical fact of being in the southern hemisphere, in the opposite agricultural cycle as its main trade partners, helps Chile's position as stable suppliers of agricultural goods in the northern hemisphere. An interesting fact is that most of those products fall within trade agreements with little to no tariffs. Finally, the service sector is the largest contributor to the value

Table 5.4: Economic structure (percentage of GDP).

	Agriculture	Industry	Services
Chile	4.2	32.8	63.0
Colombia	7.2	30.8	62.0
Peru	7.6	32.7	59.7
Uruguay	6.2	24.1	69.7
Central America	*10.5*	*23.4*	*66.1*
Latin America	*9.0*	*28.3*	*62.8*

Source: World Bank (2020) and United Nations Development Programme (UNDP) (2018).

---

22 At the end of 2019, *Albemarle*, the world's leading lithium producer, predicted the production of lithium to nearly triple by 2025 with a global demand that could even quadruple during that period.

added of the economy, accounting for approximately 63 percent of GDP. The main services comprise tourism, maritime and aeronautical services, retail, financial services, transport and communication services, informatics, and health and education. This sector has grown in the last decades, particularly after Chile became more involved in trade agreements, and currently captures about 68 percent of total employment.

Colombia has traditionally been an agricultural economy, rich in natural resources, with a high degree of population (about 77 percent of total population) living in the three main urban areas. The main agricultural products include fruits, flowers, sugar, and, of course, coffee. In fact, Colombia's production of coffee represents about 10 percent of the total world production, only behind Brazil and Vietnam. The share of the agricultural sector in GDP used to be higher in the 1970s but it currently represents about 7.2 percent and captures just 17 percent of the total labor force. Similar to Brazil, the production of coffee and banana operate in enclaves with coffee mainly produced on the Andean slopes and bananas in the Urabá and Santa Maria regions.

The urbanization observed in terms of the population is not surprising. After all, about two-thirds of the country's total manufacturing output is produced in the five main cities (Bogota, Medellin, Cali, Cartagena, and Barranquilla). Furthermore, a significant share of that production is concentrated by three local economic conglomerates that cover a variety of products: food, energy, finance, cement, soft drinks, and sugar, among others. The state-owned firm is the one in charge of the five oil refineries and alcoholic drinks. All this accounts for an industrial sector that struggled during the early 1990s due to infrastructural and labor challenges and today employs 20 percent of the total labor, and represents about 31 percent of GDP (see Table 5.4). Finally, the service sector in Colombia has increased since the 1970s, becoming the central player of the Colombian economy. It is responsible for about 62 percent of total labor and 55 percent of the GDP. Tourism and information technology services, like call centers and software development, are the most important services in Colombia.

Peru has been one of the most stable growing economies in Latin America for the last decades, particularly from 2002 to 2013. The economic performance of the Peruvian economy has been the result of a continuum of exports that sustained a vigorous demand for imports and enabled the possibility of debt repayments. The country balances a strong agriculture sector with its natural resources for mining and fishing industries, and a flourishing tourism sector. The variety of climates and geographical regions make it a leader in agriculture production, with most of the Peruvian coast dedicated to the production of goods for exports. The main agricultural products include fruits, sugarcane, coffee, rice, potatoes, and cotton. This sector, which used to be approximately 17 percent of GDP in the

1970s, is currently about 8 percent of GDP, employs 28 percent of the total labor, and is well-integrated into the exporting manufacturing industry. For instance, the Peruvian fishing industry is one of the leading ones in the world, producing almost 10 percent of all the world's supply. However, the most important aspect of the Peruvian industry is the mineral sector: it is a major source of economic growth and places Peru among the leaders in the production of silver (first worldwide), gold (fifth worldwide) and copper (second worldwide), and among the top producers of lead and zinc. The mining regions are mainly located in the coastal central area and southern area of the country. The industry sector represents almost 33 percent of GDP, employs about 16 percent of total labor supply, and is heavily tied to mining, fishing, metal mechanics, textiles, and pharmaceuticals.[23] Finally, the services sector in Peru has increased in the last 30 years, currently accounting for 60 percent of GDP, and is responsible for about 77 percent of total labor.

Uruguay has been traditionally considered an economy based on the production and processing of agricultural commodities. Most of its land is used for the farming of cattle, sheep, horses, dairies, and forage. Specifically, approximately 77 percent of Uruguay's land is used for cattle breeding and almost 7 percent for the cultivation of crops. Interestingly, most of the farms associated with cattle breeding are family-managed, of which the great majority have beef and wool as their main sources of income. That is probably why almost 35 percent of total exports are associated with meat or animal products. In fact, Uruguay is one of the leaders in the production of greasy wool and horse meat, and, to a lesser degree, of soybeans and beeswax. The main crop is rice, followed by wheat, maize, sugar cane, and soybeans. This export-oriented agricultural sector used to represent almost 15 percent of GDP in the 1970s but today accounts roughly for 6 percent of GDP and employs almost 9 percent of the total labor (see Table 5.4). Similar to other countries in this group, the industrial sector in Uruguay is mainly linked to the agriculture. Basically, agriculture and animal food processing account for half of the industrial activity. Overall, the industry sector used to be larger in the 1970s, but now represents approximately 24 percent of GDP and employs about 19 percent of total labor supply. Manufacturing activities also include wine, textiles, construction materials like cement, chemicals, oil, coal, and gold. Furthermore, recently, Uruguay also embarked on the production of wood pulp through mills from Finnish and Swedish investors.

---

23 As a consequence of the War of the Pacific (which will be discussed in the chapter about Bolivia) between Chile and allies Peru and Bolivia from 1879 to 1904, Peru lost the minerals-rich (in nitrates and guano) providence of Tarapacá.

Not without controversy, the production of these paper mills contributes about 20 percent to total exports (approximately 3 percent of Uruguay's GDP). Finally, the service sector today represents almost 70 percent of GDP, employs about 72 percent of the total labor, and is mainly focused on tourism, software and consulting, and financial services.

In all cases there has been a common pattern for the last 40 years: the agricultural sector shrunk, the industry has stayed about the same size, and services increased. Second, the relative increased share of services could be a constraint for long run growth. Arias-Ortiz et al. (2014) explain that in Latin America, there is low productivity at the firm level but also misallocation of workers across firms. In particular, they highlight how serious this problem is in the service sector as opposed to the manufacturing sector and alerted that institutional factors are an important determinant of productivity growth and resource allocation. This issue has been relevant for many Latin American countries, but particularly for Uruguay. Below, we will further discuss this.

Foreign Trade

Let us start our discussion understanding the context of the ability of countries to move financial flows. According to the Chinn and Ito (2006) index presented in Table 5.5, during the 1990s, Chile, Colombia, and Peru were at a low level of financial integration, only comparable with South Asia.[24] Uruguay is the exception, since early in the 1990s it implemented reforms that reduced the controls on capital flows. The coming of the 2000s marked two different types of financial integration strategy. Chile and Colombia, on the one hand, still lagging compared to the rest of the world, and Peru and Uruguay on the other, leading the trend of financial liberalizations. Although Chile fully liberalized the flow of capitals in about 2005, more recently there was a new wave of reforms that slowly started reestablishing some regulation on capital controls. In a similar fashion Colombia opted for more regulation of its capital flows throughout the period of analysis. Peru and Uruguay followed a different strategy with reforms at the end of the 1990s, which eliminated most regulations regarding inflows and outflows of capitals.

Interestingly, there is a striking contrast with trade openness, measured by the ratio of exports plus imports to GDP. Figure 5.3 presents the measure of trade

---

24 The Chinn and Ito (2006) index takes higher values the more open a country is to cross-border capital transactions. In particular, the normalized version ranges from 0 to 1.

Table 5.5: Capital account openness.

	1990	2000	2010	2018
Chile	0.00	0.17	0.82	0.70
Colombia	0.17	0.17	0.42	0.42
Peru	0.17	1.00	1.00	1.00
Uruguay	0.72	1.00	1.00	1.00
Latin America	0.26	0.53	0.56	0.53
East Asia and Pacific	0.55	0.49	0.68	0.61
Europe and Central Asia	0.52	0.62	1.00	1.00
Sub-Saharan Africa	0.23	0.29	0.30	0.23
South Asia	0.19	0.27	0.29	0.32

Source: Chinn and Ito (2006) index, where higher values indicate a country is more open to cross-border capital transactions.

openness for Chile, Colombia, Peru, Uruguay, and the average for Latin America. On the one hand, since 1990, Chile has been the leader of this group, with a very similar ratio to the average of Latin America at about 60 percent of GDP, even higher during some periods. The rest of the countries show a lower degree of openness compared to Chile and the average for Latin America. On the other hand, after almost 30 years, and even with some highs and lows, these ratios have not changed significantly. Chile was about 60 percent of GDP in 1990 and was about the same in 2018. Colombia and Uruguay were about 35 and 40 percent of GDP, respectively, in 1990, and were about the same in 2018. Peru is relatively an exception with 30 percent of GDP in 1990 and almost 50 percent of GDP in 2018. Although this group of countries has higher ratios than Argentina and Brazil, it is still below the average for Latin America. That means that those countries are also vulnerable or with limited scope to mitigate a financing shortage from an external shock to their current accounts. As expected, this group also faces the consequences of exports being highly concentrated in commodities. But how are these countries performing relative to the rest of the region?

From this group of countries, Chile is the country with the highest concentration of its exports in commodities, about 86 percent, of which copper and its subproducts represent almost 60 percent of exports. The main countries demanding Chilean products are China, the United States, and Japan, totaling about 60 percent of total exports. The rest of the countries in this group also concentrate their

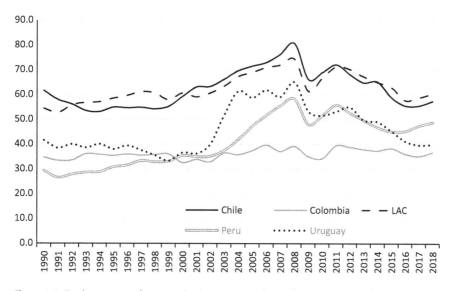

Figure 5.3: Trade openness (exports plus imports as a share of GDP, percentage).
Source: World Bank (2020).
Note: LAC is the simple average of 17 countries in Latin America, excluding the Caribbean.

exports in commodities but have a relatively low ratio compared to Chile. Uruguay, Colombia, and Peru have a ratio of 80, 74, and 73 percent, respectively, compared to 61 percent for the average of Latin America (see Table 5.6). Uruguayan exports are mainly concentrated in three areas that capture more than 65 percent of exports: (i) animal products, including meats and milk; (ii) wood pulp products associated with the pulp mills; and (iii) vegetables, including rice, soybeans, and malt. The main destinations for their exports are China, Brazil, Argentina, the United States, Turkey, and the Netherlands, representing almost 60 percent of total exports. More than 60 percent of Colombian exports are associated with petroleum, coal, or other mineral products, while another 18 percent is vegetable products. Colombian's main trade partners are the United States, China, Panama, Ecuador and Mexico, accounting for more than 50 percent of total exports. Peruvian exports are mainly concentrated in copper, gold, and other mineral products, representing almost 70 percent of total exports. The main destinations for those exports are China, the United States, India, South Korea, and Japan, accounting for almost 60 percent of Peru's exports. This is the result of Peru's active agenda on free trade agreements: with the United States in 2006, with China in 2009, with Japan in 2011, and with the European Union in 2012.

Given the high volatility of commodity prices, the concentration of exports on these types of products speaks to the vulnerability of these countries to the cycle associated with commodities. Clearly, this vulnerability creates challenges for governments since a commodity supercycle can easily expose a country's reliance on export-led growth. Furthermore, these challenges are even more stringent the higher the dependency on these commodities exports for their GDP. In that aspect, all these countries are in a particular situation: they all have a relatively high share of commodity exports in GDP. Chile has the highest share in Latin America with 21.5 percent of GDP, while Peru, Uruguay, and Colombia have 15.6, 11.2, and 9 percent of GDP, respectively. These figures, in Table 5.6, compare to a 11.8 percent of GDP for the average country in Latin America. Hence, particularly Chile and Peru, and to a lesser degree Uruguay, are subject to swings in commodity prices.

Table 5.6: Commodities' share of exports and GDP in Latin America.

	Commodity exports (mill of USD)	Exports (merchandise) (mill of USD)	Commodity/ Exports	Commodity Exports/GDP
Venezuela	72,277	74,714	96.7	15.0
Ecuador	17,772	19,122	92.9	17.0
Paraguay	7,702	8,680	88.7	19.4
Chile	59,621	69,230	86.1	21.5
Bolivia	6,423	7,846	81.9	17.1
Uruguay	6,305	7,888	79.9	11.2
Colombia	28,168	37,881	74.3	9.0
Peru	33,007	45,275	72.9	15.6
Argentina	39,072	58,622	66.7	6.1
Brazil	134,706	217,826	61.8	6.6
Guatemala	6,358	11,001	57.8	8.4
Nicaragua	2,493	5,170	48.2	18.0
Costa Rica	4,298	9,556	45.0	7.5
Honduras	3,351	8,675	38.6	14.6
El Salvador	1,374	5,760	23.9	5.5
Mexico	67,085	409,401	16.4	5.8

Table 5.6 (continued)

	Commodity exports (mill of USD)	Exports (merchandise) (mill of USD)	Commodity/ Exports	Commodity Exports/GDP
Panama	1,050	11,093	9.5	1.7
Central America			*37.2*	*9.3*
Latin America			*61.3*	*11.8*

Source: World Trade Organization (2020).

Country Specific Details

Chile: Copper, Lithium, and the Economy

The economic development of the Chilean economy has been closely related to the mining sector since the early periods of the country. Initially, the drivers of the economy were mostly silver and copper reserves, and later nitrates. For the last 25 years, the mining sector has accounted for 46 percent of the country's exports. Copper alone accounts for almost 40 percent of those exports. The Chilean copper production is organized with Codelco (Corporación Nacional del Cobre de Chile), a state-owned enterprise, producing about 32 percent, and private foreign-owned companies (some of whom have joint ventures with Codelco) that account for the remaining 68 percent.[25] The biggest fourteen private companies produce almost 60 percent of the total production of copper in Chile, with Escondida in the Atacama Desert producing almost 10 percent of the world output of copper and 20 percent of Chilean production. All profits from Codelco are returned to the government, and foreign companies pay the specific mining tax on their operations in Chile. Copper prices are extremely volatile, and can affect the entire economy. In fact, De Gregorio and Labbé (2011) and Fuentes et al. (2018) found a strong relationship between the fluctuations of copper prices and the business cycle in Chile, although such relationship became weaker in the last years when Chile adopted a more flexible exchange rate system. In a similar vein, Borensztein et al. (2010) argue that the weaker relationship is also a result of some of the mechanisms that the government established to smooth the effect of copper prices on fiscal performance.

---

25 According to Fuentes et al. (2018).

Additionally, in the northern part of Chile lies the "lithium triangle" with Argentina and Bolivia, a region containing one of the largest reserves of lithium in the world. In fact, although Australia is currently the top producer, the lithium triangle, which includes the Salar de Uyuni in Bolivia, the Salar de Atacama in Chile, and Argentina's Salar de Arizaro, is believed to have more than half of the existing lithium reserves in the world. Lithium is used in batteries for electric cars, laptops, and mobile phones. Thus, it is becoming increasingly relevant. Both top lithium producers, Albemarle (an American firm) and SQM (a Chilean firm), have a deal with the Chilean government to expand its production at the Salar de Atacama salt flat in the northern part of the country. Lithium is certainly a promising endeavor for Chile, but some caution is worth noting. Aside from the environmental concerns associated with the use of water, lithium prices are also quite volatile.[26] For instance, they plummeted in 2019, as a result of an oversupply and a slow growth of demand for the production of electric vehicles. Furthermore, current Chilean regulations (associated with nuclear concerns) affect production, and could impact future expansions. As a result, the share of Chile in global production of lithium has declined from 40 percent to 23 percent. However, according to a recent report by the World Bank (2020), global demand for lithium could increase by nearly 500 percent by 2050, to meet the growing demand for clean energy technologies.

Macroeconomic policy is crucial for a country were metal commodities, such as copper and lithium, are an important part of exports and GDP. Fiscal revenues from copper have always been an important source of resources to finance public spending in Chile. The main device Chile has developed to deal with commodity-related macroeconomic instability has been a rule for fiscal policy. While the fiscal rule has not succeeded in completely insulating the economy from effects of changes in commodity prices, it has created a buffer against unexpected events in a country prone to commodity price cycles and natural disasters.

Colombia: Economic Growth with an Internal Struggle

For more than the last two decades, Colombia has shown strong macroeconomic fundamentals with significant social improvements. In fact, from a long run perspective, GDP per capita has steadily grown since 1960, with the last two decades at a rate of 3.0 percent. Sound macroeconomic and social policies sustained a strong GDP growth that contributed to a reduction of poverty from about 50 percent

---

26 It takes approximately 70,000 liters of water to mine a ton of lithium.

of the population at the beginning of 2000 to about 27 percent in 2018. The agenda of reforms also reduced informality and improved the business climate. There are, of course, areas to improve, but in this section we want to bring the attention to something that has been running in the background of the Colombian economy: the internal conflict. For more than 50 years, Colombia has been dealing with internal struggle, which can be characterized by triangular conflicts among drug cartels, guerrillas, and paramilitaries inflicting considerable levels of violence on the society. At risk of simplifying this enormously intricate conflict we will just highlight the main organizations that participated in this struggle. (i) The guerrilla movements, particularly the Fuerzas Armadas Revolucionarias de Colombia (FARC) (Revolutionary Armed Forces of Colombia), emerged in 1966 with a Marxist ideology and an agrarian focus. They rapidly shifted towards tactical alliances with narcotraffickers, the cultivation of coca leaf, marijuana, and opium, and by the early 1990s they were the most powerful guerrilla group of Colombia. Some years before the creation of the FARC, in 1962, the Ejército de Liberación Nacional (ELN) (National Liberation Army) was created by intellectuals inspired by the Cuban revolution and the liberation theology, with a Marxist ideology. Initially, this organization captured the attention of young activists from cities, something different to the FARC who were essentially peasants. After surviving a heavy military defeat in 1973, they have regrouped several times. They carried out kidnaps and extortions as their way of financing operations and were responsible for repeated attacks on US-owned oil pipelines. The M-19 was another guerrilla movement that emerged after the election of April 19, 1970 (named for the date of the election). They were urban in their origin with a nationalist ideology, influenced by other guerrilla moments from Argentina (Montoneros) and Uruguay (Tupamaros). Eventually, M-19 ended their period as a guerilla movement deciding to participate in civilian politics at the end of the 1980s. (ii) The drug cartels, particularly from Medellin and Cali, weakened institutions in Colombia. They combined the use of violence and intimidation towards leaders, politicians, and public servants and bribery of government authorities with an active social role to improve their communities and raise public support. Their alliances with the guerrilla movements were mainly tactical and changeable. (iii) The paramilitary groups, mainly the Autodefensas Unidas de Colombia (AUC) (United Self-Defense Forces of Colombia), emerged as a self-defense organization that would employ violence for many reasons. They viewed themselves as vigilante units playing the role of protection, something that the government was unable to provide. With a right-wing ideology, as opposed to the Marxist guerillas, these paramilitaries play an active role in drug trafficking and have been the subject of many violations to human rights against civilians. It is in this context that the homicide rates in Colombia climbed from about 30 per 100,000 people in the 1970s (a relatively high rate compared to other Latin American countries), to almost 85 during the 1990s (mostly due to intense activities of drug cartels in Medellin). Since then, and as a result of a very complex peace process led by the Colombian government, the rate depicted in Figure 5.4 is now about 24 per 100,000 people, which is not far from 20 per 100,000 people, the average for Latin America.

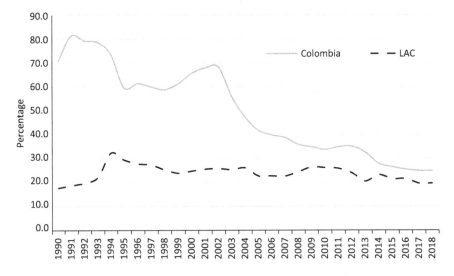

Figure 5.4: Homicides in Colombia and Latin America (per 100,000 people).
Source: World Bank (2020).
Note: LAC is the simple average of 17 countries in Latin America, excluding the Caribbean.

Colombian governments have struggled to deal with these challenges, and, in some cases, progress was clouded by scandals of corruption or violence. However, after more than 50 years and a complex peace process Colombia is now at the verge of being a democratic state without the threats of guerrillas and paramilitaries. Following early peace negotiations with the Colombian government in 1990 and 1991, the M-19 was the first guerrilla movement to demobilize and surrender its weapons in exchange for blanket amnesty. More than a decade after that, during the government of President Álvaro Uribe, Colombia passed the Justice and Peace Law that was the legal framework for the demobilization of paramilitary groups from 2003 to 2008. This demobilization was in exchange for reduced jail terms and protection from extradition. It was not until November 2012 that the government of President Juan Manuel Santos and the FARC finally initiated the peace process in Cuba. This long process involved as main issues: the negotiation of the land reform, the transition to political participation, the disarmament of the rebels, drug-trafficking activities, the rights of the victims, and the end of the conflict with implementation of the peace deal. After a failed referendum in 2016 where some of these points were contested (particularly the rights of the victims), the Congress ratified a revised peace agreement in November 2016. Finally, in June 2017, the FARC surrendered its weapons to the United Nations in Cuba and ceased to be an armed group, ending a 50-year conflict. Although the ELN did not join the peace process with the FARC, they have been negotiating one with the Colombia government for more than 15 years. The last negotiations were held by President Santos in September 2017 with a truce until January 2019 when they became active again, and President Iván Duque suspended the dialogue. In recent years, the ELN has been involved in Venezuelan politics, receiving the support of the governments of President Hugo Chavez and President Nicolás Maduro, as well as the Tupamaro movement.

There is broad agreement that the peace process will bring major social and economic dividends in the form of investments in agriculture, mining, oil, infrastructure, and energy. However, such transition will also bring long-term challenges to make sure the benefits are equally distributed for the whole population.

Peru: Silent, Successful, and Good Policies

Since the early 1990s, Peru has shown strong economic growth, with one of the highest rates in Latin America (behind Chile and Uruguay). In fact, in the past two decades Peru's growth rate was on average 5 percent, and its GDP per capita (measured in 2005 PPP dollars) doubled during that period (see Figure 5.5). Even though most of the strong growth is concentrated from 2002 to 2012, Peru was able to increase its income levels, from a lower middle-income country to a high middle-income one. The unemployment rate went from 5.7 in 2000 to 2.9 in 2019, consistent with a period of economic expansion. Similarly, the ratio of people living in poverty went from 48 percent of the population in 2000 to almost 20 percent in 2018. Inequality, measured by the Gini index, improved from 0.52 at the beginning of the 2000s to 0.42 in 2018. Both trends for poverty and inequality were not really affected by the GFC. That is, the distribution of income in the Peruvian economy showed an improvement in the last two decades. Additionally, during this period, Peru has also been able to expand its middle-class (population with an income of 13 to 70 US dollars per day, adjusted by PPP). According to Melguizo et al. (2017), the middle class in Peru was about 15 percent of the population in 2004, and reached almost 35 percent in 2017, a similar figure to the average Latin American country. Next, we will address the reasons behind this performance and some of the challenges ahead.

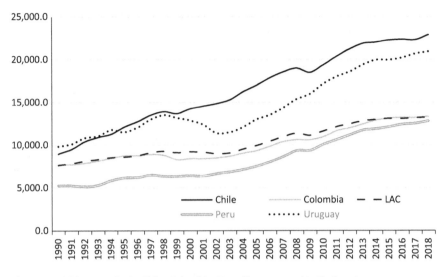

Figure 5.5: GDP per capita in Chile, Colombia, Peru, Uruguay, and Latin America
(2005 PPP dollars).
Source: World Bank (2020).
Note: LAC is the simple average of 17 countries in Latin America, excluding the Caribbean.

There are at least two main reasons behind this performance: (i) the international context, and (ii) the domestic policies implemented by Peru. Let us start with the international context. The mineral sector in Peru is a major source of economic growth, placing the country among the leaders in the production of silver, gold, copper, lead, and zinc. The export of these metal commodities with favorable terms of trade during the supercycle of commodities helped the Peruvian economy considerably until 2012. After 2013, during the slowdown of the cycle there was a deterioration of the terms of trade, but the new normal of mineral commodities has since slightly improved to pre-2011 levels. A strong performance of commodities brought a steady increase in general government tax revenues that enabled an improvement in the fiscal position and public debt of Peru during these years. Capital flows are an additional element of the international context. From 2000, the economic expansion in Peru was accompanied by steady financing inflows in the form of FDI and financial investments, only interrupted by the GFC in 2009 and in 2014. In fact, Peru moved up in the ranking as one of the top FDI destinations in Latin America, behind Brazil, Mexico, Chile, and Colombia according to ECLAC (2015). This abundance of flows benefited the credit market with more funds available to the private sector, and contributed to the appreciation of the real exchange rate, helping a highly dollarized economy.

For the last two decades there has been a slow pace of reforms in Latin America with Peru not being an exception. According to Lora (2012), only Trinidad and Tobago reformed more rapidly in the 2000s than in the 1990s. Nevertheless, there has been a set of domestic policies that contributed to macroeconomic stability in Peru. Regarding monetary policy, in the aftermath of the Asian and Russian crises, the central bank adopted an inflation-targeting framework with a credible commitment of maintaining price stability given the high level of domestic dollarization. This way, Peru was able to keep a low inflation target throughout this period until 2019 significantly reducing its degree of private credit dollarization to about 39 percent, according to BCRP (2019). To this end, the central bank also accumulated high levels of international reserves (from 17 percent of GDP in 2000 to 29 percent in 2019) that acted as insurance in cases of exchange rate volatility. Regarding the fiscal front, the main reform was the introduction of the Law of Fiscal Prudence and Transparency of 1999 (later renamed as the Fiscal Responsibility and Transparency Law in 2003) that aimed at generating savings to pursue counter-cyclical policies to alleviate the business cycle. This fiscal rule was indeed instrumental during the GFC. Mostly as a consequence of Peruvian monetary, fiscal, and debt management, JP Morgan's Emerging Markets Bond Index (EMBI) spread (a broad measure of the economic and political risk) for Peru (in Figure 5.6) has been steadily lower than that of the average of Latin

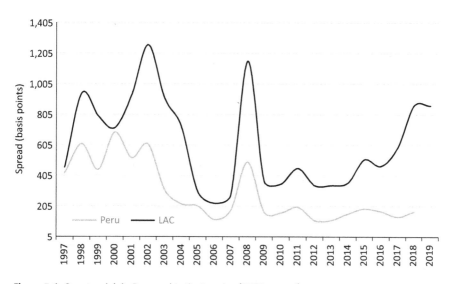

Figure 5.6: Country risk in Peru and Latin America (EMBI spread).
Source: Inter-American Development Bank (2020).
Note: LAC is the simple average of 17 countries in Latin America, excluding the Caribbean.

America throughout the 2000s, reaching the lowest point in 2017, and currently about 168 basis points. This means that Peruvian sovereign bonds are among the safest in Latin America, only close to Chile.[27]

This robust performance in the last two decades has also been reflected in the emergence of new challenges for an economy like Peru. That is, moving on to a higher level of development requires new improvements that go beyond macroeconomic stability. In particular, Melguizo et al. (2017) list some of the key areas of work for a country like Peru to move on to a higher level of development. Among those, they listed the rule of law, quality of education, tax revenues, economic complexity (amount of productive knowledge implied in the country's export structure), and the financial sector (domestic credit).

Uruguay: Institutions Matter

It is not difficult, and usually not enough, to emphasize the importance of institutions for economic development. After all, references to the quality of institutions appear in the works of classic authors, but also in the more recent literature by North (1990, 1991) and Acemoglu et al. (2001, 2002, 2005, 2006), just to name a few. In fact, Acemoglu et al. (2005, 2006) developed an organized framework of analysis that helps explain (i) the differences in economic institutions as a fundamental cause of differences in economic performance, and (ii) the reasons why these institutions vary across countries. Their main argument is that institutions help shape the incentives of crucial economic actors in a society (such as individuals and enterprises) influencing investment, technology, and production. Without neglecting the effects of geography and culture on economic performance, these authors claim institutions are the key source in explaining differences in economic growth and prosperity. Here, we briefly discuss the role of institutions for the Uruguayan economy in the last few years.

Among Latin American countries, Uruguay shows a conspicuous set of characteristics that makes it stand out. For the most part, it is considered a modern society with high income per capita (about $ 17,300 dollars), and the lowest levels of inequality (0.40 Gini index) and poverty (8.1 percent of the population) in the region. As a result, Uruguay has the largest middle class in Latin America with about 60 percent of its population, according to Duryea and Robles (2016). The reasons behind this performance can probably be linked to the quality of institutions.

---

27 We are not addressing it here, but the situation for private bonds is not necessarily same, and involves a higher risk.

Corruption and the rule of law are two key elements that have been associated with economic growth. For instance, Dreher and Herzfeld (2008) argue how less corruption enhances income growth in Latin America, while Dollar and Kraay (2003) stress the importance of the rule of law for economic development. Along these lines we can also include the positive influence of political institutions, which capture the quality and stability of the rules of the game over time, on economic growth. A more comprehensive summary of indicators is presented in Table 5.7 with data from the Worldwide Governance Indicators from the World Bank. This table presents each individual index, capturing different aspects of the institutional quality of the country, ordered by percentile rank from 0 to 100. Among countries from Latin America, Uruguay stands out particularly in *Voice and Accountability* (captures perceptions of the extent to which citizens can participate in selecting their government, as well as freedom of expression), *Political Stability* (measure the perception of the likelihood that the government will be destabilized or overthrown), *Control of Corruption* (measures the extent to which public power is exercised for private gain), *Rule of Law* (measures the perception of the extent to which agents have confidence in and abide by the rules of society), and *Government Effectiveness* (measures the perception of the quality of public services and civil service), but also in terms of *Regulatory Quality* (measures the perception of the ability of the government to implement policies and regulations that promote private sector development).

The fact that Uruguay is at the top of almost every indicator suggests that, within Latin America, it is the country with the strongest institutions. The intricacies with these indexes can be a matter of debate, but the ranking marks a clear trend. There is a generalized perception that in Uruguay contracts will be enforced, that there is a trustworthy and independent legal system, that there is no obvious favoritism in the decisions by government officials, with a relatively high level of public trust in the government, where bribes are not common, and where the political system is mostly insulated from the violent attempts to be overthrown. When all these are combined what we have is a country whose institutions promote public policies that are of good quality, are stable, and are coherent in time. Furthermore, if we include more aggregated indexes, such as the Human Development Index or the Economic Freedom Index, Uruguay is also at the top of Latin American countries.

Acemoglu et al. (2005) explain that the impact of strong institutions is not limited to economic growth; they also determine many economic outcomes, including physical and human capital, and the distribution of income. As they put it (2005: 390), "they influence not only the size of the aggregate pie, but how this pie is divided among different groups and individuals." Another way of looking into this is by using the Human Opportunity Index constructed by the

Table 5.7: Institutions in Latin America (2018).

Voice and Accountability		Political stability		Control of corruption		Rule of law		Government effectiveness		Regulatory quality	
Uruguay	89.2	Uruguay	87.6	Uruguay	87.5	Chile	83.7	Chile	81.7	Chile	88.9
Costa Rica	84.7	Costa Rica	62.4	Chile	81.7	Uruguay	73.6	Uruguay	73.1	Peru	71.2
Chile	82.3	Chile	61.4	Costa Rica	70.7	Costa Rica	69.2	Costa Rica	67.8	Uruguay	69.7
Panama	68.5	Panama	56.2	Argentina	54.3	Panama	52.4	Argentina	54.8	Costa Rica	69.2
Argentina	67	Dominican Republic	47.6	Colombia	44.7	Argentina	45.7	Panama	51.9	Panama	66.3
Brazil	60.6	Argentina	46.7	Brazil	40.4	Brazil	44.2	Colombia	50	Colombia	65.4
Peru	55.2	Ecuador	43.3	Peru	34.6	Dominican Republic	38.9	Mexico	47.6	Mexico	60.6
Colombia	52.7	Paraguay	42.4	Ecuador	32.7	Colombia	38.5	Peru	44.2	El Salvador	53.8
Dominican Republic	51.2	Bolivia	38.1	Panama	32.2	Peru	32.7	Ecuador	42.8	Dominican Republic	50.5
Paraguay	49.3	Peru	37.1	El Salvador	29.8	Paraguay	32.2	Bolivia	39.9	Paraguay	48.6
El Salvador	48.3	El Salvador	33.3	Honduras	29.3	Ecuador	28.8	Dominican Republic	39.4	Guatemala	45.7

Ecuador	47.3	Brazil	31.9	Bolivia	28.8	Mexico	27.4	El Salvador	36.5	Argentina	42.3
Mexico	45.8	Guatemala	27.1	Dominican Republic	24.5	El Salvador	19.7	Brazil	36.1	Brazil	39.9
Bolivia	44.3	Honduras	26.7	Guatemala	22.1	Honduras	16.3	Paraguay	34.1	Honduras	34.6
Guatemala	35.5	Mexico	25.7	Paraguay	20.7	Nicaragua	14.9	Honduras	27.9	Nicaragua	25
Honduras	31.5	Nicaragua	18.1	Mexico	18.8	Guatemala	13.5	Guatemala	23.6	Ecuador	16.3
Nicaragua	18.7	Colombia	17.6	Nicaragua	13	Bolivia	9.6	Nicaragua	19.2	Bolivia	15.9
Venezuela	10.3	Venezuela	9	Venezuela	4.8	Venezuela	0	Venezuela	4.8	Venezuela	0.5

Source: World Bank (2018).

World Bank. This index of essential goods/services measures how individual circumstances (such as gender, nationality, education, location, etc.) can affect a child's access to basic opportunities such as education, water, electricity, and sanitation. Based on this index, Uruguay is ranked among the top countries of Latin America in terms of primary school completion, access to water, electricity, and sanitation.

This institutional foundation gives Uruguay a solid ground to continue and deepen policies to address the educational and infrastructural gap – a common challenge in Latin America.

Chapter 6
The Laggards: Bolivia, Ecuador, Paraguay, Venezuela

The Basics

Bolivia covers a total area of 1,098,581 square kilometers, which makes it the sixth largest country in the region, has a population of approximately 11 million, and is ranked in 14th place (out of 17 countries) in Latin America in terms of GDP with $40 billion. Situated between the Andes and the Amazon Basin, Bolivia has a high level of biodiversity and a variety of climates in its several ecoregions, such as the *Altiplano* (widest area of the Andes), the Amazon rainforest, the dry valleys, and the tropical savanna. It is endowed with a remarkable amount of minerals, particularly tin, silver, copper, natural gas (the second largest reserves in South America), and lithium. It has borders with Brazil, Paraguay, Argentina, Chile, and Peru. Here is where the details are particularly important. Bolivia has a history of territorial losses to its neighbors, but maybe the one that changed its destiny the most is the one against Chile and Peru in the context of the War of the Pacific in 1879. This war ended up with a treaty in 1903 in which Bolivia lost its coastal territories and access to the Pacific Ocean, becoming a landlocked country. We will discuss the details of this war at the end of this chapter. As a landlocked country, Bolivia is the largest in South America and in the Southern Hemisphere. Most of its population (about 70 percent) lives in the urban areas of La Paz, Santa Cruz, and Cochabamba. Although Spanish is the official and predominant language, there are other indigenous languages that are spoken in Bolivia, such as Guarani, Aymara, and Quechua. According to the World Bank, Bolivia is considered a lower middle-income level country, with a GDP per capita of $3,500 (see Table 6.1).

Ecuador has a total area of 283,561 square kilometers, a population of about 17 million, and is ranked in 7th place (out of 17 countries) in Latin America in terms of GDP with $108 billion.[1] It has land boundaries with Colombia to the north, and with Peru to the eastern and southern area. The Andes are the prevailing geographical feature that defines the regions of the country from north to south. The coast (La Costa) is the region to the west of the Andes until the Pacific Ocean. This is the most fertile area of the country, with large plantations

---

1 Ecuador also controls the Galapagos Islands, situated in the Pacific Ocean about 1,000 kilometers west of the mainland.

https://doi.org/10.1515/9783110674934-006

of banana (one of Ecuador's main exports) and rice. The highlands (La Sierra) is the Andean region with most of Ecuador's volcanos (such as Cotopaxi and Mount Chimborazo, its tallest mountain), and traditional crops of potato, maize, and quinoa. The capital city, Quito, is in this region. The east (El Oriente) is the Amazon jungle to the east of the Andes. This is the area with the largest reserves of petroleum. Ecuador is considered by the United Nations as one of the countries with the highest biodiversity per square kilometer of the world.[2] It includes the Amazon rainforest, highlands, grassland, islands, and coastlines. Additionally, the Galapagos Islands host many endemic plants and animals, only found in that region of the planet. Ecuador is endowed with a variety of natural resources, including petroleum and agricultural products, such as bananas, flowers, cocoa, coffee, rice, and potatoes. According to the World Bank, Ecuador is considered an upper middle-income level country, with a GDP per capita of $6,300.

Bordered by Brazil, Argentina, and Bolivia, Paraguay is the other landlocked country in South America. It covers an area of 406,752 square kilometers, has a population of almost 7 million, and is ranked in 15th place (out of 17 countries) in Latin America in terms of GDP with approximately $40 billion (similar to Bolivia). Despite being a landlocked country, Paraguay has access to the Atlantic Ocean through the Paraguay and Paraná rivers. In fact, the Paraguay river divides the country into two very different regions. The western region, known as the Chaco, consists of a vast plain and foothills that cover about 60 percent of the country. The eastern region, known as Paraneña, is a mix of rolling hills, valleys, and lowlands, which borders with Argentina and Brazil. Unlike the western region, the eastern side is drained by both the Paraguay and Paraná rivers, two powerful rivers, making this region more apt to agriculture. Thus, it is not surprising that almost 95 percent of the population of Paraguay lives in this eastern side of the country. Similar to Bolivia, Paraguay has had territorial losses to its neighbors, with the most significant one after the War of the Triple Alliance against Argentina, Brazil, and Uruguay in 1870. Below, we will discuss more about this. Additionally, Paraguay has a heavy influence from the Guarani culture, where both Spanish and Guarani are the official languages (spoken by more than 90 percent of the population). According to the World Bank, Paraguay is considered an upper middle-income level country, with a GDP per capita of $5,800.

Finally, with an area of 916,445 square kilometers and a population of almost 29 million, Venezuela is located on the northern coast of South America, bordering

---

2 See the United Nations Development Programme on The Biodiversity Finance Initiative (http://www.biodiversityfinance.org/).

Colombia, Brazil, and Guyana.[3] Out of 17 countries in Latin America, Venezuela is ranked in 10th place in terms of GDP with about $200 billion. The regions of the country are mostly defined by its geographical features. To the northwest, there are lowlands around Lake Maracaibo, defining a foreland basin. The northern mountains are the last section of the Andes, which borders Colombia and reaches the Caribbean Sea. The Guiana highlands that include the last border of the Amazon basin, are situated in the southeastern region of the country. The llanos (plains) are extensive plains that cover from the Andes to the Guiana highlands, around the delta of the Orinoco river. In fact, the Orinoco river, the largest in the country, creates an important river system, with the largest watersheds in this part of the continent. Venezuela is also considered one of the most biodiverse countries of the world, ranging from the mountains of the Andes, the Amazon rainforest, the extensive plains, coastlines, and the Orinoco river delta. With an arable land of 3.1 percent, similar to Peru and Bolivia, Venezuela is mostly endowed with natural resources such as petroleum, natural gas, gold, and iron. As a matter of fact, since 2010, Venezuela is the country with the largest proven oil reserves, only seconded by Saudi Arabia. Interestingly, before petroleum became the main export, Venezuela used to rely on agricultural commodities such as coffee and cocoa. Below, we will get into the details of how a country with such abundance of natural resources collapsed struggling with inflation, unemployment, poverty, shortages, malnutrition, crime, and corruption. According to the World Bank, Venezuela is currently considered a low middle-income level country, with a GDP per capita of $7,000 (see Table 6.1).

All countries combined in this group cover 13.5 percent of Latin America's land and represent 10 and 6 percent of the region's population and GDP, respectively. Figure 6.1 shows that for the last two decades, Bolivia, Ecuador, and Paraguay have been growing at 4.1, 3.3, 3.2, respectively, while Venezuela contracted at an average of 1.4 percent (until 2018), compared to a rate of 3.1 for Latin America.[4] Interestingly, from 1999 to 2019, GDP per capita (measured in 2005 PPP dollars) increased about 47 percent for the region, while Bolivia, Ecuador, and Paraguay increased 65 percent, 42 percent, 45 percent, respectively, and Venezuela decreased 35 percent (until 2018). In terms of aggregate growth performance we clearly have three different trajectories: Bolivia's evolution has some similarities to the Colombian case, Ecuador and Paraguay appear conspicuously similar, while Venezuela is a story of mischiefs. Let us try to understand the details of these performances.

---

3 Venezuela also controls a group of small islands in the Caribbean Sea.
4 If we consider the unofficial local estimates for 2019 GDP, the average contraction of the last two decades is 3.0 percent per year.

Table 6.1: Population, GDP, GDP per capita, poverty, and inequality in Bolivia, Ecuador, Paraguay, Venezuela, and Latin America.

	Population (millions)	GDP (billions of USD)	GDP per capita (USD)	Poverty ($5.5 per day)	Poverty percentage (year)	Income inequality (Gini coefficient)	Inequality-adjusted education index
Bolivia	11.4	40	3,549	23.1	36.4	0.42	0.55
Ecuador	17.1	108	6,296	24.2	23.2	0.45	0.60
Paraguay	7.0	40	5,806	17.0	24.2	0.46	0.52
Venezuela	28.9	202	6,997	36.7	96.0	0.51	0.64
Central America	*47.8*	*257*	*6,656*	*30.5*	*36.7*	*0.47*	*0.46*
Latin America	*644.1*	*5,972*	*9,272*	*23.3*	*33.8*	*0.46*	*0.56*

Source: World Bank (2020), Economic Commission for Latin America and the Caribbean (ECLAC) (2019), United Nations Development Programme (UNDP) (2019).

Notes: Population, GDP, GDP per capita from 2018. Poverty from 2018, excepting Guatemala, Nicaragua, and Venezuela from 2014. Poverty percentage from 2018, excepting Bolivia, Chile, and Panama from 2017, Guatemala from 2014, Nicaragua from 2015, and Venezuela from 2019. Income inequality from 2018, excepting Guatemala, Nicaragua, and Venezuela 2014. Inequality-adjusted education index from 2018.

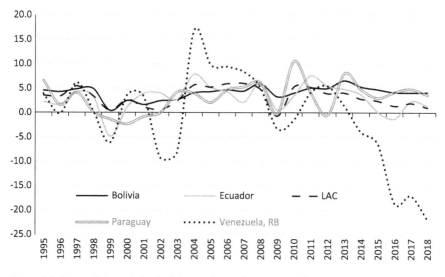

Figure 6.1: Economic growth (real GDP annual growth, percentage).
Source: World Bank (2020).
Note: LAC is the simple average of 17 countries in Latin America, excluding the Caribbean.

After the Asian and the Russian crises of 1997 and 1998, the Bolivian economy entered a deceleration period, with a sudden stop of capital inflows and a deterioration of the terms of trade. Most of what the Bolivian economy suffered from during the onset of both crises can be the result of contagion effects. Jemio (2006) and Jemio and Nina (2010) argue that from the onset of the crisis, there was a reduction of the international demand for Bolivian products, particularly crude petroleum, causing a drop in export incomes, reducing cash flow, and as a result, fewer fiscal revenues and a decline of the economic activity. The *credit crunch* associated with the lack of external financial resources and the cost of credit, also affected the stock of international reserves and money supply, further decreasing economic activity. To make things worse, the devaluation of the Brazilian real in January 1999 and the Argentinian crisis of 2001–2002 additionally deteriorated the Bolivian terms of trade.[5] The impact of these crises was felt in a fast deceleration of Bolivia's growth trend from 4.9 percent in 1998 to a 0.42 percent growth rate in 1999. During the first part of the 2000s, Bolivia experienced a mild recovery from this crisis, with positive but low growth rates. All of these events were posing challenges for the already weakened Bolivian financial system. At the beginning of 2003, the external

---

5 During these years, the coca eradication program Dignity Plan (Plan Dignidad) of President Hugo Banzer was also coming to an end.

conditions changed and Bolivia was faced with increasing export prices for its hydrocarbon and mineral exports, in particular commodities prices for natural gas and oil exports to Brazil. This led to a strong growth performance from 2003 to 2007 at an average rate of 4.4 percent per year, which enabled an increase of GDP per capita of 20 percent.

Interestingly, the global financial crisis (GFC) did not affect Bolivia as much as it did other Latin American countries. That is, Bolivia was one of the few countries with strong growth at the beginning of this crisis, at a rate of 5.9 in 2008, only to experience a slow down to 3.3 percent in 2009. Most of this behavior can be attributed to the fact that the export prices of oil and natural gas were still strong until the third quarter of 2008. Additionally, during this crisis, the Bolivian government was able to implement a moderate counter-cyclical fiscal policy to support domestic demand, such as increases in public spending for infrastructure, housing, and support for strategic sectors.[6] Just one year after the GFC, in 2010, the prices of mineral commodities increased again during the last phase of the supercycle that ended in 2014–2015. For the past ten years, Bolivia has been growing at an average of 4.7 percent and its GDP per capita increased 36 percent. These figures compare to the average of Latin America at a rate of 3.1 for GDP growth and an increase of 15 percent in terms of GDP per capita.

At the end of 1996, Ecuador started a period of political instability, facing challenges to control inflation and a newly elected president who was soon stripped from office on the grounds of mental incapacity. Not before long, Ecuador faced a sequence of external negative shocks. First, the Asian crisis unleashed, affecting the financial system bringing a sudden stop of short-term capital. Soon after that, in late 1997 and beginning of 1998, an El Niño weather phenomenon affected the agricultural sector in the form of extremely heavy rainfall that caused floods and landslides with disastrous consequences.[7] By mid-1998, the Russian financial crisis and the Brazilian devaluation of 1999 also affected the country. To make things worse, oil prices plunged, partly as a response to the global economic slowdown, hurting even further the Ecuadorian's public finances and exchange rate market. The impact of these shocks resulted in a fast deceleration of Ecuador's growth rate in 1998. Just by 1999, the banking system started showing evidence of fragility that eventually led to the largest financial crisis in the history of Ecuador. In fact, 1999 ended with a 4.9 contraction of GDP, an inflation of about 52 percent, and a depreciation of more than 100 percent of the domestic currency (the sucre).

---

6 The resources to finance these counter-cyclical measures were mostly the result of high commodities prices and the Hydrocarbon Law of 2005.

7 It destroyed a significant agricultural area, affecting roads, reducing exports, and assets of banks from the Coastal region.

The beginning of 2000 started with a drastic measure: President Jamil Mahuad decided to adopt the US dollar as the official currency of Ecuador. This was an unusual move at that time, and we will discuss it more in the last section of this chapter. During the period from 2000 to 2014, Ecuador experienced strong economic growth: GDP grew by 83 percent at an average rate of 4.2 percent, while the average country in Latin America expanded 67 percent at an average rate of 3.7 percent. Additionally, GDP per capita increased 48 percent, while the average for Latin America was 41 percent. Similar to other Latin American countries, Ecuador was affected by the GFC, experiencing a decline of the external demand for its products and remittances from abroad. Wong (2012) estimated that the fall in the value of total exports in 2008 and 2009 was about 26 percent, mainly as a consequence of the decrease in the price of oil. Remittances, which represented 5 percent of GDP, also experienced a drop of approximately 11 percent in dollars in 2009. As a result, there was a deceleration in the growth rate of GDP, from 6.4 percent in 2008 to 0.6 percent in 2009. However, Ecuador managed to quickly recover and returned to pre-crisis output levels by 2010. Following a similar response in the region at that time, Ecuador was able to pursue a variety of counter-cyclical measures to contain the crisis. Kacef and Jiménez (2009) list among other measures, tax policies to alleviate corporate income tax and external trade, as well as government spending on infrastructure. The period 2015–2019 marks the end of the boom of commodities but also the 2016 earthquake and subsequent contraction.[8] This last period is marked by a low average growth of 0.4 per year, and only a 2 percent increase in its GDP per capita.

By the end of 1994, Paraguay started showing signs of weakness in its financial system when a group of local banks, with almost 15 percent of the deposits of the financial system, were having liquidity problems. As Charotti et al. (2019) explain, insufficient banking supervision and regulation were at the heart of this episode. The central bank of Paraguay resorted to act as lender of last resort, trying to prevent a massive bank run, eventually covering all deposits.[9] However, by rescuing these banks without a proper deposit insurance system, the central bank gave the impression that more banks could be assisted if needed. In an effort to counterbalance this impression, the government approved a banking law (establishing a deposit insurance), and an assistance program by the central bank. Despite these efforts, the feeling of another wave of problems was already in

---

8 The result of the 2016 earthquake was more than 670 deaths, and damages for approximately 3 percent of GDP.

9 By the end of 1995, Amieva Huerta and Urriza González (2000) estimated the cost of rescuing these banks at about 4 percent of GDP, while Santos (2009) at 5.6 percent of GDP.

place. At the end of 1997 and in 1998, additionally to the effect of the Asian and Russian crises, a second round of instability affected the financial system with more bank runs and closures. Santos (2009) described this situation in the banking system as a *fly to quality* since foreign banks, which were perceived as more reliable, increased their participation to more than 80 percent by 1998. According to Charotti, el al. (2019), the assistance provided by the central bank and the government during this period (to 13 national banks and 35 financial institutions that ended up closed) represented approximately 7.2 percent of GDP. In 1998, GDP growth decelerated to almost a zero-growth rate. Unfortunately, this was just the beginning of a four-year recession period that lasted until 2002. Let us get into the details.

On the one hand, the Asian and Russian crises dried up capital inflows to developing countries around the globe. On the other hand, Paraguay's main trade partners and neighbors were also in distress. The devaluation of the Brazilian real in 1999 and the collapse of the Argentine economy at the end of 2001 were contributing to a sharp devaluation of Paraguay's exchange rate and loss of international reserves (as the central bank was intervening to defend the currency). The year 2002 came with a third wave of financial instability and more bank closures. The freeze on bank deposits withdrawals in Argentina (known as *corralito*) and the financial crisis in Uruguay were affecting the liquidity and solvency of banks that operated in Paraguay, representing almost 12 percent of the total deposits of the system. Santos (2009) quantified the accumulated cost of financial crises from 1995 to 2002 at 15.5 percent of GDP.[10] To put things in perspective, from 1991 to 1995, Paraguay grew at an average rate of 4.3 percent and GDP per capita increased 10 percent while the average Latin American country grew at 4.2 percent and GDP per capita increased by 12.5 percent. However, during the period of the financial instability, from 1996 to 2002, the average growth rate of Paraguay was 0.2 percent and the GDP per capita declined 12.6 percent, while the average country in Latin America grew 2.5 percent and increased its GDP per capita by 4.6 percent.

The Paraguayan economy recovered in 2003 as a combination of a strong international demand for its exports and domestic reforms. This period of strong performance would last until 2018 with the exception of two years: 2009 and 2012. In 2009, GDP declined by 0.26 percent as a result of a drop in external

---

[10] As a reference, Santos (2009) estimate the costs of the financial crises in Ecuador (1998–2000), Argentina (2002–2003), and Uruguay (2001–2002) at 20, 11.4, and 20 percent of GDP, respectively. Additionally, the IMF (2015) calculated a higher cost for Ecuador, at about 30 percent of GDP.

demand from the GFC and a drought that affected the agricultural production. Interestingly, the government was able to pursue counter-cyclical fiscal policies to rapidly revert this situation. During 2012, GDP declined 0.54 percent since Paraguay was severely affected by another drought. From 2003 to 2018, Paraguay grew at an average rate of 4.3 percent while GDP per capita grew 55 percent, compared to 3.6 percent and 46 percent, respectively, for the average of Latin America.

The beginning of the 1990s found Venezuela with a recently elected president, Carlos Andrés Pérez, that implemented structural reforms to open the economy through privatizations of state-owned companies and liberalization of trade. From 1990 to 1992, GDP managed to grow at an average rate of 7.2 percent per year, but unemployment was still at almost 10 percent. In this context, in February of 1992, Venezuela received the first signs of *Chavismo*, when Hugo Chávez led an unsuccessful first coup. The second unsuccessful attempt happened in November 1992, while Chávez was arrested (although he was later released, and pardoned in 1994). This political instability lasted until 1993 when President Rafael Caldera was elected after President Pérez was impeached. Additionally, the price of oil was following a declining trend since the beginning of the 1990s, wearing down fiscal revenues. In fact, understanding the key role of oil for the economy is utmost important when analyzing the performance of Venezuela. We will discuss this at the end of this chapter.

A set of elements came together during the years 1993 to 1998. On the one hand, there were domestic factors, such as the fracture of the political system, a severe banking crisis (1994 and 1995) that ended with the government bailing out 17 banks, a rampant inflation that even reached 100 percent by 1996, and a considerable increase in poverty affecting more than 60 percent of the population. On the other hand, there were external factors, such as the decline in the price of oil (with the exception of 1996) that eroded fiscal revenues and oil exports, and the Asian and Russian crises that were causing significant outflows of capitals along with currency depreciations. During this period, Venezuela grew at an average rate of 1.3 percent while GDP per capita declined 2.5 percent, compared to 4.1 percent and a growth of 11.5 percent, respectively, for the average of Latin America.

The year 1999 marks the start of a new era for Venezuela: Hugo Chávez took office after being elected in December 1998. During the first year, the new government implemented a series of reforms and a new constitution that would set the ground for the next 14 years of *Chavismo*. With this context, in the aftermath of the Asian and Russian crises, and experiencing low oil prices, the Venezuelan economy contracted 6.1 percent. With low prices and oil earnings at modest levels, during the first years of the 2000s, President Chávez moved to gain control of the petroleum industry. This contributed to increasing political instability and an oil strike by the state-owned company, PDVSA (Petróleos de Venezuela, S.A.). As a consequence, from 2001 to 2003, Venezuela's GDP dropped 8.6 percent per year. However, from 2004 until 2008, Venezuela enjoyed an increase in the price of oil not seen in many years. This feature, combined with the fact that the government changed the distribution policy of oil revenues to obtain a larger share, led to an expansionary period where GDP grew at an average rate of 10 percent while GDP per capita increased 52 percent, compared to 5.5 percent and a growth of 25 percent, respectively, for the average of Latin America. The GFC affected Venezuela mainly through the drop in the price of oil, but worked as an indicator of how dependent the economy was on oil. As Restuccia (2018) explains, the transmission of this oil shock to economic activity was through fiscal policy. The expansionary fiscal policy during the years before the GFC left the government with no space for counter-cyclical policies. In fact, Weisbrot and Johnston (2012) report that to weather this crisis, taxes were increased in 2009. GDP fell by 3.2 and 1.5 percent in 2009 and 2010 while GDP per capita dropped by 4.6 and 3.0 percent during those years. The end of the supercycle of the price of oil ended in 2014, a year after President Chávez died and was succeeded by President Nicolás Maduro. Soon after President Maduro took office, the price of oil collapsed from almost 100 dollars a barrel in 2014 to barely 48 dollars a barrel in 2015. With an economy where petroleum revenues represent about 95 percent of export earnings, it is not difficult to imagine the collapse. Since 2014 the Venezuela economy has been in a deep full-blown crisis that has brought the entire country down, only comparable with going through a war. In free-falling mode, the GDP contracted approximately 66 percent since 2014 while GDP per capita dropped by 65 percent during that period. We will discuss more about this fall in the last section of this chapter.

Let us now compare the performance of this group of countries in terms of their income gap relative to the rest of the world, following Birdsall et al.'s (2008) methodology. Panel A in Table 6.2 traces the evolution of this gap relative to the world's most advanced economies (in terms of health, education, and income).[11] Relative to most developed countries, there seems to be a slight increase of Bolivia's and Paraguay's level of development. Ecuador seems to be almost at the same level since 1990, after going through a decrease in the 2000s

---

11 Based on the Human Development Index, we first construct an equally weighted subindex of health, education, and income. The most developed countries are those in the top decile of this subindex. Countries are classified as having similar level of development if they are ranked in the same decile of this subindex. Finally, Latin American countries is the average of the 17 countries within Latin America. A greater figure implies a better performance with one being the threshold when the comparison renders the same.

and an improvement in the 2010s. Finally, Venezuela is the one that catches more attention, since their level of development has significantly decreased compared to 1990. It is worth mentioning that during the 2010s there was an improvement during the supercycle period of commodities. Panel B in Table 6.2 traces the evolution of this gap relative to countries with a similar level of development. Since 2000, Bolivia, Ecuador, and Paraguay have been able to reduce their gaps with countries of similar levels of development, without closing those gaps. Venezuela, however, has followed quite the opposite trend, widening the gap. Finally, Panel C in Table 6.2 traces the evolution of this gap relative to the average of Latin America. In this case, we observe two distinct patterns. First, Bolivia slightly increased relative to the average in Latin America by 2018. Second, Paraguay remained practically at the same levels, relative to the average country in Latin America, for the past three decades. Third, Ecuador and Venezuela were above the average for Latin America in 1990, but experienced a deterioration of their conditions and now face a wider gap. This situation is particularly remarkable in the case of Venezuela, since the country is experiencing an unprecedented crisis that is bringing the economy down.

Table 6.2: Income gap based on relative GDP per capita.

	1990	2000	2010	2018
Panel A: Most developed countries				
Bolivia	0.08	0.08	0.12	0.12
Ecuador	0.21	0.14	0.22	0.20
Paraguay	0.13	0.10	0.16	0.17
Venezuela	0.31	0.20	0.37	0.18
Panel B: Similar level of development				
Bolivia	0.44	0.44	0.41	0.50
Ecuador	0.34	0.36	0.65	0.40
Paraguay	0.60	0.52	0.56	0.67
Venezuela	1.38	1.04	1.13	0.70
Panel C: Latin American countries				
Bolivia	0.38	0.42	0.46	0.48
Ecuador	1.05	0.72	0.82	0.79

Table 6.2 (continued)

	1990	2000	2010	2018
Paraguay	0.67	0.50	0.62	0.65
Venezuela	1.55	0.99	1.42	0.67

Source: World Bank (2020), United Nations Development Programme (UNDP) (2019) based on Birdsall et al. (2008).
Note: A value of 1 represents absence of income gap, while a value smaller (greater) than 1 implies a negative (positive) gap. Individual GDP per capita in 2011 dollars at purchasing power parity relative to the average of each comparison group of countries. *Most developed countries* refers to the group of countries in the top decile of a subindex of health, education, and income of the Human Development Index. *Similar level of development* refers to the group of countries in the same decile of a subindex of health, education, and income of the Human Development Index. *Latin American countries* refers to the group of countries from Latin America in a subindex of health, education, and income of the Human Development Index.

The last 20 years have witnessed a declining trend of poverty and inequality in Bolivia, Ecuador, Paraguay, and Venezuela. There is, however, some heterogeneity in this behavior. Bolivia experienced an increase of its poverty rates at the beginning of the 2000s, mostly as a consequence of a period of high income inequality, but later turned for a downward trend (benefiting from natural gas and oil prices) until 2018. Since the start of the dollarization process, Ecuador has been able to reduce its poverty steadily, with a mild increase during the GFC. Remittances have been an important source of income for Ecuador, contributing to such reduction, particularly after the 2000s. In fact, in the period 2000 to 2019, the number of remittances tripled, and currently represent more than 3 percent of GDP. Paraguay was in the middle of a crisis at the beginning of the 2000s, with poverty consequences until 2002. However, with the recovery of the economy, the poverty levels declined consistently until 2018, with no interruption by the GFC. Cruces et al. (2015) argue that rising labor incomes is the main reason for this reduction in poverty, particularly after 2006. Interestingly, Bolivia, Ecuador, and Paraguay observed reductions in their population living in poverty conditions throughout the last 20 years, with little to no consequences from the GFC. Moreover, similar to Ecuador, Venezuela also started the 2000s in the midst of a crisis (during 2002 and 2003) with increases in its poverty levels. The reduction in poverty came after the economy recovered its growth trend and labor incomes, with the exception of the period of the GFC. However, the recent debacle and collapse of the Venezuelan economy changed the landscape, since poverty conditions are now the new reality of almost everyone in the country.

The downward trend in poverty rates observed in all countries seems to be consistent with increases in labor earnings, as well as government programs that supported the vulnerable population. Cash transfer programs have played an important role in the fight against poverty across Latin America, particularly those targeted to the vulnerable population. For instance, conditional cash transfer programs such as Bono Juancito Pinto (established in 2006) in Bolivia, Bono de Desarrollo Humano (established in 1998) in Ecuador, and the *Tekoporã* (established in 2005) in Paraguay, contributed to explaining the reduction in poverty and income inequality. In the case of Venezuela, the Sistema Nacional de Misiones (active since 2003), mostly financed by PDVSA, are the main social programs focusing on health, education, and work programs. In Table 6.1, using the absolute measure of 5.5 dollars per day, a global standard of poverty, Bolivia and Ecuador show similar rates with 23.1 and 24.2 percent, respectively, of their population living in poverty, while Paraguay has the lowest of the group with 17 percent of its population.[12] In the case of Venezuela, almost 37 percent of the population falls below this standard of poverty, compared to about 23 for the entire region. When using the official poverty line (instead of the 5.5 dollars per day measure), the figures are similar for Ecuador with 23 percent of the population, while Bolivia and Paraguay jumped to 36.4 and 24.2 percent, respectively, of their population falling below this standard of poverty. These poverty trends usually follow the evolution of the economy, particularly that of GDP. However, as Cruces et al. (2017) report, the differences between these poverty lines could also be due to fluctuations in food prices, key elements in official poverty lines. The unofficial poverty line results for Venezuela are particularly alarming. Based on the Encuesta Nacional de Condiciones de Vida (Encovi) 2019–2020, the Universidad Católica Andrés Bello (UCAB) from Venezuela computed a measure of poverty at 3.2 dollars per day and a measure of poverty line, both based for 2019–2020. They found that 75.8 percent of the population falls below the threshold of 3.2 dollars a day, while 96.2 percent of the population is below the official poverty line. These disturbing statistics are only comparable with the poorest regions of the world and are the last outcome of a rapid deterioration process of the economy that started in 2014, with the end of the boom of the price of oil.

---

12 The World Bank has an international poverty line for upper middle-income countries (most Latin American countries) that captures the concept of absolute poverty by setting a threshold of 5.5 dollars a day (in 2011 PPP terms). Absolute poverty is defined as the lack of monetary resources to meet certain basic needs of human existence. Official poverty lines are based on household surveys with population weighted averages and include more comprehensive structures of basic needs. Despite considerable improvement and harmonization of household surveys in Latin America, comparison across countries might not be perfect.

Furthermore, income inequality, measured by the Gini coefficient, also experienced a relative decline in the last 20 years but still remains high.[13] In particular, Ecuador and Paraguay have similar coefficients at 0.45 and 0.46, respectively and similar to the average for Latin America, while Bolivia is at 0.42 and Venezuela at 0.51 (one of the highest in the region, similar to Honduras). The distribution of income can be influenced by the distribution of human capital. Hence, the distribution of human capital is influenced by the distribution of educational opportunities. Using the inequality-adjusted education index, Table 6.1 also shows Venezuela and Ecuador with the highest scores, 0.64 and 0.60, respectively, followed by Bolivia and Paraguay with 0.55 and 0.52, respectively.[14] This means, Venezuela and Ecuador have less unequal distribution of education compared to Bolivia and Paraguay, and to the average of Latin America. However, note that this statistic is purely based on the number of years (*quantity*) of education obtained, but less informative about the quality of education.

The Macroeconomic Record

As expected, not all countries in this group went through similar experiences with inflation. We first have Bolivia (after the period of hyperinflation) and Paraguay sharing similar experiences after 1990, then Ecuador that experienced high inflation at the beginning of the 1990s, and finally, Venezuela, which is still living an unprecedented hyperinflation. Let us first put things in context. At the beginning of the 1990s, Bolivia was in a new phase of stabilization, after experiencing one of the worse hyperinflations in the world from 1982 to 1986, with a record of 11,750 percent in 1985. Antelo (2000) describes that during this

---

13 Income inequality is usually measured using the Gini coefficient. The Gini coefficient is a measure of the deviation of the actual income distribution from perfect equality. It ranges from 0 to 1, 0 being perfect equality and 1 implying perfect inequality. No country in the world conforms to either extreme. There are at least two caveats regarding the use of the Gini coefficient. The Gini coefficient does not capture subgroup (region, ethnic group, etc.) changes and puts equal weight to the entire distribution. That means that the lower end of the distribution has a similar weight in the index than the upper end. This feature could be masking important changes in the dynamics of the distribution.

14 The inequality-adjusted education index is the HDI education index value adjusted for inequality in the distribution of years of schooling of the adult population, drawn from household surveys (UNDP, 2019). The inequality dimension is estimated by the Atkinson measure, capturing subgroup (region, ethnic group, etc.) changes and putting more weight to the lower end of the distribution. This index is constructed by the UNDP and ranges from 0 (most inequal) to 1 (most equal) in terms of education equality.

period, Bolivia implemented structural reforms following the Washington Consensus under the stabilization plan known as the New Economic Policy (Nueva Politica Economica) (NPE).[15] The NPE included, among other things, a commitment to price stability and financial liberalization. In this context, the central bank unified the exchange rates and adopted a crawling-peg regime. As part of this financial liberalization, transactions and deposits in dollars were re-established. Given the history of inflation in Bolivia, it was not unexpected the increase in dollarization of deposits from about 60 percent at the beginning of the 1990s to 92.4 percent in 1998. That is, there was an overwhelming trend to save in a "hard" currency rather than in domestic currency (the boliviano). The NPE also contemplated a tighter monetary policy, preventing public lending. As a result, in the period from 1990 to 1997, inflation decreased from 17 percent to 4.7 percent in 1998 while the economy was growing at an average of 4.0 percent per year and GDP per capita increased 19 percent. This growth was mostly the result of privatizations of public enterprises that brought large inflows of foreign direct investment (FDI) in sectors such as oil, energy, and telecommunications.

Although the Bolivian economy was affected during the Asian and Russian crises of 1997 and 1998, there was not a noticeable impact on export prices. The GFC affected the economy and the inflation rate jumped to 14 percent in 2008, but rapidly reverted to 3.3 percent in 2009. Two elements are worth noticing in this context. First, the history of high dollarization of the Bolivian economy made its monetary policy quite challenging and sometimes not responsive. Second, dollarization can be seen as an extreme case of a fixed exchange rate regime. In fact, this happened in 2011, when the central bank adopted a fixed rate. While Garcia-Escribano and Sosa (2011) found that the exchange rate appreciation played an important role in the de-dollarization of the Bolivian economy, there is recent evidence suggesting that some macroprudential policies could have helped as well. Specifically, deposit dollarization declined from almost 90 percent in 2003 to less than 15 percent in 2018. During this last period, from 2010 to 2019, Panel A in Table 6.3 shows that the inflation rate in Bolivia has been averaging 4.3 percent, which is slightly below the average for the region without Venezuela (4.7 percent).

---

15 The Washington Consensus refers to a loose collection of economic policies that has been promoted by multilateral institutions in Washington, DC, such as the World Bank, the IMF, and a number of think tanks. The main point was a movement away from the import substitution industrialization paradigm toward a more market-based economy. These reforms included an efficient tax system, a fiscal policy appropriate for macroeconomic conditions, improvement to basic services to promote economic growth, capitalization through privatization, liberalization of goods and financial markets, and promotion of exports to generate foreign resources.

Table 6.3: Inflation rate and Central Bank independence.

	1990–1999	2000–2009	2010–2019*
Panel A: Inflation rate, percentage			
Bolivia	10.5	4.9	4.3
Ecuador	39.0	17.8	2.6
Paraguay	16.5	8.3	4.3
Venezuela	47.4	21.0	26,636.7
Central America	*15.4*	*6.6*	*3.6*
Latin America	*140.1*	*8.2*	*483.9*
*Latin America***	*145.5*	*7.5*	*4.7*
Panel B: Central Bank independence index (Garriga, 2016)			
Bolivia	0.55	0.80	0.80
Ecuador	0.88	0.80	0.47
Paraguay	0.50	0.62	0.62
Venezuela	0.67	0.76	0.60
Central America	*0.51*	*0.64*	*0.64*
Latin America	*0.57*	*0.59*	*0.62*
*Latin America***	*0.56*	*0.59*	*0.61*

* = 2010–2014 in Panel B; ** = without Venezuela
Source: World Bank (2020) and Garriga (2016).
Note: The Garriga (2016) index goes from 0 to 1, with 0 being completely dependent and 1 being independent.

The Alto Cenepa War (a military conflict between Ecuador and Peru) in 1995, brought uncertainty about the soundness of the Ecuadorian economy fueled by the increase in military spending. That year, inflation reached 23 percent and the exchange rate devaluated about 17 percent, much more than the expected figures of the stand-by-agreement with the IMF. By 1996, Ecuador was then living a period of instability that was aggravated by the election of President Abdalá Bucaram and the challenges to control inflation. The combined negative shocks of the Asian crisis, the El Niño effect, the drop in oil prices, and the Russian crisis contributed to further increase the pressures on inflation and on the sucre, which depreciated 36 percent in 1998. During this time, the central bank went through a series of reforms included in the Constitution of 1998. It was granted with technical and administrative independence – a major reform at that time – with the explicit purpose to safeguard the stability of the currency, and even barred the possibility of lines of credits to the public sector or the financial system (except in the case of crises). Panel B in Table 6.3 shows that during this period, Ecuador was the country with the highest degree of independence from this group, about 0.88 in the Garriga (2016) index that goes from 0 to 1, with 0 being completely dependent and 1 being independent. As a point of reference, the Latin American average during this period was 0.57. However, by the end of 1998, the financial system was already under stress, mostly as a result of external shocks but, as Jácome (2004) argues, also as a consequence of inadequate banking supervision. The modifications to the central bank charter were rapidly put to the test. By acting as lender of last resort, the central bank tried to contain the bank run. This caused a considerable increase in lending to the financial system as well as in monetary aggregates that ended up contributing to more inflation. In 1999, Ecuador entered its worst economic crisis with a freeze on deposits and, a significant reduction of the financial system.[16] The exchange rate regime was abandoned, moving to a floating scheme, unleashing a devaluation of almost 180 percent by the end of 1999 with inflation reaching 65 percent.

The decision to adopt the dollar as the official currency of Ecuador in 2000 was mainly motivated by a ramping inflation and a domestic currency that was devaluating at a worrisome pace. After peaking at 96 percent in 2000, the inflation rate declined, reaching a single digit in 2003. Throughout the period of boom of commodities and beyond (until 2019), the average inflation rate has been 3.1 percent, with 2008 (during the GFC) as an exception year with 8.4 percent.

During 1995 and 2003, the period of financial crises in Paraguay, inflation was under control at a yearly average rate of 10 percent, below the rate of 12.5 percent for Latin America. This is not unusual; throughout its history, Paraguay has shown moderate levels of inflation at about 11 percent (from 1960 to 2019). During this same period, the exchange rate followed an "intermediate regime" of managed flotation. Alonso (2018) argues that the exchange rate policy and the central bank management of monetary aggregates were the main reasons behind the low-inflation performance. The year 1998 came with the Asian and Russian crises and an episode of financial instability with bank runs. This period of volatility brought a sudden stop of capital flows that pressured the exchange rate with an unusually high depreciation of the domestic currency (the guarani) of almost 25 percent (by the end of 1998). By 2002, after Argentina and Uruguay were in the

---

16 Naranjo (2003) reports that 15 out of the 40 banks and two financial companies, were closed or taken over by the state.

midst of financial crises, another wave of instability affected Paraguay's financial system with new bank interventions and runs on deposits. This time the outflow of capital represented almost 10 percent of GDP, according to Santos (2009), and even with the central bank intervention, the exchange rate depreciated 38 percent in 2002. In fact, Santos (2009) argues that the relatively low financial development and the sound macroeconomic base at the beginning of the crises were key in preventing a generalized contagion and containment of the effects within the economy. Nevertheless, the economy contracted and a first round of reforms were implemented in the context of an agreement with the IMF.

By 2003, the government approved a new framework of regulation and supervision for the central bank that included an insurance deposit and began laying out the fundamentals of an inflation-targeting regime. Under this intermediate regime, the government was able to maintain an average inflation rate of 6.6 percent from 2004 to 2010. Even though the GFC brought a drop in the demand for Paraguayan exports and a temporary fall in commodity prices, and the drought of 2009 impacted agricultural production, there was not a significant impact in terms of inflation. It was in 2011 when the central bank officially announced the adoption of a full-fledged inflation-targeting framework establishing a target of 5 percent (that was later changed to 4 percent). During this period from 2011 to 2019, the monetary authority managed to consolidate credibility and predictability with inflation averaging 4.2 percent while the guarani depreciated about 3 percent.

The analysis of inflation in Venezuela is closely tied to its exchange rate policy. Let us get into the details. At the beginning of the 1990s the government established a floating system for the exchange rate consistent with an IMF program that aimed at recovering macroeconomic stability through market liberalization policies. The transition to this new regime led to a large devaluation, which combined with the elimination of price controls, brought increases in prices of public goods and wages. GDP grew from 1990 to 1993, and this adjustment process initially helped to keep inflation at about 40 percent per year. However, the political instability of that time, including two unsuccessful coup attempts of 1992, the impeachment of President Pérez in 1993, and the major financial crisis of 1994, contributed to an environment of uncertainty and capital flight. To prevent a massive sudden stop of capital flows, the government introduced capital controls with a fixed exchange rate system. The new exchange restrictions had a direct negative impact on domestic demand, pressuring inflation. Additionally, a parallel (black-market) exchange rate suggested implicit depreciation expectations for the currency (the bolivar), contributing even further to inflation expectations. As it is always the case, these expectations soon materialized when the government adjusted the (fixed) exchange rate leading to a significant devaluation of the currency at the end of 1995, with consequences on inflation through 1996.[17] By mid-1996, the central bank eliminated exchange controls on capital transactions and a crawling band was adopted as the exchange rate regime. These policies reduced inflation and depreciation to pre-1990s levels, with inflation reaching 12.5 percent in 2001, the lowest rate since 1986. By this time, after just two years of electing President Chávez, Venezuela was living through increasing political uncertainty following the new constitution of 1999, the reform of institutions, and capital outflows.[18] After a significant reduction of almost $6 billion (3.4 percent of GDP) in international reserves by 2002, the government eventually abandoned the crawling band and moved to a floating system without capital controls. This system was just a transitory measure. After more political instability associated with the oil strikes of 2002–2003 and low oil prices, the GDP contracted, unemployment increased to more than 18 percent, and there was a massive stop of capital inflows that depreciated the currency and ignited inflation (again). In this context, by 2003, the government decided to reestablish a fixed system (with a single exchange rate) and strict capital controls. Despite this system created a parallel market of foreign currency, the strong performance of the price of oil, during the period 2003 to 2008, was enough to put the economy on a solid growth path.

The GFC brought instability and maybe a first alert that things were about to get complicated. With a low price of oil and continued outflows of capital, the Venezuelan authorities moved to defend its fixed exchange rate system losing foreign reserves. The large depreciation of almost 100 percent came in 2010 after two years with a new currency (the bolivar *fuerte*) and a wave of multiple exchange rates. Kulesza (2017) argues that the combination of corruption scandals associated with the foreign currency system, the large misalignment with the parallel market (that caused an increase in the cost of production), capital flights, and reduced real wages, resulted in a consistent acceleration of the rate of inflation. By 2014, the Venezuelan government stopped publishing statistical data on a regular basis. Soon after that, by 2016, Venezuela entered a grim period of hyperinflation when the rate reached 274 percent. With growing expectations of a new devaluation, the dollar in the parallel market kept increasing, pushing inflation to unprecedented levels. Moreover, the reliance of the government on the foreign exchange system with multiple exchange rates brought even more uncertainty and capital outflows, that contributed to shortages, and extreme poverty,

---

17 The inflation rate reached 100 percent in 1996.
18 In fact, capital outflows increased the pressure on the exchange rate regime and the central bank decided to defend it with international reserves.

to the point that the domestic currency (now, the bolivar *soberano*) and prices were just irrelevant. In fact, by mid-2019, the central bank published its consumer price index showing that the inflation rate reached 863 percent, and 130,060 percent in 2017 and 2018, respectively, and an accumulated inflation between 2016 and mid-2019 of 53,798,500 percent.

The other components of the macroeconomic record are the fiscal and debt dynamics. These are closely related with what we discussed above. During the mid-1990s, Bolivia was in the midst of reforms (in the context of the NPE) that tried to improve efficiency and reduce the fiscal deficit. Unsurprisingly, the main challenge during this time was the management of public debt. In 1996, Bolivia joined the Heavily Indebt Poor Countries (HIPC) initiative, along with another 39 developing countries that were eligible for special assistance from the IMF and the World Bank.[19] According to Kehoe et al. (2019), through this initiative, Bolivia was able to reduce its external debt over a period of 15 years. However, as a result of the international crises (Asian and Russia) and regional crises (Brazil, Argentina, and Uruguay), the fiscal deficit went from 3.2 percent in 1997 to almost 7 percent of GDP in 2001 (see Panel A in Figure 6.2). Additionally, after a (new) default (on its multilateral and bilateral debt), Bolivia's public debt reached 60 percent of GDP in 2001. Fortunately, by 2003, Bolivia started a recovery phase. Kehoe et al. (2019) explain this recovery was based on the improvements of international economic conditions, an increased demand for natural gas and hydrocarbons, and rises in prices of commodities.[20] Soon after that, by 2005, the Congress passed the Hyrdocarbons Law to return the legal ownership to the state of all hydrocarbons and natural resources. It was essentially a nationalization that would anticipate the tone of Evo Morales's presidency that started in 2006. By maintaining the royalty rate paid on hydrocarbon production but increasing the taxes, the government was able to substantially increase its fiscal revenues. This enabled a sustained fiscal surplus throughout the commodity boom from 4.5 percent in 2006 to 0.6 percent of GDP in 2013. It also created savings that were used as a buffer to pursue counter-cyclical fiscal policies to support domestic demand during the GFC. Most of the reduction of public debt during the boom of commodities was due to the HIPC initiative and external conditions. Specifically, public debt was reduced from 90 percent in 2004 to 37 percent of GDP by 2014. Once

---

19 The HIPC initiative provided financial support by reducing the debt of developing countries that were heavily in debt and poor, to prevent them from being overwhelmed by the debt burden. In a first step (HIPC I) the idea was to reduce the debt/export ratio to less than 200 percent while in a second step (HIPC II) the aim was to reduce the ratio to 150 percent.

20 All this happened in the aftermath of an election process that created political instability when the president did not have the needed support of Congress.

the supercycle of commodities was ended, things started reverting to the previous dynamic with a fiscal deficit hovering at about 8 percent of GDP and public debt fast approaching 60 percent of GDP in 2019.

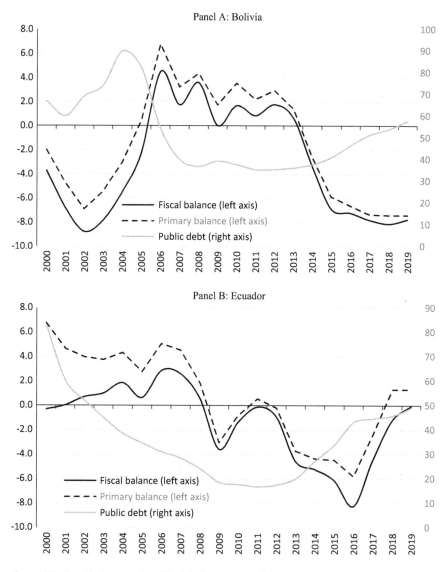

Figure 6.2: Fiscal balance and public debt (percentage of GDP).
Source: World Bank (2020) and International Monetary Fund (2020b).

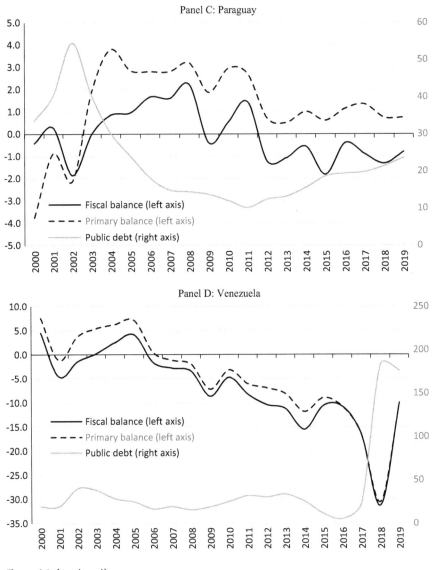

Figure 6.2 (continued)

During 1999, at the peak of the financial crisis in Ecuador, public debt reached a maximum of 94 percent of GDP, with some Brady bonds in default. The dollarization proposed by President Mahuad, and confirmed by President Gustavo Noboa by the end of 2000, came with some reforms to ensure its sustainability. Cueva (2008) and Diaz (2018) provide a detailed analysis of the fiscal responsibilities laws that were approved during that time. Among those reforms, the Ecuadorian government limited public expenditure to 3.5 percent of GDP, the debt to GDP ratio to 40 percent, and created stabilization funds to force savings from oil production. Regarding public debt, the government managed to restructure the defaulted foreign debt, reducing the face value by approximately 40 percent, according to Cueva and Diaz (2018). The first years following the dollarization (2000–2006) were when most of the new measures started taking place in the context of prudent fiscal policies and sustainable debt management. The fiscal result improved from a deficit of 0.3 to a surplus of almost 3 percent of GDP in 2006, while the public debt declined from a debt to GDP ratio of 83 percent of GDP in 2000 to 31 percent in 2006 (see Panel B in Figure 6.2). The election of Rafael Correa in 2007 as president of Ecuador, coincided with the beginning of the supercycle of commodities, but also marked a change in terms of economic policies.[21] President Correa's first two terms were characterized by an increase in the role of the public sector, terminating the negotiations for a free trade agreement with the United States, and reverting much of the policies and reforms from the post-dollarization era. The fiscal result deteriorated from a surplus of 2.6 percent of GDP in 2007 to a deficit of 4.6 percent of GDP in 2013, mainly as a result of public expenditures outgrowing revenues. This performance occurred in the context of a boom in commodities, particularly in oil prices that increased fiscal revenues, and a sequence of tax reforms (aimed at increasing collection). Interestingly, during this time there was a slight decline of the debt to GDP ratio from 28 percent in 2007 to 20 percent in 2013, mainly driven by a strong GDP.[22] The years 2013–2016 were marked by the burst of the oil boom, the 2016 earthquake, and the end of President Correa's third terms as president of Ecuador.[23] With oil prices having plunged, a low demand for

---

21 Together with Hugo Chavez of Venezuela and Evo Morales of Bolivia, President Correa became part of the "pink tide", a phrase to denominate leftist governments in Latin America.
22 To understand why this happened, let us back up and do the math. To finance the new deficits, the Ecuadorian government increased its borrowing from about $14.5 billion in 2007 to $19.1 billion in 2013, which implies an increase of 31.2 percent, while nominal GDP increased 86.5 percent, during the same period. In other words, the reduction in the ratio debt to GDP during that period was driven by the increase in GDP.
23 The 2016 earthquake was of magnitude 7.8, and it is estimated that more than 670 died, 4,600 people were injured, and the total damage climbed to 3 percent of GDP, according to national authorities and ECLAC.

exports, the lack of fiscal buffers, and limited access to international financing (with the exception of multilateral organizations), Ecuador ended 2016 with a contraction of GDP of about 1.2 percent. By the end of this period, the fiscal deficit and public debt substantially increased, reaching more than 8.0 percent of GDP and 43 percent of GDP, respectively. In fact, from 2007 to 2016, the public debt tripled, from about $14 billion to approximately $43 billion while nominal GDP doubled, thus the debt to GDP ratio increased from 28 to 43. In recent years (2017–2019), after the burst of the commodity supercycle, with a "new normal" state of external prices, growth has decelerated in Ecuador. However, the administration of President Lenín Moreno reached agreements to pass laws to regulate the central bank, a new fiscal framework capping the growth of public spending, and an oil stabilization fund to smooth the commodity cycle. At the end of the period of analysis, the fiscal deficit was almost zero and public debt hovered at 49 percent of GDP.

The end of the 1990s, after a decade of reforms to modernize the state, found Paraguay in the middle of a sequence of domestic banking crises, the Asian and Russian crises, and the Brazilian devaluation, which affected growth and tax revenues. Consequently, the year 2000 was the first time that the Paraguayan economy experienced a fiscal deficit (0.4 percent of GDP) in more than 20 years. As Charotti et al. (2019) explain, during this time, the government relied on public debt to finance public infrastructure, resulting in an increase of indebtedness from 33 percent of GDP in 2000 to 54 percent in 2002. Moreover, during 2002, the contagion from the Argentine crisis combined with a weak agriculture production caused a sharp fall in economic activity in Paraguay. The fiscal deficit reached 2 percent of GDP and the government accumulated large payment arrears mainly from foreign debt. However, in 2003, the administration of President Nicanor Duarte received the financial support of the IMF to start a wave of reforms to strengthen the fiscal front, the debt management, and the supervision and regulation of financial institutions. From 2003 to 2008 the fiscal result went from −0.01 to 2.2 percent of GDP, while public debt declined from 40 to 14.5 percent of GDP (see Panel C in Figure 6.2). This performance enabled fiscal savings that soon were used as buffers during times of distress.

The GFC of 2008, the decline of the price of commodities, and the drought of 2009 were all contributing factors for the decline of activity in Paraguay. Similar to other Latin American countries, the government was able to implement counter-cyclical policies, such as temporary housing projects, increases of public infrastructure, support for small and medium enterprises, and support to agriculture to weather the consequences of the crisis. By 2010, the economy was back on its growth trend with prudent macroeconomic policies that resulted in a fiscal surplus of 0.5 percent of GDP and a public debt of 12 percent of GDP. Unfortunately, not long after, this Paraguay received a new shock in the form of a severe drought in 2012, which prevented meat exports and negatively affected all sectors of the economy. Despite the fact that growth bounced back fast, fiscal revenues did not manage to recover immediately, leading to fiscal deficits the following years. Nevertheless, the government of President Horacio Cartes approved a fiscal responsibility law in 2015, which contributed to macroeconomic stability with prudent fiscal policies. Under this framework, the fiscal deficit was capped at 1.5 percent of GDP (with a medium-term outlook of 1 percent of GDP), there was a cap on the amount of government spending, and a temporary freeze of public wages. Hence, since 2015 the average fiscal deficit has stabilized at about 1 percent of GDP, while public debt has increased from 18.6 to approximately 24 percent of GDP. This macroeconomic and fiscal management of the economy has helped Paraguay lessen, to some extent, large swings associated with the supercycle of commodities.

At the end of the 1990s, Venezuela was concluding a decade with a positive fiscal result of 0.7 percent of GDP and a public debt hovering at 24 percent of GDP. Hugo Chávez was elected and took office in 1999, with a wide range of reforms that contributed to political turmoil. After the Russian crisis and with low oil prices, the government embarked on an endeavor to control the petroleum industry as a way to secure fiscal resources. Following the oil strikes of 2002–2003, President Chávez managed to control the oil rents and reform the tax structure, pursing a program that promoted the role of the state with an expansionary fiscal policy. In fact, from 2003 to 2008, Venezuela's public spending was the driving force behind fiscal policy, increasing from 31 percent of GDP to an average of almost 35 percent during that period, with a peak of 39 percent of GDP in 2006. As a result of the government's reforms in oil regulation and taxation, fiscal revenues also increased from about 29.5 percent of GDP in 2002 to an average of 34.4 percent from 2003 to 2008. This period of unusually strong oil prices, generated these high fiscal revenues, that combined with the expansionary fiscal expenditure policy, brought the Venezuela economy from a fiscal surplus of 0.17 percent of GDP in 2003 to a deficit of 3.5 of GDP in 2008 (see Panel D in Figure 6.2). Since 1914, when crude oil was discovered, Venezuela has been an economy with a strong reliance on the price of oil.[24] Benefited by the increase in the prices of oil and the strong performance of the economy, the public debt to GDP ratio declined from almost 40 percent in 2002 to about 15.5 percent of GDP by 2008.

---

24 Based on Ríos et al. (2012), during the 1990s, with a price of oil of about 20 dollars per barrel, 59 percent of fiscal revenues were generated by oil production and 71 percent of total exports were coming from oil, while during the 2000s, with an average price of 57 dollars per

Similar to other countries in Latin America, the GFC adversely affected the economy of Venezuela, mostly through the decline in the price of oil. Unlike other countries in Latin America, Venezuela did not save for bad times during the boom, preventing the government from pursuing counter-cyclical policies. In fact, public spending was reduced and taxes increased in 2009, in a clear example of procyclical fiscal policy. However, after a brief two-year period, the economy had gone back to pre-GFC levels by 2012 with a recovery of the price of oil and new increases in public spending and fiscal deficits. As Ríos et al. (2012) explain, most of these deficits were associated with oil taxation, a significant increase in spending, and the fact that PDVSA was undertaking official fiscal activities, as a parallel national office. Specifically, fiscal spending in 2009 was about 35 percent of GDP and increased to more than 50 percent of GDP by 2014 while fiscal revenues after 2010 stayed at about 30 percent of GDP. Most of the increases in public debt during this period are attributable to PDVSA that since 2010 was, among other things, operating the government's social spending programs.

The end of the supercycle of petroleum combined with years of inconsistent fiscal and exchange rate policies, financial constraints, and increasing external debt, led to an explosive fiscal deficit of 31 percent of GDP by 2018, mostly as a result of the collapse of the economy and thus of fiscal revenues (4.2 percent of GDP).[25] Unsurprisingly, the public debt also followed an explosive trajectory reaching more than 182 percent of GDP by 2018. Even though the traditional credit markets have been closed for a while for Venezuela, this increase in public debt is mostly the result of arrears (even with multilateral banks), bilateral loans, and legal arbitration cases.[26]

Economic Structure

Bolivia is particularly rich in mineral resources such as tin, gold, silver, zinc, and iron. More importantly, it also has reserves of natural gas, lithium, and oil. In fact, Bolivia's proven reserves of natural gas are estimated at approximately

---

barrel, oil fiscal revenues were about 48 percent, and more than 90 percent of total exports were coming from oil activities.

25 The IMF is estimating a deficit of 10 percent by 2019, but these figures are unclear due to the lack of official statistics.

26 The Heritage Foundation and the Institute of International Finance estimate the Venezuelan public debt to reach 176 percent of GDP by 2019.

300 billion cubic meters according to data from the Organization of the Petroleum Exporting Countries (OPEC). This places Bolivia behind Venezuela, Peru, Brazil, and Argentina in Latin America in terms of proven natural gas reserves. Most of the production of natural gas happens in the eastern part of the country and is shipped through pipelines to Argentina and Brazil. Accounting for about 8 percent of Bolivia's GDP, natural gas certainly is one of the nation's main energy resources and exports, with a history of privatization and nationalizations.[27] Oil production is mostly for domestic consumption in the form of vehicle gasoline, liquid propane and butane, jet fuel, and diesel oil for use in the industry.

Jointly with Argentina and Chile, Bolivia's Salar de Uyuni is part of the "lithium triangle," a region containing a large portion of the world's lithium reserves. Notice that lithium is used in small batteries but most importantly in batteries for hybrid and electric vehicles. Hence, the Bolivian government has an intricate balance to maintain at the Salar de Uyuni. It is a unique natural landscape – the world's largest salt flat – with constant tourism in the region and with the second largest known concentration of lithium.[28] Nevertheless, lithium mining requires significant technological investments, not easily available domestically. Moreover, since Bolivia has a history of nationalizations it is not surprising that foreign firms might require some reassurances before committing to such a venture. Considering those mineral resources with the processing of food, beverages and tobacco, cotton and woolen, and the production of synthetic fibers, the Bolivian industrial sector represented approximately 38 percent of GDP and employed 20 percent of the labor force in 2018. Table 6.4 presents the economic structure of the economy.

Agriculture is challenging in Bolivia due to the topography and climate, and in the rural regions it is mainly a form of subsistence with crops such as potatoes, corn, barley, quinoa, wheat, alfalfa, and oats. The leading agricultural exports are soybeans, followed by cotton, sugarcane, and coffee. However, the most lucrative crop is coca, with an estimated cultivation area of approximately 32,900 hectares (behind Colombia and Peru) and a cocaine production potential of 254 metric tons, according to the United States Office of National Drug Control Policy (ONDCP) (2019). Overall, agriculture's share has steadily declined since the 1970s, and today represents about 14 percent of GDP but employs 32 percent of the country's labor force. Finally, the service sector is the largest contributor to the value added of the economy, accounting for approximately 49 percent and

---

27 During the structural reforms of the mid-1990s, the natural gas sector was privatized, and later re-nationalized in 2006.
28 See the USGS (2019) summary for "Lithium."

Table 6.4: Economic structure (percentage of GDP).

	Agriculture	Industry	Services
Bolivia	13.8	38	49
Ecuador	6.7	33	60
Paraguay	17.9	28	55
Venezuela	4.7	40	55
Central America	*10.5*	*23.4*	*66.1*
Latin America	*9.0*	*28.3*	*62.8*

Source: World Bank (2020) and United Nations Development Programme (UNDP) (2018).

employing about 49 percent of the labor force. Nevertheless, this is a sector that suffers from weak demand and informality.[29] The main industries from this sector are tourism, retail, and financial services.

Ecuador has traditionally been an agricultural economy; rich in natural resources, it is the world's leading exporter of bananas, but also an exporter of flowers, cocoa, coffee, sugar, tuna, and shrimp. The share of the agricultural sector in GDP used to be about 26 percent in the 1970s but currently represents about 6.7 percent and captures about 28 percent of the total labor force. Interestingly, while the major crops from the highlands, like corn, wheat, potatoes, and soybeans, are for domestic consumption, most of the agriculture of the coast is oriented toward exports.

During the late 1960s, foreign companies found oil in the Ecuadorian Amazon rainforest, and with this the promise of modernization and progress. By 1972, Ecuador finished the construction of the Andean pipeline that brought oil from the Amazon region to the coast, making Ecuador the second largest oil exporter of the region after Venezuela. The state-owned company Petroamazonas EP currently produces more than 80 percent of total production. The remaining production comes from fields operated by foreign oil companies from Spain, Italy, Argentina, and China. Today, Ecuador is largely dependent on petroleum resources (producing about 550,000 barrels per day of petroleum and other liquids), which represent about 30 percent of government revenues, almost 40 percent of export earnings, and 76 percent of the country's total energy consumption. The

---

29 Half of production in Bolivia comes from the informal sector, according to estimations from Medina and Schneider (2018)

manufacturing sector mainly comprises the petroleum industry and its deriva-tives. With the development of new technology and changes in global de-mand, Ecuador has also been able to develop other sectors like processed food, textiles, metal work, flowers, and paper products. However, with the ex-ception of oil, of which 70 percent of the production is exported, most of the industrial activity is for the domestic market. All this accounts for an indus-trial sector that has been increasing its share to about 33 percent of GDP and employs 19 percent of the total labor force. Finally, the service sector in Ecua-dor accounts for 60 percent of the GDP and is responsible for about 53 percent of total labor. The tourism sector accounts for a significant share of the service industry along with transportation, communication, and financial services. Although at similar levels to the average for Latin America, the size of the in-formal economy (about 30 percent of GDP) is one of the main challenges for the development of a strong service industry in Ecuador.

Traditionally, Paraguay has been an economy highly dependent on agricul-ture, with soybeans as the leading crop (one of the largest producers in the world) followed by beef, corn, and rice. According to the World Bank, the arable land of Paraguay represents about 12 percent of the country, mostly surrounding cities such as Asunción, Encarnación, and Ciudad del Este, in the eastern region. Simi-lar to the region's trend, the share of agriculture has declined since the 1970s and today represents about 18 percent of GDP, employing 20 percent of the country's labor force. Paraguay has all the disadvantages of a landlocked country, with higher transportation costs that affect its exports, but with access to the Atlantic Ocean through the Paraná and Paraguay rivers, crossing Argentina. In fact, along the Paraná River lies an important component of the Paraguayan economy: the Itaipu Dam. Constructed jointly by Paraguay and Brazil in 1984, it is a hydroelec-tric dam (the second largest in the world based on generation capacity) along the Paraná River between both countries. Under an agreement dated from 1973, both countries have the right to use half of the dam's production. According to the US Energy Information Administration (EIA), Paraguay's Itaipu and Yacyretá dams produce approximately 63 billion kWh/year while the domestic consumption is about 11 billion kWh/year. That is, all of Paraguay's domestic electricity comes from hydroelectric power and the rest (about 83 percent of the production) is ex-ported to Argentina, Brazil, and Uruguay. A matter of current dispute under the agreement with Brazil is that the energy produced from Itaipu and sold to Brazil is paid at the cost of production instead of the market price of electricity, potentially affecting Paraguay's revenues.

Although manufacturing in Paraguay has traditionally been based on the processing of agricultural and animal products for export, it is currently more di-verse. In particular, it includes the production of cement, steel, textile industry, wood products, and pharmaceutical and chemical goods. All this accounts for an industrial sector that currently employs 19 percent of the total labor and is responsible for about 28 percent of GDP. Finally, the service sector in Paraguay is mainly comprised of transportation, technology services, banking and finance services, and a small tourism industry. The development of this sector has been particularly challenged by the business cycle and the high level of informality, currently estimated by Medina and Schneider (2018) at 32 percent of GDP. Overall, the service sector in Paraguay represents about 55 percent of GDP and employs nearly 61 percent of total labor.

For more than a century, Venezuela has been an economy centered on the production of petroleum. In fact, since 2010, Venezuela is the country with the largest proven oil reserves in the world, estimated at 302,809 million of barrels in 2019. Production of oil has plummeted in recent years, from a maximum of 3.3 million in 1997 to about 0.8 million barrels per day in 2019. This is mostly the result of the new management at PDVSA after President Chavez took control of the firm, but also due to the changes in the rules of the agreements between the government and foreign companies producing oil.[30] In other words, the oil reserves are there but there is no installed capacity, or foreign interest to produce it. This decline in the production of oil seems to have little correlation with its international price and more with the complex process of extracting oil in Venezuela. Nevertheless, currently, the petroleum sector accounts for about 25 percent of GDP and almost 90 percent of exports. Additionally, Venezuela has other natural resources such as natural gas, gold, iron, and nickel. The manufacturing sector includes steel, cement, aluminum, textiles, apparel, and food and beverages production. Overall, the sector approximately contributes to 12 percent of GDP. However, if we include the petroleum refining (most of petroleum is exported as crude oil), which is a major industry, the sector accounted for 40 percent of GDP and employed about 22 percent of the total labor in 2013.[31]

Interestingly, before petroleum became the main export, Venezuela used to rely on agricultural commodities such as coffee and cocoa. More recently, rice, corn, fish, and beef extended the list of agricultural production. However, a key element of agriculture is that Venezuela is not self-sufficient and needs to import most of the food. This is a particular challenge that has exacerbated the impact of shortages during past and the present crises.[32] Employing about

---

30 Venezuela has petroleum deposits that are considered extra-heavy and requires special technology to be extracted.

31 2013 is the last year reported to the World Bank.

32 In fact, food scarcity has been a constant theme in Venezuela, but with the recent fallout of the economy this rate has skyrocketed. The UN World Food Programme (2020) estimates that

7 percent of the labor force, the agricultural sector in Venezuela accounts for approximately 5 percent of GDP. Finally, the service sector is the one with the largest share in the economy contributing approximately 55 percent and employing 71 percent of the labor force. Within this sector, retail, banking and finance, real estate, government agencies, and tourism are the most important subsectors. Poverty and a considerable degree of informality are by far the largest problems in this sector.

Foreign Trade

Let us briefly discuss the ability of countries to move financial flows. According to the Chinn and Ito (2006) index presented in Table 6.5, by 1990, Bolivia was at high levels of financial integration, relative to this group of countries, but also relative to Latin America and other regions.[33] At that time, Venezuela was not far from those levels of financial openness. These magnitudes were probably the result of the structural reforms in both countries. Ecuador and Paraguay, on the other hand, were at relatively low levels of financial integration, only comparable with South Asia. By the year 2000, all countries from this group increased their financial integration at different paces, but most of them as a consequence of more recent reforms. With the exception of Ecuador, the rest of the countries were considerably above the average for Latin America and other regions. The turn came by 2010. At about this time, the only country that kept this trend of increasing integration with financial markets was Ecuador, which was above the average for the region and most other places. Although Bolivia and Paraguay introduced some restrictions to the flow of capitals, they averaged at similar levels to the region. However, Venezuela marked a different experience with a total closure of its accounts for financial transactions. By 2018, the trend observed for Bolivia, Paraguay, and Venezuela continued, putting them at a situation of low financial integration relative to the rest of the world. These restrictions on the free flow of capital can be controversial. Some of the literature views capital controls as causing more harm in terms of limiting growth than it provides in benefits of some protection against exchange rate shocks. More recent

---

roughly a third of the population has moderate or severe food insecurity. However, Encovi 2019–2020 from the Universidad Católica Andrés Bello (UCAB) reported this figure to be almost 80 percent of Venezuelans.

33 The Chinn and Ito (2006) index takes higher values the more open a country is to cross-border capital transactions. In particular, the normalized version ranges from 0 to 1.

research indicates that the cost–benefit analysis may be more complex and dependent on other factors of the economy, such as the financial development of the country and its institutions.[34]

Table 6.5: Capital account openness.

	1990	2000	2010	2018
Bolivia	0.55	0.75	0.51	0.45
Ecuador	0.18	0.42	0.88	0.70
Paraguay	0.17	0.75	0.57	0.45
Venezuela	0.42	1.00	0.00	0.00
Latin America	0.26	0.53	0.56	0.53
East Asia and Pacific	0.55	0.49	0.68	0.61
Europe and Central Asia	0.52	0.62	1.00	1.00
Sub-Saharan Africa	0.23	0.29	0.30	0.23
South Asia	0.19	0.27	0.29	0.32

Source: Chinn and Ito (2006) index, where higher values indicate a country is more open to cross-border capital transactions.

The picture looks different with respect to trade openness, measured by the ratio of exports plus imports to GDP. Figure 6.3 presents the measure of trade openness for Bolivia, Ecuador, Paraguay, Venezuela, and the average for Latin America. Since 1990, Paraguay has been the leading country in this group and in Latin America, with a ratio of about 100 percent of GDP throughout the decade; even higher during some years. The rest of the countries show a degree of openness closer to the average of Latin America – but usually below – from 1990 until 2005. In all cases, they felt the shock of the GFC, since their demand for exports and imports decreased during that time. However, when commodities gained momentum during their last boom, Bolivia and Ecuador experienced increases in their ratios. In the case of Bolivia, this ratio reached 85 percent of GDP by 2014, after which it decreased to almost the regional average of 60 percent. In the case of Ecuador, the ratio returned to pre-GFC levels, but after the price burst, it declined further to the levels of 1998. Venezuela reached the Latin American average in 2013, at the peak of the oil boom, and then declined

---

34 For instance, see Rodriguez (2017).

considerably to a historical low during the first years of the current crisis, reaching 48 percent of GDP in 2018, according to Venezuela's central bank. This group of countries currently has higher ratios than Argentina, Brazil, Chile, Colombia, Peru, and Uruguay, and, with the exception of Ecuador and Venezuela, they have a trade ratio hovering around the average for Latin America. Although these figures might be giving the impression of less vulnerability, these countries face more volatility since their exports are highly concentrated on commodities. Let us look into the details.

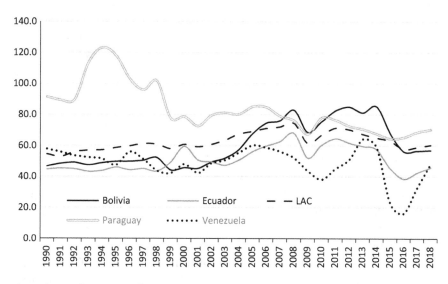

Figure 6.3: Trade openness (exports plus imports as a share of GDP, percentage).
Source: World Bank (2020).
Note: LAC is the simple average of 17 countries in Latin America, excluding the Caribbean.

In fact, the countries from the current group are the ones with the highest concentration of their exports in commodities from the entire region. In all cases, their ratios of exports that are commodities are always above 81 percent, compared to the average of 61 percent for Latin America (see Table 6.6). This might not come as a surprise. After all, one of the main barriers for growth in Latin America is the high dependency on commodities. Venezuela is the country with the highest concentration with almost all of its exports being commodities. About 86 percent of Venezuelan exports are associated with petroleum, while another 11 percent are associated with gold and iron. Just by these figures one can imagine the level of reliance of the Venezuelan economy on the oil cycle. The main trade partners of Venezuela are the United States, India, China, United Arab

Emirates, and Turkey, accounting for approximately 90 percent of total exports. Ecuador comes in second place with 93 percent of its exports as commodities. In particular, the main exports are led by petroleum and its derivatives, bananas, crustaceans, and processed fish, which capture more than 76 percent of its exports. The main destinations for those exports are the United States, Peru, China, Chile, Panama, and Vietnam, accounting for almost 62 percent of Ecuador's exports. Paraguay comes next in this ranking, with almost 89 percent of its exports concentrated in commodities. However, unlike Venezuela and Ecuador, most of these exports are non-fuel commodities associated with food and fertilizers. This is particularly relevant since Ocampo (2017) shows that the last supercycle for non-fuel commodities was shorter and weaker than that for oil commodities. In particular, approximately 67 percent of Paraguay's exports are soybeans and its derivates, and animal products associated with bovine meat. The main destinations for its exports are Argentina, Brazil, Russia, Chile, and India, representing almost 64 percent of total exports. Lastly, in the case of Bolivia, 73 percent of its exports are led by natural gas, zinc, gold, soybeans, and precious metals. The main countries demanding Bolivian products are Brazil, Argentina, India, Japan, South Korean, and the United States, totaling about 60 percent of total exports.

The price volatility associated with commodities naturally translates into volatility in overall exports. When these exports represent a relatively high percentage of GDP, then the growth rate of real GDP can be substantially impacted by changes in commodity prices. In this aspect, all countries in this group have a high share of commodity exports in GDP. Paraguay has the second highest share in Latin America with 19.4 percent of GDP, while Bolivia, Ecuador, and Venezuela have 17.0, 17.1, and 15.0 percent of GDP, respectively. These figures, in Table 6.6, compare with a 11.8 percent of GDP for the average country in Latin America. Hence, for this group of countries, fluctuations in commodity prices can have significant impact on the volatility of their real GDP, and therefore their economic growth.

Table 6.6: Commodities' share of exports and GDP in Latin America.

	Commodity exports (mill of USD)	Exports (merchandise) (mill of USD)	Commodity/ Exports	Commodity Exports/GDP
Venezuela	72,277	74,714	96.7	15.0
Ecuador	17,772	19,122	92.9	17.0
Paraguay	7,702	8,680	88.7	19.4

Table 6.6 (continued)

	Commodity exports (mill of USD)	Exports (merchandise) (mill of USD)	Commodity/ Exports	Commodity Exports/GDP
Chile	59,621	69,230	86.1	21.5
Bolivia	6,423	7,846	81.9	17.1
Uruguay	6,305	7,888	79.9	11.2
Colombia	28,168	37,881	74.3	9.0
Peru	33,007	45,275	72.9	15.6
Argentina	39,072	58,622	66.7	6.1
Brazil	134,706	217,826	61.8	6.6
Guatemala	6,358	11,001	57.8	8.4
Nicaragua	2,493	5,170	48.2	18.0
Costa Rica	4,298	9,556	45.0	7.5
Honduras	3,351	8,675	38.6	14.6
El Salvador	1,374	5,760	23.9	5.5
Mexico	67,085	409,401	16.4	5.8
Panama	1,050	11,093	9.5	1.7
Central America			*37.2*	*9.3*
Latin America			*61.3*	*11.8*

Source: World Trade Organization (2020).

Country Specific Details

Bolivia: The War of the Pacific and the Struggle of Being Landlocked

Since its inception, Bolivia has dealt with tensions along its borders with Brazil, Paraguay, Argentina, Chile, and Peru. A lingering problem following independence along the coast of South America was the borders among Bolivia, Peru, and Chile, which led to one of the most significant conflicts of the time: the War of the Pacific (1879–1904).

During some time, Bolivia and Chile attempted to settle their disputes by treaty in 1866 and 1874. However, distrust of Chile moved Bolivia and Peru to form a (secret) defensive alliance in 1873, to mutually defend themselves. The tensions were exacerbated by economic interests around the Antofagasta region.

The province of Antofagasta (then in Bolivia) is a high mountain desert rich in nitrates. In this period, these nitrates, in the form of saltpeter used to produce explosives and guano used for fertilizer, were extremely valuable. In addition, the region contains an incredible amount of copper. The resources were being exploited by British capital backing Chilean companies. Bolivia and Chile had reached an agreement on the taxation of Chilean companies in 1874, but in 1878 Bolivia attempted to increase taxes beyond the previously agreed upon rates. Bolivia and Chile entered a dispute about the legality of such tax until Bolivia threatened to confiscate the mining company in February 1879. That was the time when Chile occupied the port of Antofagasta. When Bolivia declared war on Chile in March 1879, the defensive alliance immediately brought Peru into the war. To hold Antofagasta, Chile first controlled the naval access to the province. Following the naval campaign, the Chilean Army led a successful ground campaign. The military conflict ended in 1883 when Chile and Peru signed the Treaty of Ancón while Bolivia signed a truce with Chile in 1884. However, it was not until 1904 when Chile and Bolivia finally signed the Treaty of Peace and Friendship, establishing definite boundaries. From this conflict, Chile gained not only Antofagasta province (a nitrate-rich coastal territory) and the Litoral department from Bolivia, but two provinces in Peru (Tacna and Arica). Under the treaty, the status of these two Peruvian provinces was supposed to be determined by a plebiscite to be held in 10 years. Disagreement over the terms of the plebiscite resulted in the dispute continuing until 1929. Through US mediation, the Tacna–Arica compromise of 1929 gave Arica to Chile and Tacna to Peru.

As a result of this conflict, Peru lost a war and a province, while Bolivia lost a war and its access to the sea, becoming a landlocked nation. Although Bolivia has ceded land to most of its neighbors, either through diplomacy or treaties that followed military conflicts, the ill will generated by the War of the Pacific lingers into the 21st century. On the one hand, because the region still is important for its resources: while saltpeter and guano are part of its economic history, substantial revenues accrue to Chile from copper and, more recently, lithium. On the other hand, because the lack of access to the sea became an exceptionally sensitive subject. The 1904 treaty established boundaries that rendered Bolivia into a landlocked country but also covered Bolivian demands associated with railways, education, customs, and financial independence. Nevertheless, for more than a century, Bolivia and Chile remained in disagreement about the compliance of each country regarding the terms of the treaty. In fact, the Bolivian national sentiment is still sour towards Chile and nostalgic for the days when Bolivia had access to the sea. For instance, Bolivia celebrates the *Día del Mar* (Day of the Sea) on March 23, which observes the loss of the Litoral Department in the War of the Pacific. Additionally, Bolivia still maintains a navy that serves as a river and lake patrol force, hoping to also operate in the Pacific port someday. Moreover, in 2013 President Evo Morales filed a lawsuit (that was rejected in 2018) with the International Court of Justice demanding Chile to cede coastal territory to Bolivia.

With a few exceptions, most landlocked countries are among the poorest in the world. Coastal countries, as a group, have much higher average income levels than landlocked countries. Based on data from the Penn World Table, the GDP per capita of landlocked countries is 40 percent lower than their costal neighbors. They also export an average of 30 percent less than coastal countries.[35] An obvious impact of being landlocked is that moving goods to and from ports is more expensive, just because more distance has to be covered to get to the port. In that sense, Arvis et al. (2010) conclude that landlocked economies are affected not only by a high cost of freight services (approximately 50 percent more), but also by the unpredictability associated with transportation times. Along the same line of argument, Faye et al. (2004) discuss how landlocked countries depend on their neighbors' infrastructure, their political relations, and administrative practices. Carmignani (2015) expands the list of effects on landlocked countries by arguing that they also have weaker institutions. That is, the flow of cultures and new ideas that brought innovation to coastal countries largely bypassed landlocked ones. Even though Bolivia has tariff-free access to the ports of Arica and Antofagasta, it also struggles with the consequences of being landlocked. In fact, in a report for the UN Office of the High Representative for the Least Developed Countries, Landlocked Developing countries and Small Island Developing States (UN-OHRLLS) (2014), Carmignani estimates that Bolivia's GDP would be almost one-fifth higher if it had not lost access to the Pacific Ocean.

Ecuador: The Process of Dollarization

There is one distinctive issue, almost impossible not to notice upon arrival to Ecuador: you do not need domestic currency for transactions. The US dollar is legal tender; that is, the official currency used in Ecuador. Not many other countries share this characteristic. In fact, El Salvador is the other (non-island) country of the world in this particular situation.[36] Here, we will briefly explore the details of the dollarization and some of its consequences for Ecuador.

The adoption of the US dollar as the domestic currency and unit of account in Ecuador was preceded by a combination of domestic and external shocks

---

35 According to estimates from Limao and Venables (2001).
36 Zimbabwe was also using the US dollar as legal tender from 2009 until 2019.

that once combined put the country in its worst economic crisis. Let us first understand the domestic situation. After the 1995 war against Peru, Ecuador was left with a fiscal deficit of almost 2 percent of GDP and a low stock of international reserves that was used to defend the sucre due to the uncertainty created. Inflation was not as severe as during periods of hyperinflation but it was certainly a concern. In this context, President Bucaram (inaugurated in August 1996) suggested tackling this issue with a currency board, á la Argentina. This proposal never materialized since President Bucaram was declared mentally incapable, and quickly removed from office in February 1997, increasing political instability. In fact, between this episode and the announcement of the dollarization (January 9, 2000), Ecuador lived through a new constitution (August 1998), two interim presidents (Rosalia Arteaga and Fabián Alarcón), and one president (Jamil Mahuad) that lasted only 12 days (after the official announcement of the dollarization).

Nevertheless, the external shocks were also key determinants of the crisis that preceded the dollarization. During 1997 and 1998, Ecuador suffered floods and destruction due to a El Niño phenomenon. Additionally, fiscal revenues were also in distress due to low international oil prices. By October 1998, the Asian and the Russian crises were palpable and affecting the cost of credit and its availability for developing countries. During these days, the first signs of concerns with the financial system were emerging. Initially with a bank failure (mostly associated with El Niño) that created solvency uncertainty, but ending with a bank run on the entire financial system. The central bank acted as lender of last resort, expanding the money in circulation, further decreasing the international reserves and adding uncertainty about the defense of the exchange rate. To prevent losing the already low stock of international reserves, the central bank shifted to a floating exchange rate regime for the sucre by February of 1999. The banking crisis escalated, and a freeze on deposits was dictated for one year by March 1999. The exchange rate was under continued pressure, depreciating approximately 180 percent during 1999 and pushing inflation to pre-hyperinflation rates. The combination of banking and exchange rate crises with the uncertainty from the political system fueled a debt crisis that materialized when Ecuador defaulted on some of its sovereign debt (Brady bonds) in August 1999. By the end of 1999, as Naranjo (2003) and Cueva and Díaz (2018) discuss, almost half of the financial system disappeared or was nationalized, the non-performing loans rose to 45 percent of all loans, and the IMF (2015) estimated the total cost of the banking crisis was about 30 percent of Ecuador's GDP. Based on the analyses of de la Torre et al. (2002), Jácome (2004), and Borensztein and Ruiz-Arranz (2018) the main issues that contributed to this crisis can be summarized as: (i) insufficient banking supervision (particularly associated with offshore activities), (ii) lack of banking regulation and the role of the central bank as lender of last resort, (iii) *moral hazard* in lending practices, and (iv) high degree of credit dollarization (about 80 percent by 1998). The consequences of El Niño added more pressure to an already fragile financial system.

With an economy severely affected by the crisis and the sucre in free falling mode, on January 9, 2000, President Mahuad announced the intention to officially adopt the US dollar as the currency of Ecuador.[37] Just 12 days after this announcement President Mahuad resigned, in the midst of considerable demonstrations and social and political turmoil. Nevertheless, the process to dollarize was rapidly ratified by his successor, President Gustavo Noboa.[38]

Dollarization in Ecuador came with a mix of policies to ensure its sustainability. Cueva and Diaz (2018) summarize them as follow. First, there were reforms to the central bank to ensure a smooth transition of assets and liabilities to a system centered on the use of the dollar. Second, authorities successfully renegotiated the defaulted foreign debt extending maturity and decreasing its face value. Third, since authorities gave up the capacity to finance deficits by printing money, the government focused on promoting fiscal discipline as the main instrument of policy. In this spirit, Ecuador approved laws to limit government spending and the debt to GDP ratio, and created oil stabilization funds to save for future crises. The dollarization process brought back the economy to its growth path, managed to decrease the inflation rate to one digit by 2003, and reestablished stability and credibility in the banking system.

Paraguay: The War of the Triple Alliance

Two major events are the exceptions to the general peacefulness of the region during the second part of the 19th century: the War of the Pacific and the War of the Triple Alliance. We discussed the former in the first part of this section, and here we will address the latter. Many things have been written about the origins of the war, receiving considerable attention from a historical point of view. However,

---

37 The exchange rate was fixed at 25,000 sucres per dollar, such that the amount of international reserves was enough to cover the money in circulation.

38 The discussion to fully dollarize an economy was a matter of academic debate at that time. Calvo and Reinhart (2001, 2002), among other scholars, argued that the combination of the "fear of floating," the credit constraints of an unofficially dollarized economy to play the role of lender of last resort, and the "sudden stops" of capital flows were arguments that made dollarization a sensible choice for some Latin American countries.

there is a consensus that this conflict was the result of the struggle for hegemony in the region and one of the bloodiest in the history of Latin America.

The war began when Paraguay invaded Brazil in 1864 after a long dispute regarding boundaries in Uruguay between Argentina, Brazil, and Uruguay. Within a year, after the invasion, Argentina, Brazil, and Uruguay united into a Triple Alliance against Paraguay (Bethell, 1996). Although Paraguay entered the war with a larger military force than the Allies and managed some initial victories, they were badly equipped and eventually outnumbered (Salles, 2003). The war lasted until President Solano López was killed in battle in March 1870, after fighting and losing a war and more than a year of a guerrilla resistance. There has been some debate about the motivations of President Solano López to enter the war and to keep fighting in a guerrilla-type resistance, however the consequences are undisputed but profoundly damaging. Paraguay permanently lost 140,000 square kilometers of territory (over a quarter of the country) to Argentina and Brazil. The human cost was staggering. Based on the 1871 census, the population dropped from approximately 525,000 to 221,000, due to military losses, malnutrition, and diseases. Based on that figure, Potthast-Jutkeit (1991) estimated that there were 106,000 women, 86,000 children, and 28,000 men still alive in the country. This implies a sex ratio of four women for every man, which is remarkably high.[39]

The overall consequences of this war are not easy to estimate and the aftermath of it left the country with enormous challenges. In fact, one needs to keep in mind that Paraguay suffered a catastrophe on a scale not seen since the Spanish conquest. In a recent article, Alix-Garcia et al. (2020) managed to analyze the short-, medium-, and long-term impacts of an extraordinarily large sex ratio shock using the case of the War of the Triple Alliance. In the short and medium term, these authors find that, as a consequence of the war, there were higher out-of-wedlock birth rates than in comparable municipalities of Argentina and Brazil. Furthermore, the closer to the conflict zone, the higher the sex ratio, the school attendance for girls, and the share of out-of-wedlock births. It is worth mentioning that the sex ratios for cohorts born after the war quickly converged to unity. Regarding long-term impacts, Alix-Garcia et al. (2020) found that 100 years later, women who lived in regions with skewed sex ratios as a result of the war were more likely to be unmarried living with a child, be the head of the household, have higher education outcomes, and were more likely to be employed. Interestingly, these authors find that Guarani cultural traditions from the pre-colonial era were not leading to more persistent effects.

---

39 However, Carrasco (1905) documents that using the 1899 census this ratio was closer to 1.16.

These findings show the magnitude of the implications of the war for Paraguay. On the one hand, they highlight how this conflict altered gender roles for generations, affecting the role of women in the household and labor market in Paraguay. On the other hand, the improvement in educational outcomes for women might have leveraged their potential labor earnings. Nevertheless, after more than 150 years since the war has ended, one cannot help but notice that Paraguay still is one of the least developed countries in the region. Hence, the extent of the long run impacts for the development of the country could be traced back to this historical event.

Venezuela: The Economic Implosion

Venezuela was once a "normal" country in Latin America. In 2014, the population was approximately 32 million, producing a GDP of about $500 billion. At nearly $16,000, GDP per capita was among the highest in the region. In the middle of the 20th century, Venezuela had a standard of living that was easily equivalent to the poorer countries in southern Europe. This should have been the case. Venezuela has oil reserves that are among the highest in the world. A large and stable oil industry was providing the country with a standard of living that was relatively high. The collapse of the economy since the middle of the last decade is hard to come to grips with. The fact that the government quit publishing the usual economic statistics in 2014 is relating that something is deeply wrong. Unofficial local estimates are that GDP has fallen somewhere between 66 and 75 percent and that nearly all Venezuelans live in poverty (96 percent). For a country not at war, this is an unfathomable number. In addition, the country is racked by hyperinflation to the extent that prices are virtually meaningless and money is almost useless. In addition, supplies of both food and medicine have created a situation where most of the population is hungry and common illnesses can be dangerous. A final statistic is the most telling. Since the middle of the last decade about 6 million Venezuelans have fled the country. The official count is 5.4 million but the UN Refugee Agency (UNHCR) estimates this figure at about 6.5 million Venezuelans living outside the country by 2020. As Bahar and Dooley (2019) describe, the speed of this displacement outpaced that of Syria. Although not associated with a conventional war or conflict, the case of Venezuela is a migration crisis in modern history; it is not just the affluent who are leaving but large numbers of average citizens.

Let us discuss how this happened in economic terms. Hugo Chávez took office in 1999 after winning the 1998 elections. Skidmore et al. (2010) argue that the Chávez's victory was almost a consequence of the frustration with the traditional leadership in Venezuela.[40] The political system was going through a crisis of parties, the banking system was coming out of a massive crisis with 17 banks bailed out by the government, inflation was increasing again after reaching 100 percent in 1996, and poverty was affecting about 60 percent of the population. In his first year, President Chávez consolidated power by calling a referendum to enact a new constitution that permitted reelection, increased executive powers (allowing to rule by decree), and reduced the Congress to a unicameral National Assembly, weakening traditional political parties. By 2001, under the new constitution, President Chávez put in place 49 laws by decree to implement his plan, including a hydrocarbons law to restructure PDVSA and a land reform. Seeking redistribution, the land law reformed commercial farms, seized property and land, expropriated companies, and passed the ownership to local cooperatives. Unfortunately, most of these cooperatives lacked technical knowledge and managerial skills leading to a food production collapse and difficulties associated with doing business. Initially with low oil prices (26 dollars per barrel), modest levels of rent but with a high level of production (the highest was about 3.3 million barrels per day in 1997), President Chávez also moved to gain control of the petroleum industry as a source of revenue. Social and political tension started to build up, and by late 2002 an oil strike started, lasting 2 months until February 2003 when President Chávez fired approximately 20,000 employees of PDVSA (including technical positions), according to Rapier (2017), and replaced them with workers loyal to the government. Naím and Toro (2018) report that, this represented a considerable loss of technical knowledge since the appointed employees knew little about the oil business. It is worth nothing that Venezuela's oil reserves consist of extra-heavy crude oil that is considerably capital intensive to produce, hence, investment in maintenance was one of the most important factors to keep production steady. However, President Chávez's strategy was based on transferring resources out of PDVSA into social programs. Hence, government spending grew rapidly but the tax base in the private sector did not, creating large mismatches between tax revenues and expenditures. This problem was mitigated in the short run by high oil prices. As long as oil prices were high, the decline of the private sector was manageable.

With the surge in global oil prices in 2003, the lack of capital investment was not immediately noticeable, but, by 2005, it was clear that something was not right when news came out reporting technical workers from PDVSA started leaving the firm. Anecdotal evidence from 2005 suggested about 1,000 former

---

40 In fact, McCoy and Myers (2006) explain that the election of President Caldera in 1994 can be considered the end of traditional parties in Venezuela.

high-skilled PDVSA workers left Venezuela to work at oil companies in Mexico, the United States, Russia, or Saudi Arabia.[41] With a record price of 100 dollars per barrel in 2007, the government sought more resources from foreign oil companies by changing agreements, creating new taxes, increasing royalties, and in some cases seizing assets. Regarding this point, Johnson (2018) suggests that President Chávez seemed more focused on channeling resources to keep his social plan running than investing to keep PDVSA healthy. From 2003 to 2010, the production of oil stayed at about 2.5 million barrels per day (see Figure 6.4), but the boom in the price of oil exhibited extraordinary profits for some time, masking the need for a major capital investment to keep PDVSA up to date. Without a major renovation of the industry and unable to keep up with the production of oil, PDVSA reclassified 200 billion barrels as proved reserves. The level of production still remained constant until the end of the commodity boom when the price of oil dropped below 40 dollars per barrel in 2016 after years of fluctuating at about 95 dollars per barrel. This was the beginning of the debacle. With an economy heavily dependent on oil (representing more than 90 percent of exports), the drop in its price brought the economy to a full-blown crisis with almost no options to counter the crisis. In one of the last years that statistics were available, the government budget deficit was 24 percent of GDP. The deficits were being financed by printing money and the rest is history. This is the recipe for all most great inflations of history. In addition to the hyper-inflation, imports were being controlled and producers could not secure adequate supplies of raw materials and intermediate goods. In this context, the production of oil plummeted to a historical low of 0.8 million barrels per day (see Figure 6.4). This was mainly due to the fact that before PDVSA can export its heavy crude oil, imported inputs are needed for its extraction, but the required cash to purchase those inputs was simply not available. Increasing the production of oil seems like a minimum condition to restart the economy and get new resources. However, resurrecting the oil industry requires a considerable amount of investment that the government is currently unable of doing by itself.

With inflation spiraling upwards, investment and total production in the economy have been rapidly falling. Political instability has added pressure to an already weakened economic system. This downward spiral of rising prices and falling production continues today. Unfortunately, after some years with these conditions, the basic infrastructure of the country is now deteriorating at a rapid pace. Furthermore, there is no hint of any change in economic policy.

---

41 Based on union officials, Johnson (2018) reports that in 2017, about 25,000 workers have resigned from PDVSA, and that some offices have refused to accept more resignations.

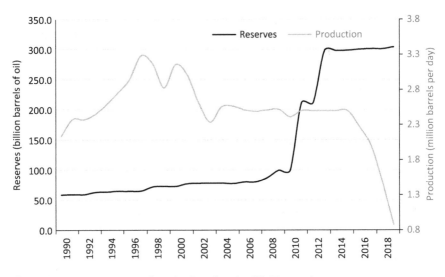

Figure 6.4: Proven reserves and production of crude oil in Venezuela.
Source: US Energy Information Administration (2020).

This contraction of the economy might not be easily reversed and recovery will probably take some time since the basic structure of the economy has been seriously affected.[42] Further, the government seems incapable of providing basic services such as reliable electricity, clean water, basic health care, or basic education, what fuels the flow of people fleeing the country. Without further changes to the current business arrangements, the country seems to be heading to a catastrophic state. Venezuela has become an economic black hole in the heart of Latin America. At this point, unfortunately, there is no clear end in sight and the challenges still persist for a reconstruction of the economy.

---

42 As Bahar and Dooley (2019) argue, the Venezuelan collapse was not the result of a war or external forces but a consequence of decisions from those in power.

Chapter 7
Mexico and Central America

The Basics

Behind Brazil and Argentina in terms of land size, with an area of 1,972,550 square kilometers, Mexico is the second largest country in Latin America in terms of population (approximately 126 million) and GDP ($1.2 trillion).[1] It is the 11th largest economy in the world and currently has a GDP per capita of $9,700, slightly above the average for Latin America (see Table 7.1). It is the only Latin American country entirely in North America and has shorelines on the Gulf of Mexico and the Caribbean Sea on the east coast, and the Pacific Ocean and the Gulf of California on the west coast. Mexico has two major mountain ranges, the Sierra Madre Oriental (running from the east side) and the Sierra Madre Occidental (running from the west side), with the Mexican Altiplano in between, along with the Transvolcanic Belt that covers the central-south area of the country and the Sierra Madre del Sur in the south. Considered one of the top countries in terms of biodiversity, Mexico is also endowed with an array of climates, ranging from tropical, rainforest to desert, and with natural resources, particularly petroleum, silver, copper, and lead. In fact, it used to be the fourth-largest oil producer in the world, but currently stands in 11th place with about 2.3 million barrels per day. Mexico is considered an upper middle-income economy with high levels of human development. Nevertheless, its stable macroeconomy and growing private sector coexist with high levels of informality, poverty, and inequality. Mexico was the first country from Latin America to join the Organisation for Economic Co-operation and Development (OECD) in 1994.

The region to the south of Mexico and to the north of Colombia is what we know as Central America. It includes seven countries: Belize, Guatemala, El Salvador, Honduras, Nicaragua, Costa Rica, and Panama. For this chapter, we exclude Belize because as a former British colony with a relatively short history as an independent country, is culturally identified as West Indian rather than Central American.

Under Spanish colonial rule, most of Central America was governed as one area. In fact, after declaring independence from Spain and separating from Mexico, the United Provinces of Central America was created as a sovereign state,

---

1 Mexico also controls several small islands along the Gulf of Mexico, the Pacific Ocean, and the Gulf of California.

https://doi.org/10.1515/9783110674934-007

Table 7.1: Population, GDP, GDP per capita, poverty, and inequality in Mexico and Central America.

	Population (millions)	GDP (billions of USD)	GDP per capita (USD)	Poverty ($5.5 per day)	Poverty percentage (year)	Income inequality (Gini coefficient)	Inequality-adjusted education index
Costa Rica	5.0	61	12,112	10.9	21.1	0.48	0.61
El Salvador	6.4	26	4,068	25.7	26.3	0.39	0.40
Guatemala	16.3	73	4,473	48.8	60.0	0.48	0.35
Honduras	9.6	24	2,506	50.3	62.0	0.52	0.37
Mexico	126.2	1,221	9,673	25.7	49.0	0.45	0.56
Nicaragua	6.5	13	2,021	34.8	30.0	0.46	0.42
Panama	4.2	65	15,593	12.7	20.7	0.49	0.61
Central America	*47.8*	*257*	*6,656*	*30.5*	*36.7*	*0.47*	*0.46*
Latin America	*644.1*	*5,972*	*9,272*	*23.3*	*33.8*	*0.46*	*0.56*

Source: World Bank (2020), Economic Commission for Latin America and the Caribbean (ECLAC) (2019), United Nations Development Programme (UNDP) (2019).

Notes: Population, GDP, GDP per capita from 2018. Poverty from 2018, excepting Guatemala, Nicaragua, and Venezuela from 2014. Poverty percentage from 2018, excepting Bolivia, Chile, and Panama from 2017, Guatemala from 2014, Nicaragua from 2015, and Venezuela from 2019. Income inequality from 2018, excepting Guatemala, Nicaragua, and Venezuela 2014. Inequality-adjusted education index from 2018.

consisting of the contemporary countries of Guatemala, El Salvador, Honduras, Nicaragua, and Costa Rica. This independent state did not last long, and by 1840 it was dissolved into the current countries. The region has a combined area of 499,413 square kilometers, a population of almost 50 million, and a GDP of approximately $275 billion. To put this in context, the area of Central America is slightly greater than that of Paraguay, its population about the same as that of Colombia, and its combined GDP about the size of Chile. Along its territory, from north to south, Central America has the Sierra Madre del Sur from Mexico, a mountain range that crosses Guatemala, El Salvador, and Honduras, along with the Cordillera Isabelia in Nicaragua, and the Cordillera de Talamanca in Costa Rica and Panama. With a rainy summer and a dry winter, this region has a climate defined by the winds from east to west, and is endowed with natural resources such as nickel, iron, and oil. Although bananas and coffee dominated the Central American economy for decades, representing about 65 percent of exports in 1960, they now account for just 11 percent.[2]

In order to provide some context, let us briefly highlight some key elements and challenges of each country of Central America. Honduras and Guatemala are the poorest countries of Latin America, with half of their population living with less than 5.5 dollars per day (see Table 7.1). In fact, according to official surveys, that figure is more than 60 percent of the population. Although an imperfect measure, the Gini coefficient places Honduras and Guatemala at a high degree of inequality of 0.52 and 0.48, higher than the average for Latin America.[3] Guatemala is the largest economy of the region (with a GDP of approximately $73 billion and a GDP per capita of $4,400) and the only oil-producing country with almost 9,000 barrels per day, while Honduras (with a GDP of about $24 billion and a GDP per capita of $2,500) is highly dependent on the textile demand from the United States.[4] Nicaragua is the country with the lowest GDP and GDP per capita of Latin America, with approximately $13 billion, and $2,000, respectively, has 30 percent of the population living in poverty, and also depends on the

---

2 For Guatemala this figure is 22 percent while for El Salvador just 2 percent of exports.

3 Income inequality is usually measured using the Gini coefficient. The Gini coefficient is a measure of the deviation of the actual income distribution from perfect equality. It ranges from 0 to 1, 0 being perfect equality and 1 implying perfect inequality. No country in the world conforms to either extreme. There are at least two caveats regarding the use of the Gini coefficient. The Gini coefficient does not capture subgroup (region, ethnic group, etc.) changes and puts equal weight to the entire distribution. That means that the lower end of the distribution has a similar weight in the index than the upper end. This feature could be masking important changes in the dynamics of the distribution.

4 Almost half of textile exports from Honduras is demanded by the United States.

demand from the United States. El Salvador is the smallest country (with 21,040 square kilometers) but has the highest population density of the region. Its GDP is estimated at $26 billion with a GDP per capita of $4,000. It is, jointly with Ecuador, the other country in Latin America that officially adopted the US dollar as its currency since 2001. Crime and violence are, however, one of the big challenges for development in El Salvador. It has one of the highest homicide rates in Latin America and in the world, with a rate of 66 reported homicides per 100,000 population, according to the United Nations Office on Drugs and Crime (UNODC) (2019). As one of the most stable democracies in Latin America jointly with Uruguay, Costa Rica is quite a different story. It is ranked in fifth place in Latin America, jointly with Panama, with a high human development index (HDI). Costa Rica's GDP amounts to $61 billion with a GDP per capita of approximately $12,000. Interestingly, almost all of the electricity (approximately 98 percent) of Costa Rica is generated from renewable resources and was recognized in 2019 by the United Nations for its efforts to become a zero-carbon country. Finally, Panama is the country with the highest degree of development in Central America according to the HDI. Its GDP is similar to Costa Rica's, at about $65 billion, but has a GDP per capita of almost $16,000. In fact, Panama's GDP per capita has more than doubled in the last 20 years, partly due to the Panama Canal that accounts for almost 20 percent of its GDP, and attracts most of the investment flows coming to Central America.

All countries combined in this group cover 12.3 percent of Latin America's land and represent 28 percent and 26 percent of the region's population and GDP, respectively. For the last two decades, Mexico and Central America have been growing at 2.1 and 3.6 percent, respectively, compared to a rate of 3.1 for Latin America. Interestingly, from 1999 to 2019, Latin America's GDP per capita (measured in 2005 PPP dollars) increased 47 percent, while that of Mexico and Central America increased 16 percent and 67 percent, respectively. It is worth noting that the simple average for Central America inevitably contains some degree of heterogeneity. For instance, during the last 20 years, Panama's GDP increased at an average rate of 5.7 percent, while El Salvador's GDP grew at approximately 2.0 percent. Similarly, Panama's GDP per capita more than doubled during that period, increasing 119 percent, while Guatemala's GDP per capita only increased 30 percent. Figure 7.1 shows the evolution of the growth rate for Mexico, and the averages for Central America and Latin America. One thing that stands out is the synchronicity of the business cycles between Mexico and Central America, and of course with Latin America. Periods of booms and busts occur simultaneously, with Mexico showing more pronounced episodes and Central America following the cycle of the whole Latin American region. Let us analyze the details.

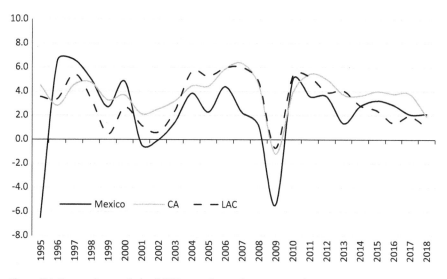

Figure 7.1: Economic growth (real GDP annual growth, percentage).
Source: World Bank (2020).
Note: LAC is the simple average of 17 countries in Latin America, excluding the Caribbean. CA is the simple average of the 6 countries of Central America.

From 1988 to 1994, in the preamble to the 1994–1995 crisis, Mexico went through many reforms including privatizations, a process of financial liberalization, the signing of the North American Free Trade Agreement (NAFTA), and a sequence of laws that strengthened the independence of the central bank. Kehoe (1995) and Meza (2018) provide a detailed timeline of the events that led to this crisis. In fact, the crisis of the Mexican peso in 1994 is probably a natural starting point to understand the economy of Mexico. It was an election year, charged with increasing political instability, depleted international reserves, a shortage of capital inflows, a rising stock of debt indexed to the dollar, and a collapsed exchange rate regime that ended with the peso left to float, unleashing a considerable devaluation. With the newly elected President Ernesto Zedillo in 1995, the Mexican economy navigated its worst contraction since the Great Depression in the 1930s: its GDP declined 6.5 percent while GDP per capita contracted 8 percent. Furthermore, this crisis was one of the first episodes to shed light about the risks associated with the sudden stops of capital flows for developing countries. After adopting a free-floating regime (which has remained in place for more than 25 years) and consistent macroeconomic policies, with a bailout organized by the United States, Mexico was able to rapidly overcome this crisis. However, soon after this recovery, the Asian and the Russian crises of 1997 and 1998 hit the economy again, affecting capital inflows and deteriorating the terms of trade. From 1996 to 1999, the growth rate slowed down from 6.5 percent to 2.7 percent.

For the last 20 years, but particularly during the first years of the 2000s, Mexico has had an unusually volatile growth performance. A contributing factor for this performance has been the increasing *co-movement* of their business cycles between Mexico, the United States, and Canada (after the inception of NAFTA). This has been particularly relevant for the manufacturing and financial sectors. In other words, when the economy of the United States goes through ups or downs, such effects tend to be felt in Mexico, and usually with some degree of amplification. In fact, in 2001, the United States went through a recession after the burst of the dot-com bubble.[5] As a consequence, after growing at approximately 5 percent in 2000, Mexico suffered a slowdown during 2001 and 2002, contracting an average of 0.2 percent per year. Interestingly enough, no synchronization was evident between the supercycle of commodities and the Mexican economy after 2002. After all, commodities in Mexico represent just 16 percent of exports, compared to the regional average of 61 percent. The recovery after the dot-com crisis lasted until the arrival of the global financial crisis (GFC) in 2007. Based on the close relation with the United States, Kehoe and Meza (2011) explain how Mexico was the country from Latin America that suffered the most from the GFC. Basically, Mexico experienced a decline of its external demand (the United States accounts for about 80 percent of Mexican exports), a drop in the price of oil exports, and a reduction in the flow of remittances.[6] Additionally, due to a (new) sudden stop of capital inflows, there was an increase in the cost of credit and a depreciation of the peso. The slowdown of the economy, which started in 2007 and continued throughout 2008, ended with a contraction of 5.4 percent of GDP by 2009. Overall, during the 2000s, Mexico grew at an average rate of 1.8 percent per year (only better than El Salvador) while the average for Latin America was 3.6 percent. Thus, GDP per capita increased 3.6 percent in Mexico when Latin America grew 27.5 percent. It was an unusually jarring decade. After a fast recovery based on the government's counter-cyclical policies, the rebound of manufacturing exports to the US, and

---

5 This was a stock market crisis associated with an unprecedented speculation in Internet-based firms, which initially created a boom in the technological industry but rapidly crashed after the September 11 attacks and the accounting scandals of Enron in October 2001 and World-Com in June 2002.

6 Based on data from the World Development Indicators from the World Bank, Mexico received the largest share of remittances from the United States before the GFC, accounting for approximately $10 billion (1.2 percent of Mexican GDP).

the inflows of capital seeking higher rates of return, Mexico returned to its long run growth rate of 2.8 per year, and a 12 percent increase in its GDP per capita, for the period from 2010 to 2019.

At the aggregate level, Central America follows a similar growth trend to the entire region of Latin America. That is, whenever the region goes through periods of booms or busts, Central America follows a similar pattern. This particular resemblance is noticeable in Figure 7.1 where all periods of crises can be spotted. This is not surprising for a group of countries that represent almost one-third of Latin America's GDP. During the sequence of crises of 1998, 2001, and 2008, Central America suffered a slowdown of its growth rate trend, from an average of 4.7 percent in 1998, to 2.0 percent in 2001, to a contraction of 1.2 percent in 2009. Moreover, the slowdown experienced by Latin America after 2010 was also present in Central America, when the growth rate declined from an average of 5.4 in 2011 to 1.62 in 2019.

There are, however, heterogeneous behaviors at the individual level. For instance, in 1994, Costa Rica suffered a banking crisis mostly as a result of supervision problems, affecting growth and contributing to inflation until 1996. After quickly recovering from this episode (helped by Intel's investment on a microchip plan), Costa Rica faced the following crises (except the GFC) in the form of a slowdown in economic growth. El Salvador and Honduras were both experiencing banking crises with severe to moderate inflation and growth effects in the years before the Asian and Russian crises. Given their level of integration to capital markets, Jácome (2008) explains that the slowdown of economic activity during this period was mostly a combination of solvency problems associated with banking crises and international external shocks. Honduras additionally suffered the consequences of Hurricane Mitch in 1998, which devasted the country, contributing to a contraction of the economy in 1999. Interestingly, during the early 2000s, Guatemala and Nicaragua also went through financial crises associated with solvency problems that aggravated the external context. However, with the exception of Honduras in 1999, no Central American country experienced a severe contraction of activity from 1995 to 2008. In fact, from the dot-com bubble to the GFC, most countries in this region benefited from increases in the prices of their exports. Furthermore, countries like Guatemala, Nicaragua, Honduras, and El Salvador also experienced an additional boost in private consumption funded by remittances.

Remittances are not a new phenomenon in Latin America; they have been occurring from the United States to Mexico and Central America for quite a long period. What is new is the rapid increase in their relative size. Let us be more specific. Based on Table 7.2, by 2000, in El Salvador, Guatemala, Honduras, and Nicaragua, remittances represented about 15, 4, 7, and 6 percent of GDP, respectively.

This is money that migrants working in the United States sent to their families and relatives in Central America, to assist with their levels of consumption. At the beginning of 2008, the amount of remittances to El Salvador, Guatemala, Honduras, and Nicaragua was significantly larger, accounting for approximately, 22, 12, 21, and 10 percent of GDP, respectively.[7] Acosta. et al. (2008) explain that these flows to the region are larger than the flows of official development assistance to these countries. Weighing the boom in commodity prices and the increase in the level of remittances, Central America experienced a period of steady resources. The average yearly growth from 1995 to 2008 was 4.1 percent (ranging between 2.2 and 5.4 percent for El Salvador and Panama, respectively) and the increase in GDP per capita was, on average, 40 percent (ranging between 19 and 63 percent for El Salvador and Panama, respectively).

Table 7.2: Remittances in Central America (percentage of GDP).

	1995	2000	2005	2010	2015	2019
Costa Rica	1.1	0.9	2.1	1.4	1.0	0.9
El Salvador	11.9	15.0	20.6	18.8	18.2	20.9
Guatemala	2.7	3.5	11.3	10.2	10.3	13.2
Honduras	2.3	6.8	18.7	16.6	17.5	21.6
Mexico	1.2	1.1	2.6	2.1	2.2	3.0
Nicaragua	1.8	6.3	9.7	9.4	9.4	13.2
Panama	1.3	0.1	0.8	1.4	1.0	0.8
Central America	3.2	4.8	9.4	8.6	8.5	10.5

Source: World Bank (2020).

Things were different with the arrival of the GFC and the major disruptions it caused in the region. The impact was mainly in terms of exports, incomes from tourism, a drop in foreign direct investment (FDI), and contraction of remittances. In all cases, there were slowdowns in 2008, and negative growth rates in 2009 (except for Guatemala and Panama), and quick recoveries in 2010. In some sense, things were different this time. All Central American countries implemented counter-cyclical policies to weather the crisis, preventing a major disruption and helping a V-shaped recovery. The growth rates for the region in the post-GFC

---

[7] Besides the GFC, Honduras also experienced political instability stemming from a military coup in 2009.

period have been buoyant but fairly constant between 2.3 and 3.6, with the exception of Panama and Nicaragua. The initial acceleration of the growth rate of Panama (with some double-digit growth rates) coincided with the construction of the expansion of the Canal, which officially began in 2007, and the Colon-Free Zone, a (public investment) free port dedicated to re-exporting merchandise to Latin America. The culmination of the expansion of the Canal and low activity in the Colon-Free Zone, due to foreign exchange restrictions in Venezuela and tariffs in Colombia according to the IMF (2014), led the annual growth rate to slow down and currently hovers at about 3.6 percent. The case of Nicaragua is associated with the economic consequences of political and social unrest. After a period of five years of strong growth performance from 2012 to 2017, at an average of 5 percent, things took a turn for the worse. At that point, the Nicaraguan Social Security Institute (INSS) was experiencing exponential deficits, and without any reform the IMF (2017) concluded that it was on the verge of depleting its reserves by 2019. To make things worse, in 2017, Venezuela (a longtime ally) retracted its oil collaboration support in the midst of its own economic crisis. In April 2018, President Daniel Ortega, announced measures to reform the INSS, slashing benefits and increasing contributions. This sparked a series of protests and violent policing of demonstrators that led to President Ortega dropping of the reform. However, the social crisis was already triggered. What followed was widespread violence, road blockades, accusations of human rights violations, and a continuum of demonstrations that paralyzed the country during the second half of 2018. With tourism, construction, and retail seriously affected, and job losses estimated at 20 percent of the formal sector by the IMF (2020a), the Nicaraguan economy shrunk by 4 percent in 2018 and in 2019, and is expected to fall 5.9 percent in 2020.

Let us now analyze how this group of countries performed in terms of their income gap relative to the rest of the world, following Birdsall et al.'s (2008) methodology. Panel A in Table 7.3 traces the evolution of this gap relative to the world's most advanced economies (in terms of health, education, and income).[8] Relative to most developed countries, Costa Rica and Panama were able to increase their level of development since 1990. El Salvador, Guatemala, Honduras, Mexico, and Nicaragua, however, seem to have stayed almost at the same level after almost

8 Based on the Human Development Index (HDI), we first construct an equally weighted subindex of health, education, and income. The most developed countries are those in the top decile of this subindex. Countries are classified as having a similar level of development if they are ranked in the same decile of this subindex. Finally, Latin American countries is the average of the 17 countries within Latin America. A greater figure implies a better performance with one being the threshold when the comparison renders the same.

three decades. Interestingly, Mexico started out in 1990 as the one closest to the most developed countries but by 2018 Panama has taken the lead while Costa Rica has managed to catch up. Panel B in Table 7.3 traces the evolution of this gap relative to countries with a similar level of development. Since 2000, Costa Rica and Panama have been able to improve but only Mexico has managed to close the gap in this category. The rest of the countries either stayed at similar levels of development or even worsened, like the cases of Nicaragua and Guatemala. Finally, Panel C in Table 7.3 traces the evolution of this gap relative to the average of Latin America. In this case, we observe a couple of patterns. First, Costa Rica, Mexico, and Panama were above the average for Latin America in 1990 and still were in 2018. Second, Panama is the country that clearly improved, relative to where it was three decades ago, while the rest of the countries stayed at a similar level and in some cases deteriorated.

Table 7.3: Income gap based on relative GDP per capita.

	1990	2000	2010	2018
Panel A: Most developed countries				
Costa Rica	0.26	0.26	0.31	0.33
El Salvador	0.09	0.12	0.15	0.14
Guatemala	0.13	0.13	0.15	0.15
Honduras	0.10	0.08	0.09	0.09
Mexico	0.41	0.37	0.37	0.39
Nicaragua	0.10	0.09	0.09	0.11
Panama	0.22	0.25	0.36	0.45
Panel B: Similar level of development				
Costa Rica	0.51	0.51	0.84	0.70
El Salvador	0.95	0.88	0.49	0.68
Guatemala	1.40	1.01	1.77	0.72
Honduras	0.59	0.64	0.42	0.43
Mexico	0.66	0.93	1.12	1.14
Nicaragua	1.15	0.71	0.43	0.50
Panama	0.44	0.48	0.49	0.88

Table 7.3 (continued)

	1990	2000	2010	2018
Panel C: Latin American countries				
Costa Rica	1.30	1.32	1.18	1.27
El Salvador	0.44	0.58	0.55	0.55
Guatemala	0.65	0.67	0.58	0.59
Honduras	0.51	0.42	0.34	0.35
Mexico	2.07	1.88	1.40	1.49
Nicaragua	0.53	0.47	0.36	0.41
Panama	1.12	1.25	1.35	1.72

Source: World Bank (2020), United Nations Development Programme (UNDP) (2019) based on Birdsall et al. (2008).
Note: A value of 1 represents absence of income gap, while a value smaller (greater) than 1 implies a negative (positive) gap. Individual GDP per capita in 2011 dollars at purchasing power parity relative to the average of each comparison group of countries. *Most developed countries* refers to the group of countries in the top decile of a subindex of health, education, and income of the Human Development Index. *Similar level of development* refers to the group of countries in the same decile of a subindex of health, education, and income of the Human Development Index. *Latin American countries* refers to the group of countries from Latin America in a subindex of health, education, and income of the Human Development Index.

In the last 20 years, poverty and inequality have relatively fallen in this group of countries. First, an improvement from 2001 to 2007, followed by a deterioration during the GFC and a later mild improvement in the post-crisis era, to a period of stagnated results. Using the absolute measure of 5.5 dollars per day, a global standard of poverty, Mexico has about 25.7 percent of the population living in poverty, while the Central American countries have an average of 30.5 percent.[9] The latter figure comprises contrasting cases like Costa Rica with 10.9 percent and Honduras with more than 50 percent of the population living in poverty, and compares to the Latin American average of 23.3 percent. When using the official poverty line, the figure for Mexico

---

9 The World Bank has an international poverty line for upper middle-income countries (most of Latin American countries) that captures the concept of absolute poverty by setting a threshold of 5.5 dollars a day (in 2011 PPP terms). Absolute poverty is defined as the lack of monetary resources to meet certain basic needs of human existence. Official poverty lines are based on household surveys with population weighted averages and include more comprehensive structures of basic needs. Despite considerable improvement and harmonization of household surveys in Latin America, comparison across countries might not be perfect.

currently reaches almost half of the population while Guatemala and Honduras reach more than 60 percent, when the average for Latin America is 33.8 percent. The trend of poverty usually follows the evolution of the economy, particularly that of GDP. However, as Cruces et al. (2017) explain, the differences between these poverty lines could also be due to extreme fluctuations in food prices. Furthermore, income inequality, measured by the Gini coefficient, also experienced a relative decline but still remains high. In particular, Mexico is at 0.45 while the average for Central America and the whole region are 0.47 and 0.46, respectively. Most of these declines can be explained, to some extent, by public spending programs and the flow of remittances from the United States. The distribution of income can be influenced by the distribution of human capital. Thus, the distribution of human capital is influenced by the distribution of educational opportunities. Using the inequality-adjusted education index, Mexico shows a score of 0.56, similar to the average for Latin America and higher than the average for Central America.[10] In fact, Costa Rica and Panama show the less unequal distribution of education in Central America, while Guatemala and Honduras the most unequal systems. However, it is worth noting that this information is based on the number of years of education obtained, but might be less informative about the quality of education.

The Macroeconomic Record

The year 1994 is, in many aspects, an inflection point for Mexico. Just the year before, the law declaring independence for the central bank of Mexico was approved establishing the protection of the value of the domestic currency as its main objective. With this new legislation in place, the central bank set the first inflation target of 19 percent. With this preamble, the Mexican economy transitioned to 1994 and the development of the crisis.[11] During this election year, political tension was building up about the economic future of Mexico. In the midst of his campaign, the candidate from the ruling party (the Partido Revolucionario Institucional [PRI]) and the one leading the

---

10 The inequality-adjusted education index is the HDI education index value adjusted for inequality in the distribution of years of schooling of the adult population, drawn from household surveys (UNDP, 2019). The inequality dimension is estimated by the Atkinson measure, capturing subgroup (region, ethnic group, etc.) changes and putting more weight to the lower end of the distribution. This index is constructed by the UNDP and ranges from 0 (most inequal) to 1 (most equal) in terms of education equality.

11 There is not a unique interpretation to explain this crisis and many theories can serve some part of the story. Meza (2018) has a comprehensive analysis of the forces at play in this crisis and the abundant literature generated by this event. In this chapter we try to circumvent this discussion as much as possible.

polls, Luis Donaldo Colosio, was murdered in Tijuana in March 1994 increasing political instability and uncertainty. The sudden stop of capital inflows was particularly pronounced during the second quarter of 1994. After defending the exchange rate regime by issuing dollar-denominated short-term debt (*tesobonos*) and by using international reserves, in December 1994 the administration of President Zedillo decided to allow the Mexican peso to float. This regime change produced a significant depreciation of the peso by more than 100 percent, unleashing a deep economic and social crisis that included inflation jumping to 52 percent by the end of 1995. President Zedillo established fiscal and monetary policies to overcome the crisis, including a bailout package organized by the United States to keep access to international markets, and a banking reform to deal with the consequences of the crisis. After this crisis, the central bank rapidly opted for a strategy to show commitment to combatting inflation, establishing tentative targets. The following years saw a considerable decrease in inflation. By 1999, the central bank announced the intention to converge to similar inflation rates as its NAFTA partners establishing tentative targets. Finally in 2001, with an inflation of about 6.4 percent, Mexico adopted a full-fledged inflation-targeting system. By 2002, the central bank defined the long-run inflation rate target of 3 percent. It was part of an integrated framework comprising a floating exchange rate, an independent monetary authority with inflation targets and transparency, and financial market openness. During the period 2003 to 2019, excluding the years of the GFC, this framework managed to keep inflation at an average rate of 4 percent per year, closer to the upper limit of its target range. Additionally, Panel B in Table 7.4 shows that during the period of analysis, Mexico slightly increased its degree of independence, from about 0.56 in the 1990s to 0.64 in the 2010s, similar to the average of Latin America, using the Garriga (2016) index that goes from 0 to 1, with 0 being completely dependent and 1 being independent. Given this improvement since the 1990s, Mexico is currently ranked only behind Panama (which in practice uses the US dollar as its currency) in this group, in terms of central bank independence.

With a flexible exchange rate system in place, a foreign exchange commission was established to restock international reserves as a measure to enhance credibility in monetary policy. As Chamon et al. (2019) explain, the interventions in the foreign exchange market were designated to manage international reserves or to control episodes of exchange rate volatility, without setting any particular target for the exchange rate. The basic mechanism relied on restricting the state oil company PEMEX (Petroleos Mexicanos) to sell dollars from oil exports to the central bank at the market exchange rate. As documented by Chamon et al. (2019), with this framework in place, PEMEX was the main source of international reserve accumulation, increasing from approximately $6 to $183 billion from 1994 to 2019.

Table 7.4: Inflation rate and Central Bank independence.

	1990–1999	2000–2009	2010–2019*
Panel A: Inflation rate, percentage			
Costa Rica	16.9	10.9	3.2
El Salvador	11.0	3.6	1.3
Guatemala	15.0	7.0	4.1
Honduras	19.7	8.2	4.7
Mexico	20.4	5.2	4.0
Nicaragua	23.5	9.0	5.6
Panama	1.1	2.4	2.4
Central America	*15.4*	*6.6*	*3.6*
Latin America	*140.1*	*8.2*	*483.9*
*Latin America***	*145.5*	*7.5*	*4.7*
Panel B: Central Bank independence index (Garriga, 2016)			
Costa Rica	0.60	0.73	0.73
El Salvador	0.34	0.76	0.76
Guatemala	0.68	0.76	0.78
Honduras	0.49	0.67	0.67
Mexico	0.56	0.64	0.64
Nicaragua	0.65	0.72	0.69
Panama	0.22	0.22	0.22
Central America	*0.51*	*0.64*	*0.64*
Latin America	*0.57*	*0.59*	*0.62*
*Latin America***	*0.56*	*0.59*	*0.61*

* = 2010–2014 in Panel B; **= without Venezuela
Source: World Bank (2020) and Garriga (2016).
Note: The Garriga (2016) index goes from 0 to 1, with 0 being completely dependent and 1 being independent.

As in most Latin American countries, the 1980s were a period of high inflation for Central America. Only after 1995, inflation in Central America has shown a declining trend (see Panel A in Table 7.4). Panama and Guatemala were running inflation rates below 10 percent from 1995 to 2007, while Nicaragua (after struggling with a considerable hyperinflation at the end of the 1980s) managed to control inflation at about 10 percent until the GFC. Let us discuss some details for Costa Rica and Honduras. In the case of Costa Rica, the inflation dynamic during the mid-1990s was mostly the result of a combination of a banking crisis in 1994 (that required central bank assistance), a crawling peg exchange rate regime (fairly popular across Latin America during that time), and a monetary policy that monetized the public debt (from the 1980s).[12] Nevertheless, by 2001, the inflation rate reached less than 10 percent and, with the exception of 2008, continued the declining trend until the current rate of 4.4 percent. This performance benefitted from moving toward an inflation-targeting framework since 2005 (although officially adopted in 2018) with a more flexible exchange rate regime. In the case of Honduras, we have two groups of factors that contributed to the dynamic of inflation. On the one hand, the series of reforms implemented by Honduras during the 1990s, accompanied by the global reduction of inflation, contributed to the decline of its inflation rate from 1995 to 2002. On the other hand, the serious effects of Hurricane Mitch in 1998 and the sequence of banking crises of 1999, 2001, and 2002, operated as igniters of inflation. However, by 2001 the rate was below 10 percent and kept its declining trend until 2019, with the exception of 2008. The close ties of Central America with the United States exacerbated the negative effects of the GFC in a variety of ways, with inflation being one of those channels. The halt in capital inflows, the increase in volatility and uncertainty were translated into price increases, with inflation rates spiking in 2008 for all countries of Central America.

There were also other factors in place that contributed to the decline in inflation and the stabilization of economies during the last 20 years. For instance, all Central American countries implemented some degree of legal independence for their central banks.[13] Using the Garriga (2016) index, Panel B in Table 7.4 shows that all countries increased their degree of independence since the 1990s, with Guatemala currently exhibiting the highest score. Another aspect that is worth mentioning is the role of the exchange rate regime. Central American countries have not been excluded from the global trend toward more flexible regimes. For instance, Costa Rica operated a crawling peg for many years until 2006 when the country started the transition, first to a crawling band, then to a managed float with an inflation-targeting framework (implemented in 2018). Nicaragua has had

---

12 The monetization of the public debt implies that the central bank buys government bonds by issuing money.

13 Jácome and Vazquez (2008) documented this for El Salvador (1991), Nicaragua (1999), Costa Rica (1995), Honduras (2004), and Guatemala (2001). However, notice that legal independence might not be enough to generate independent monetary policies.

a (pre-announced) crawling peg in place since 1993, mostly trying to safeguard competitiveness. Honduras first opted in 1999 for a crawling band where the domestic currency (the lempira) fluctuated within a 7 percent against the US dollar, then fixed the band in 2005 (a *de facto* fixed exchange rate), and finally returned to the previous system in 2011 until today. Since 1991, Guatemala has had a crawling band against the US dollar, allowing for intervention by the central bank to limit its volatility. Interestingly, since 2000 Guatemala also started a transition to an explicit inflation-targeting framework, formally adopted at the end of 2004, which has kept inflation on target, even in the face of adverse shocks. Finally, El Salvador and Panama are two interesting cases of monetary policy. In the aftermath of the consequences of Hurricane Mitch and a moderate banking crisis in 1998, and after less than a decade of operating under a pegged exchange rate, El Salvador adopted in 2001 the US dollar as its official currency. Unlike the case of Ecuador, this transition from a peg system to an official dollarization was not the result of a crisis. Inflation was already below 10 percent, the economy was slowly growing at about 2 percent per year, and there were no fiscal or debt crises. Swiston (2011) and Pinon et al. (2012) explained that the arguments for dollarization were based on the intention to tighten links with the United States to increase trade, foreign direct investment (FDI), and economic growth. The main implication of this change, other than the obvious fact that the banknotes and coins are those of the United States, is that El Salvador lost control over traditional monetary policy. That means that the government has fiscal policy as the main instrument for policies. Additionally, dollarization helped reducing inflation (after an initial increase) by importing the monetary policy credibility from the United States and increased the degree of international financial integration (Arellano and Heathcote, 2010). Panama has officially pegged its currency (the balboa) to the US dollar (at a rate of one) since its independence from Colombia in 1903. In fact, the dollar is legal tender, so in practice this means that Panama uses the dollar and the balboa as accepted currency.[14] This link with the United States for more than a century, has helped Panama maintain a long history of low inflation rates. Similar to El Salvador, Panama surrendered its capacity of conducting monetary policy and relies exclusively on fiscal policy. Unlike El Salvador, since dollarization started with its independence, Panama does not have a formal central bank. The National

---

14 An interesting detail is that there are Panamanian coins circulating jointly with US coins, but all paper currency is from the United States.

Banking Commission and the Superintendency of Banks in Panama are the institutions in charge of the oversight and regulation of the banking sector.

The other components of the macroeconomic record are the fiscal and debt dynamics, depicted in Figure 7.2. These are closely related to what we just discussed above. Let us start with Mexico and the year 1994. In the preamble to the crisis of the peso, the government was issuing *tesobonos* (denominated in foreign currency) to compensate for the loss of international reserves used to defend the currency. Additionally, the banking sector was also experiencing an increase of short-term deposits denominated in foreign currency, combined with an increase in credit, and non-performing loans. Hence, the exposure to fluctuation of the exchange rate was at the top of the list of problems. The devaluation of the peso after adopting a floating exchange rate, caused one of the worse crises in the history of Mexico. The response of the administration of President Zedillo was based on fiscal and monetary policies and a bailout organized by the United States. In fact, in January 1995, President Bill Clinton coordinated a rescue package administered by the IMF to help Mexico keep access to international financial markets.[15] This package included measures aimed at lowering the *risk premium* associated with the uncertainty from the crisis. Additionally, it helped with the bailout of the banking system when the government acted as lender of last resort. Meza (2018) estimates that the total cost of this rescue (later transformed into public debt) from 1995 to 1998 was about 13.3 percent of GDP, while Santos (2009) argues this figure was closer to 19.3 percent of GDP. Furthermore, Meza (2018) explains, that the fiscal policies implemented in the aftermath of the crisis were procyclical: an increase in the consumption tax, increases in energy prices, and a contraction of fiscal spending. While the fiscal deficit remained at about 2.4 percent of GDP by 1995, the primary balance improved from 1.9 in 1994 to 3.7 percent of GDP in 1995.[16] That means the increase in the fiscal deficit was explained by debt interest payments. In fact, benefiting from consistent primary surpluses until 2007, the debt to GDP ratio managed to remain relatively stable at about 40 percent of GDP, even throughout the Asian and Russian crises of 1997 and 1998, and the dot-com episode in the United States in 2001.

---

15 The package consisted of approximately $50 billion, of which $20 billion came from the United States, $17 billion from the IMF, $10 billion from the Bank for International Settlement, and the rest from the Bank of Canada and other Latin American countries.
16 The primary (fiscal) result is the fiscal result without the accrual of interests to be paid.

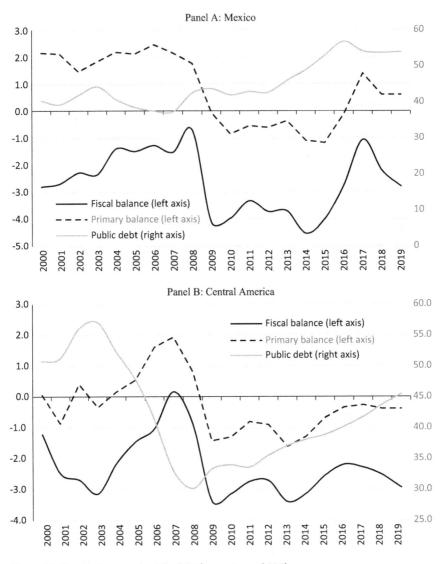

Figure 7.2: Fiscal balance and public debt (percentage of GDP).
Source: World Bank (2020) and International Monetary Fund (2020b).

As Kehoe and Meza (2011) argue, Mexico was the country that suffered the most from the GFC. Interestingly, the response to this crisis was different than that from the peso crisis of 1994. President Felipe Calderón followed counter-cyclical fiscal policies in an attempt to counterbalance the effect of the crisis. In particular, the government implemented temporary reduction of taxes and social contributions, reduction of taxes on external trade, increases in spending for infrastructure, housing, and support for agricultural producers and small and medium enterprises. According to Kacef and Jiménez (2009) the cost of these measures was approximately 2.5 percent of GDP, mostly geared as increases in government spending. Hence, during this period, the fiscal deficit increased from almost zero to 4.1 percent of GDP in 2009.[17] In terms of public debt, there was a slight increase to an average of almost 42 percent of GDP until 2012. The last period from 2012 to 2019 is characterized by a consistent increase in public debt and some improvements in terms of public finances. In the context of dwindling oil revenues at the end of the boom of commodities, President Enrique Peña Nieto introduced a fiscal reform in 2014. Among other things, this tax reform aimed to simplify the tax code, attacking inefficient taxes and creating new ones, eliminating tax deductions, and increasing the tax rate for high-income salaries. As a result, the non-oil tax revenue jumped from about 16 percent to about 20 percent of GDP by 2017. Overall, the fiscal deficit was reduced, from 4.5 percent in 2014 to almost 1 percent in 2017, and is now about 2.8 percent of GDP. An important detail is that the primary result reverted to positive 1.4 percent of GDP in 2017 and has stayed slightly below the government target of 1 percent of GDP. Nevertheless, the stock of public debt still increased after the tax reform, showing the susceptibility to swings in oil prices, but finally stabilized at approximately 54 percent of GDP by 2017.

Compared to other regions of Latin America, the group of countries from Central America has had historically low fiscal deficits (see Panel B in Figure 7.2). Let us focus on three aspects to understand this performance: (i) the role of economic growth, (ii) the cycle of commodity prices and global factors, and (iii) the public debt trajectory. For the last 20 years, Central America has been growing at a higher rate (3.8 percent per year) compared to South America (which has been growing at 2.9 percent per year). During periods of growth (contractions), it is expected that the fiscal deficit would decrease (increase) since for a given tax base, more (less) economic activity renders more (less) fiscal revenues. Panel B in Figure 7.2 shows the fiscal balance performance has been consistent with this argument. The reasons behind swings in economic growth in Latin America come from a variety of factors, some of which are summarized by Vegh and Vuletin (2018), as commodity price effects, the trend growth in developed countries, and global liquidity. As we will discuss later, the dependence on commodities in Central America is less clear than in

---

17 Kehoe and Meza (2011) argue that changes in the accounting rules of Petróleos Mexicanos (PEMEX) might have also contributed to this deficit.

other parts of Latin America. That is, they are still important drivers of the business cycle, but less so than in other countries of the region. That means the trend growth of developed countries and global liquidity play a crucial role in explaining the booms and busts in Central America. The evolution of the fiscal deficit in the first part of the 2000s reflects the dot-com crisis in the United States, which reduced foreign demand for Central American products, along with the devastating effects of Hurricane Mitch and the banking crises in El Salvador, Honduras, Nicaragua, and Guatemala. As Vegh and Vuletin (2018) argue, a key element to assess these performances is understanding if those shocks are permanent or temporary. That way, policymakers can have a strategy for a counter-cyclical fiscal policy (if the shock is temporary) or can adjust to the new normal (if the shock is permanent). Of course, realizing which is the true nature of the shock is not easy, but brings us to the experience of Central American countries in the period just before the GFC. During this period that coincides with the start of the supercycle of commodities, most countries were able to save more than in previous years, closing in some cases the fiscal gap by adopting fiscal rules, reducing public debt, and increasing foreign reserves. Thus, creating buffers for future periods of crisis. These buffers were promptly tested with the GFC. Despite some differences, all Central American countries responded with some degree of counter-cyclicality. For instance, Costa Rica, Guatemala, Honduras, Nicaragua, and Panama implemented both revenues and spending measures, some reducing income taxes or taxes on external trade, while increasing investment in public infrastructure, interest rates reductions for housing, small and medium enterprises, and agricultural producers. Additionally, Costa Rica expanded the coverage of the cash transfer program Avancemos, while El Salvador implemented a stimulus plan (Plan Global Anti-Crisis), increasing fiscal spending for housing, grants, and in-kind transfers to support strategic sectors affected by the GFC.[18]

In the absence of external factors, the dynamic of public debt is intrinsically connected with the cyclicality of fiscal spending. When the latter rises, it is (usually) financed with fiscal revenues and/or increases in public debt. From an aggregate perspective, Central America was able to reduce its public debt level since the beginning of the decade until the GFC by an average of 20 percentage points of GDP. In some cases, like Costa Rica and Panama, strong growth rates enhanced a relatively large reduction of public debt, from 39 and 56 percent of

---

[18] An interesting perspective can be found in Vegh et al. (2017) where they argue about the strong relationship between the quality of institutions in the region and the countries' ability to move away from conducting macroeconomic policy in a procyclical way.

GDP in 2000, respectively, to 24 and 40 percent of GDP in 2008. In some other cases, like El Salvador, public debt increased from 30 percent of GDP in 2000 to 47 percent of GDP in 2008, while Guatemala remained unchanged at 20 percent of GDP. Additionally, both Nicaragua and Honduras were going through the Heavily Indebted Poor Countries (HIPC) Initiative, instituted in 1996 by the IMF and the World Bank, to alleviate the debt burden of poor countries.[19] Through this initiative Nicaragua and Honduras received debt relief of about 80 and 40 percentage points of GDP, respectively, from the IMF, the World Bank, multilateral organizations, and bilateral creditors.

During the post-GFC years, all countries, with the exception of Panama, increased their stock of public debt. At the aggregate level the rise was from about 30 percent of GDP to the current level of more than 45 percent of GDP. This trajectory is mostly explained by Costa Rica, Nicaragua, and El Salvador. Specifically, Costa Rica by leaving in place the stimulus plans of 2009, contributed to a fiscal deficit of more than 6 percent of GDP. With steady fiscal revenues, the public debt soared, from 24 percent of GDP in 2008 to 57 percent in 2019. In the case of Nicaragua, where most of the external public debt is owed to multilateral creditors (with the Inter-American Development Bank accounting for the largest percent) public debt climbed from less than 30 percent of GDP in 2008 to 40 percent in 2019. This rise was mostly due to an increasing shift to domestic debt associated with financial needs after the end of the oil collaboration with Venezuela and the increasing deterioration of the balance sheet of the INSS.[20] Additionally, the economic contraction of 2018, 2019, and possibly 2020, which came as a result of the considerable social unrest and violence triggered by the announcement of reforms to the INSS, further deteriorated the debt to GDP ratio. There is now a spiral dynamic that seriously compromises the viability of the INSS, since lower growth prospects and continued weaknesses in formal employment suggest revenues are not expected to increase in the coming years. Finally, in the case of El Salvador, public debt soared from 46 percent of GDP in 2008 to approximately 70 percent in 2019, mostly as a result of running large fiscal deficits. IMF (2016) argue these high levels of public debt are also associated with debt from the pension system, unrecorded liabilities, and methodological changes to El Salvador's nominal GDP. Interestingly, both the government and political parties

---

19 This initiative was later enhanced in 1999 under the HIPC II.

20 In fact, the IMF (2017) alerted that with no reforms, the sustainability of the INSS would be jeopardized by 2019. Unfortunately, by 2018, in the midst of the social protests, the INSS exhausted its liquid reserves requiring approximately 1.2 percent of GDP in transfers from the central government.

from El Salvador reacted to this increasing trend of public debt. In fact, the signing of a fiscal responsibility law in December 2016 intended to assure the sustainability of public debt, established debt ceilings, caps on fiscal deficits, and fiscal rules for the next decade. Furthermore, this law was recently strengthened by imposing a declining path for the public debt to reach 60 percent of GDP by 2030.

Economic Structure

Mexico has traditionally produced large quantities of agricultural products, and particularly after NAFTA this production has been focused on tropical fruits, horticulture, and vegetables, such as corn, beans, coffee, sugar cane, limes and lemons, strawberries, and avocados (the leading producer in the world). The share of the agricultural sector in GDP (shown in Table 7.5) used to be larger in the 1970s but consistent with the development of Mexico, it now represents a mere 3.6 percent and captures 14 percent of the total labor force. Most of the agricultural production is concentrated in the areas of the Gulf of Mexico, the *Bajío* region, and the northwest region. Mexico is also endowed with abundant mineral resources such as gold, silver, copper, lead, natural gas, and petroleum. In fact, ranked in 11th place with approximately 2.3 million barrels per day, PEMEX is the largest company in Mexico, hence a crucial player in the economy. Oil exports still represent about 3 percent of Mexico's export earnings and due to a heavy taxation structure, PEMEX provides about one-third of tax revenues for the government.[21] Nonetheless, the other two important industries in Mexico are the automotive sector, accounting for about 3.0 percent of GDP and the food and beverages industry, representing about 4.5 percent of GDP. Benefiting from the geographic location, near the United States, the subsequent trade agreements, and the relatively convenient labor costs, many car companies (from the United States, Japan, and Germany) and food and beverage conglomerates have installed production plants in Mexico. The maquiladora is another central industry that flourished after NAFTA but suffered the dot-com crisis and has recently faced competition from other regions of the world. Overall, the industrial sector represents about 32 percent of the GDP and employs 26 percent of the labor force. Similar to Chile, Mexico ranks among the most industrialized countries in Latin America. Finally, the service

---

21 After years of efficiency and taxation problems, the company now faces a considerable underinvestment that has led to a consistent decline of production. According to standards from the OECD (2019), PEMEX has an estimated debt of about 9 percent of Mexico's GDP, the highest for an oil company.

Table 7.5: Economic structure (percentage of GDP).

	Agriculture	Industry	Services
Costa Rica	5.5	20.6	73.9
El Salvador	12.0	27.7	60.3
Guatemala	13.3	23.4	63.2
Honduras	14.2	28.8	57.0
Mexico	3.6	31.9	64.5
Nicaragua	15.5	24.4	60.0
Panama	2.4	15.7	82.0
Central America	*10.5*	*23.4*	*66.1*
Latin America	*9.0*	*28.3*	*62.8*

Source: World Bank (2020) and United Nations Development Programme (UNDP) (2018).

sector, the largest contributing factor to the value added of the economy, accounts for approximately 64 percent of GDP and employs almost 61 percent of the labor force. The tourism industry is the most important service. After all, Mexico is ranked as the seventh most visited country in the world in 2018 according to the Tourism Barometer 2019 from the United Nations World Tourism Organization (UNWTO). Other services comprise retail, financial services, and transport and communication services. A rampant problem in the Mexican economy, but particularly problematic in the service sector, is the degree of informality. Based on Medina and Schneider (2018), Mexico has had a fairly constant informal economy of about 30 percent of GDP in the last decade. This figure is not far from the average in Latin America (32 percent of GDP), but large compared to Chile or Colombia, the other OECD members.

At the aggregate level, Central America has an agricultural sector that represents about 10 percent of GDP, with the industry and the service sectors accounting for 23 percent and 66 percent of GDP, respectively. However, these figures cover some of the heterogeneity of the region. For instance, Costa Rica and Panama currently have an economic structure with an emphasis on services. Costa Rica's economy has historically been based on agriculture with bananas, pineapples, sugar, and coffee as its main crops. However, in more recent years, Costa Rica has transitioned into a service center led by its free trade zones that have attracted foreign investments (mainly from the United States) from hardware and logistics companies, medical and health laboratories, and tourism. With these changes in the last 20 years, the service sector and the industry sector now represent about 74 and 21 percent of GDP, respectively, and employs 70 and 20 percent of the labor force, respectively. Panama's economy revolves around the canal and its expansion project. For the last 20 years, the Canal has been under the administration of the Panamanian government, after the United States transferred its control to Panama. Due to its geographic location, its ties to the United States through the Canal, and the recent Panama–Unites States Trade Promotion Agreement that eliminated tariffs, Panama has developed into an economy based on services.[22] The services sector accounts for approximately 82 percent of GDP and employs 67 percent of the total labor force. Among the services, the Panama Canal plays a crucial role, contributing for about 20 percent of its GDP, jointly with the banking sector, making Panama the largest regional financial center. In fact, the financial industry accounts for about 10 percent of Panama's GDP. Other services include the Colon free trade zone, insurance companies, medical and health laboratories, and tourism.

Interestingly enough, the economies of Guatemala, Honduras, and Nicaragua have a similar structure, with the agricultural sector representing about 14 percent, industry 26 percent, and services approximately 60 percent of GDP. These are economies that historically have been based primarily on agriculture with a recent expansion of manufactures and processed food. Coffee, bananas, and sugar dominated the production of crops until the late 1980s when there was a turn toward the production of textiles and apparel (knit and woven), in some cases through maquila factories, with the United States as their main trading partner. Unfortunately, the manufacturing sector still has considerable challenges with low (and sometimes negative) productivity growth, compared to the rest of Latin America.[23] In these countries, the agricultural sector employs about 31 percent of the labor force, while the industry sector employs another 20 percent. The services sector, which employs half of the active population, includes transportation, warehousing, commerce, financial services, and tourism, which has become increasingly important for this region.

Similar to Costa Rica, El Salvador is not dependent on its primary sector, and has traditionally had the largest industrial sector in Central America, with a share of 22 percent of GDP at the beginning of the 2000s and currently almost at 28 percent of GDP. Since the beginning of the 1990s this sector has focused, first, on textiles and apparel from maquila factories with free zones, and more recently on the processing of agricultural products and electrical machines, to export to the

---

22 Panama is not a member of the Dominican Republic–Central America Free Trade Agreement (CAFTA-DR) but has had its own free trade agreement with the United States since 2012.
23 See the compilation by Pagés (2010).

United States (its main trading partner). This sector currently employs 22 percent of the active population. In a similar fashion to other Central American countries, the services sector is the largest contributor to the economy, accounting for 60 percent of GDP, employing 61 percent of the labor force. It mainly includes call centers, logistics, communications, financial services, and tourism.

Similar to other countries across Latin America, there is a common pattern from the 1970s to 2018 where the agricultural sector shrunk, industry stayed about the same size (with some exceptions), and services increased. With an increased relative importance of the service industry, challenges associated with low productivity and informality can be barriers to development. These issues are common across countries in this group with some exceptions for Costa Rica and Panama. Interestingly, both countries exhibit the highest scores for institutional quality in this region (see Table 7.6). In fact, it is not surprising given the well-documented relationship between institutions and productivity growth and resource allocation.[24]

Foreign Trade

Let us now discuss the ability of countries to move financial flows. In particular, this group of countries moved from less to more openness in the last 30 years. According to the Chinn and Ito (2006) index in Table 7.7, in the 1990s, Central America was at low levels of financial integration, comparable to the averages for Latin America and Sub-Saharan Africa.[25] Mexico and Guatemala were the exception. The arrival of the 2000s marked a considerable increase in the financial integration strategy with all countries increasing their degree of openness. In the case of Nicaragua and Panama with few regulations on capital controls. This trend of openness continued until today with most countries operating under flexible conditions in terms of inflows and outflows of capitals. In fact, with the exception of Honduras, all countries are considerably above the regional average for Latin America and the rest of the world, only behind Europe and Central Asia.

Interestingly, a similar evolution occurred with trade openness, measured by the ratio of exports plus imports to GDP. For instance, since 1990, the group of Central American countries has been leading this trend, with higher ratios than

---

24 See for instance Arias-Ortiz et al. (2014), among others.

25 The Chinn and Ito (2006) index takes higher values the more open a country is to cross-border capital transactions. In particular, the normalized version ranges from 0 to 1.

Table 7.6: Institutions in Latin America (2018).

Voice and accountability		Political stability		Control of corruption		Rule of law		Government effectiveness		Regulatory quality	
Uruguay	89.2	Uruguay	87.6	Uruguay	87.5	Chile	83.7	Chile	81.7	Chile	88.9
Costa Rica	84.7	Costa Rica	62.4	Chile	81.7	Uruguay	73.6	Uruguay	73.1	Peru	71.2
Chile	82.3	Chile	61.4	Costa Rica	70.7	Costa Rica	69.2	Costa Rica	67.8	Uruguay	69.7
Panama	68.5	Panama	56.2	Argentina	54.3	Panama	52.4	Argentina	54.8	Costa Rica	69.2
Argentina	67	Dominican Republic	47.6	Colombia	44.7	Argentina	45.7	Panama	51.9	Panama	66.3
Brazil	60.6	Argentina	46.7	Brazil	40.4	Brazil	44.2	Colombia	50	Colombia	65.4
Peru	55.2	Ecuador	43.3	Peru	34.6	Dominican Republic	38.9	Mexico	47.6	Mexico	60.6
Colombia	52.7	Paraguay	42.4	Ecuador	32.7	Colombia	38.5	Peru	44.2	El Salvador	53.8
Dominican Republic	51.2	Bolivia	38.1	Panama	32.2	Peru	32.7	Ecuador	42.8	Dominican Republic	50.5
Paraguay	49.3	Peru	37.1	El Salvador	29.8	Paraguay	32.2	Bolivia	39.9	Paraguay	48.6
El Salvador	48.3	El Salvador	33.3	Honduras	29.3	Ecuador	28.8	Dominican Republic	39.4	Guatemala	45.7
Ecuador	47.3	Brazil	31.9	Bolivia	28.8	Mexico	27.4	El Salvador	36.5	Argentina	42.3
Mexico	45.8	Guatemala	27.1	Dominican Republic	24.5	El Salvador	19.7	Brazil	36.1	Brazil	39.9

Bolivia	44.3	Honduras	26.7	Guatemala	22.1	Honduras	16.3	Paraguay	34.1	Honduras	34.6
Guatemala	35.5	Mexico	25.7	Paraguay	20.7	Nicaragua	14.9	Honduras	27.9	Nicaragua	25
Honduras	31.5	Nicaragua	18.1	Mexico	18.8	Guatemala	13.5	Guatemala	23.6	Ecuador	16.3
Nicaragua	18.7	Colombia	17.6	Nicaragua	13	Bolivia	9.6	Nicaragua	19.2	Bolivia	15.9
Venezuela	10.3	Venezuela	9	Venezuela	4.8	Venezuela	0	Venezuela	4.8	Venezuela	0.5

Source: World Bank (2018).

Table 7.7: Capital account openness.

	1990	2000	2010	2018
Costa Rica	0.16	0.72	0.72	1.00
El Salvador	0.00	1.00	0.88	0.70
Guatemala	0.37	0.72	1.00	1.00
Honduras	0.00	0.42	0.17	0.17
Mexico	0.25	0.70	0.70	0.70
Nicaragua	0.17	1.00	1.00	1.00
Panama	1.00	1.00	1.00	1.00
Central America	0.26	0.79	0.78	0.79
Latin America	0.26	0.53	0.56	0.53
East Asia and Pacific	0.55	0.49	0.68	0.61
Europe and Central Asia	0.52	0.62	1.00	1.00
Sub-Saharan Africa	0.23	0.29	0.30	0.23
South Asia	0.19	0.27	0.29	0.32

Source: Chinn and Ito (2006) index, where higher values indicate a country is more open to cross-border capital transactions.

the average of Latin America at about 73 percent of GDP; even substantially higher during some periods (see Figure 7.3). In fact, the average for Central America recorded a maximum of 105 percent of GDP just before the GFC, compared to 75 and 58 for the average of Latin America and Mexico, respectively. Mexico also shows an increasingly open economy in terms of trade, having double its ratio from 40 percent in 1990 to 80 percent today. Despite starting from quite different places in 1990, and after almost 30 years, both Mexico and Central America are now at similar levels of trade openness, above the regional average for Latin America as a whole. This trend for openness is mostly the result of these countries effectively committing to regional trade agreements with the United States. In fact, the current group of countries is significantly more opened than those analyzed in previous chapters. Although still vulnerable to financial shortages from external shocks, they are less dependent on commodity exports than the countries analyzed before. Let us discuss how these countries are performing relative to the rest of the region.

From this group, Panama and Mexico are the countries with the lowest concentration of exports in commodities, with 9.5 and 16.4 percent, respectively

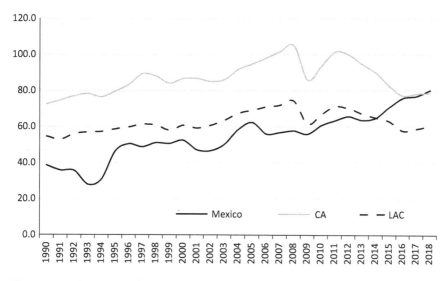

Figure 7.3: Trade openness (exports plus imports as a share of GDP, percentage).
Source: World Bank (2020).
Note: LAC is the simple average of 17 countries in Latin America, excluding the Caribbean.

(see Table 7.8). Panama's main exports are led by petroleum and its derivatives, passenger and cargo ships associated with the Canal, bananas, and gold, representing about 70 percent of total exports. However, just the oil-related products and the cargo associated with the Canal capture almost 55 percent of exports. The main destinations for those exports are Ecuador, Netherlands, United States, Costa Rica, Cyprus, and Switzerland, accounting for almost 55 percent of Panama's exports. Mexico's main exports are concentrated on machines (such as computers and telephones), transportation (such as cars, auto parts, and delivery trucks), and medical and industrial instruments, which capture more than 70 percent of the total. Unsurprisingly, the main destination is by far the United States, capturing more than 78 percent of total Mexican exports, followed by Canada with a mere 4 percent. As highlighted above, both Panama and Mexico have most of their exports concentrated on non-commodities. With a higher degree of commodity dependence, El Salvador ranks after these countries. It has most of its exports concentrated on textiles, electrical capacitors, and processed food, which account for 67 percent of total exports. The main destinations for exports from El Salvador are the United States, Honduras, Guatemala, Nicaragua, and Costa Rica, representing 80 percent of total exports.

The other countries in this group, Guatemala, Nicaragua, Costa Rica, and Honduras, have a concentration of commodities in exports of about 58, 48, 45,

Table 7.8: Commodities' share of exports and GDP in Latin America.

	Commodity exports (mill of USD)	Exports (merchandise) (mill of USD)	Commodity/ Exports	Commodity Exports/GDP
Venezuela	72,277	74,714	96.7	15.0
Ecuador	17,772	19,122	92.9	17.0
Paraguay	7,702	8,680	88.7	19.4
Chile	59,621	69,230	86.1	21.5
Bolivia	6,423	7,846	81.9	17.1
Uruguay	6,305	7,888	79.9	11.2
Colombia	28,168	37,881	74.3	9.0
Peru	33,007	45,275	72.9	15.6
Argentina	39,072	58,622	66.7	6.1
Brazil	134,706	217,826	61.8	6.6
Guatemala	6,358	11,001	57.8	8.4
Nicaragua	2,493	5,170	48.2	18.0
Costa Rica	4,298	9,556	45.0	7.5
Honduras	3,351	8,675	38.6	14.6
El Salvador	1,374	5,760	23.9	5.5
Mexico	67,085	409,401	16.4	5.8
Panama	1,050	11,093	9.5	1.7
Central America			*37.2*	*9.3*
Latin America			*61.3*	*11.8*

Source: World Trade Organization (2020).

and 39, respectively. They are still below the average of 61 percent for Latin America, but slightly above the average of 37 for Central America. Guatemala, Nicaragua, and Honduras have most of their exports concentrated on vegetables, textiles, and processed food, accounting for 70, 65, and 68 percent of total exports, respectively. The United States, Mexico, and neighboring countries in Central America are the main markets for these products, representing more than 70 percent of exports in all cases. This is not unusual given the number of regional trade agreements between countries in this region. Costa Rica is slightly different, with almost 30 percent of exports concentrated on medical instruments and the rest on fruits and vegetables (such as bananas and coffee) and processed food, for a total of 66 percent. The United States is also a key destination for exports, accounting for more than 35 percent, with the neighboring countries of Central America representing about 15 percent, and European countries demanding an average of 24 percent of total exports.

Since this group of countries has the lowest concentration of exports on commodities, they are less exposed to their high volatility of prices. Nevertheless, there are still challenges for countries following an export-led growth strategy when faced with booms and busts of commodity prices. In fact, from this group, Nicaragua and Honduras are the ones most vulnerable to swings in commodity prices given their dependency on this type of exports for their GDP. Nicaragua has one of the highest shares in Latin America with 18 percent of GDP, followed by Honduras with 15 percent of GDP. On a distant second tier, Guatemala, Costa Rica, Mexico, and El Salvador have lower ratios of 8.4, 7.5, 5.8, and 5.5 percent of GDP, respectively. Finally, Panama is the country less exposed to commodities in Latin America, with an average of 1.7 percent of GDP. All these figures compare with a 11.8 percent of GDP for the average of Latin America.

Country Specific Details

Mexico: History and Geography

Since the independence movements, Mexico's history has been influenced by its geographical proximity to the United States. Initially, that influence came in the form of losses of territory after the Mexican-American War in 1846, followed by a bitter civil war in the next decade, and an intervention of European powers in the 1860s. Later came the Tampico affair in 1913, during the faction wars of the Mexican Revolution, the Battle of Columbus (New Mexico) in 1916 after Francisco "Pancho" Villa's raid, and the first immigration disputes. That is, unlike the rest of Latin America, Mexico had to deal with not only internal turmoil but also conflicts with the United States.

Furthermore, from a more recent perspective, oil has been usually a matter of debate, and it has not been the exception between Mexico and the United States. In 1938, after some diplomatic tension, President Lazaro Cardenas nationalized the foreign oil companies (including US oil firms). Interestingly, the United States did not retaliate since President Franklin D. Roosevelt was pushing for better relations with Latin American countries, and World War II was about to begin. During 1938 President Cardenas created PEMEX granting exclusive rights of oil in Mexico. After this unusual start, PEMEX evolved into one of the world's largest oil companies. The following years found Mexico slowly distancing from the United States as the government was adopting a development strategy based on ISI. During these years, most of the relevant relations with the United States were in the form of temporary work programs for Mexican workers in the United States.

By the end of the 1960s, Mexico had a consolidated export base, the maquilas were on the rise, and the country was largely self-sufficient in manufactured goods. The Mexican government was able to maintain growth and stability through strong public investment and high tariffs, with an average annual growth rate of approximately 5 percent between 1940 to 1968. However, the inequalities embedded in the distribution of wealth within Mexico's society continued and led to social unrest, like the Tlatelolco massacre in 1968. As Meza (2018) explains, almost throughout the 1970s Mexico was running large deficits financing them via monetary emission and external borrowing. This is a recipe for high inflation. After the oil crisis of 1973 forced Mexico into a net exporter of oil, the discoveries of vast quantities of oil in the Gulf of Mexico in 1976, bolstered oil exports, bringing new sources of revenues. While the United States (under President Jimmy Carter) was pressing Mexico about the growth of unauthorized immigrants, Mexico was dealing with increasing oil exports that opened international markets for more external debt, an overvalued peso (due to the fixed exchange rate regime), and rampant inflation. As Meza (2018) argues, by 1982 Mexico was left with low oil prices, high levels of interest rates in the United States, growing fiscal and current account deficits, inflation reaching 60 percent, and was heavily indebted in foreign currency.[26] The collapse of the Mexican economy between 1981 and 1982 included an accumulated devaluation of the peso of more than 250 percent, and an increase of the debt to GDP ratio from 20 percent to almost 60 percent in 1982. This crisis pushed Mexican immigrants to the United States in search of opportunities. Facing this situation, in 1986 the United States passed a law to control immigrants, granting amnesty to almost 3 million undocumented workers.

During these years, Mexico reevaluated its approach on trade probably recognizing that keeping the Mexican economy separated from the United States was not a viable development strategy. By 1986, Mexico and other Latin American countries joined the General Agreement on Tariffs and Trade (GATT), starting an era of trade agreements and reductions of barriers to trade. Not long after, President Carlos Salinas led Mexico to enter a free-trade agreement with Canada and the United States (NAFTA) in 1994. The creation of NAFTA also brought

---

26 Meza (2018) gives a detailed chronology of these events.

cooperation between Mexico and the United States on military training, border control, environmental conservation, central bank coordination, and intellectual property rights.

The 21st century arrived with the end of the monopoly of the PRI and the election of Vicente Fox from the Partido de Accion Nacional (PAN) promising deeper cooperation with the United States to improve trade, fight drug trafficking cartels, reduce corruption, and improve the situation of Mexican immigrants. Skidmore et al. (2010) explain there was an unusual sense of optimism that Mexico might make a break from its troubled past into a brighter future. However, the terrorist attacks of September 2001 in the United States dwindled the attention towards Mexico. The following administration, of President Felipe Calderon (also from the PAN), renewed the focus to work on democracy, fight drug cartels (that were bringing cocaine from Colombia, using Mexico as the point of entry to the United States) and organized crime jointly with the United States, and improve economic conditions. Financially supported by the United States, the Mexican drug war has proven considerably challenging. It is now a conflict that has escalated in violence, with well-organized criminal organizations that generate approximately $18 billion to $39 billion each year from the United States.

The last ten years of relations between Mexico and the United States have been mainly characterized by issues related to immigration and drug trafficking. Despite growing at a rate of 2.8 per year and a 12 percent increase in its GDP per capita, for the period from 2010 to 2019, nearly half of the population still lives in poverty conditions. Now, as in the past, there are two Mexicos. One is the Mexico that is capable of producing computers and telephones, cars and delivery trucks, medical equipment, and food and beverages. In the other Mexico, poverty and personal insecurity are, unfortunately, the norm. However, now Mexico and the United States seem to be moving closer together. In 2018, Mexico was the top destination for exports from the United States, while the United States was the top destination of exports from Mexico. In terms of imports, Mexico was the second largest partner for the United States, while the United States was the top partner for Mexico. Additionally, the United States was Mexico's top contributor to FDI with approximately $12 billion in 2018, about 34 percent of total inflows. Furthermore, remittance from the United States to Mexico represent about 95 percent of total remittances received, and have increased from about $22 billion in 2013 to almost $39 billion in 2020. Mexico's potential as a world power has always been there. Unleashing that potential depends on the ability of the country to solve its old problems and turn its geography into a powerful advantage.

Central America: The Union That Never Was

Within a very small geographic area, there are seven small countries in Central America. We are not considering Belize as it is a former British colony with a relatively short history. Under Spanish colonial rule, most of Central America was governed as one area. Upon independence, the countries of the region formed a federal republic, the United Provinces of Central America. This sensible solution died in the late 1830s as tensions among various political groups erupted into civil war. By the early 1840s, Central America had splintered into five countries. Panama at the time was still a province of Colombia and became an independent country in 1903. During the 19th and 20th centuries, there have been attempts to reconstruct the union in different ways but to no avail. A substantial part of the problem has been recurring domestic political conflicts that have led to violence and civil wars in many cases. Unfortunately, these problems have not been totally solved. Central America still is the poorest part of the region. A substantial part of the problem has been the inability of the countries to form stable democratic governments. It has also been the part of Latin America that has been most prone to the attention of the United States. What follows is a brief description of some of the pertinent characteristics of these countries. One should keep in mind that, unfortunately, while poverty and inequality are still common in Central America, the resources and the people make for a compelling idea of what the region could become.

Guatemala: Waiting for Success

In terms of population, Guatemala dominates Central America with a population of more than 16 million in a region with nearly 50 million. Of this population, more than 40 percent are of Mayan descent. While it is the largest economy in Central America, the country is still trying, with limited success, to escape a troubled past. The modern history of Guatemala is inextricably tied to the position of the United Fruit Company and the support of the company by the United States government. The country has suffered from the usual political instability of the 19th century and decades of civil war (after a military coup in 1954) in the late 20th century. While the country is now stable and democratic, the past has left its mark. Export agriculture is still the mainstay of the economy with a recent expansion of processed food. Poverty and the lack of consistent economic growth have combined to produce an outflow of people, mostly to Mexico and the United States. Remittances now account for two-thirds of exports and 12 percent of GDP. As is the case of other countries in Central America, Guatemala seems to be waiting for economic management that is up to the task of developing the country. Given its importance in the region, Central America would be hard pressed to prosper without a prosperous Guatemala.

Honduras: Escaping the "Banana Republic"

Honduras has the dubious distinction of being similar to Guatemala but not as developed. It has roughly half the population of its northern neighbor but both GDP and GDP per capita are much smaller. It shares a similar history with Guatemala. American fruit companies, such as United Fruit Company, established export-oriented enclaves in the northern part of the country and their interests were supported by periodic incursions of United States troops. Sadly, the pejorative term "banana republic" was coined by O. Henry with reference to Honduras, its ruling class, and its relationship with United States corporations. This set the pattern for an economy dominated by agriculture from which the country has been struggling to escape. Unfortunately, the manufacturing sector still has considerable challenges with low productivity growth. Political reform movements began in the 1950s but true political stability has proven to be elusive: periods of democracy interspersed with military rule and United States influence. Internal strife within the country was exacerbated by military conflict with El Salvador in 1969. While traditionally the violence within Honduras has been less than that of Guatemala, economic progress under these circumstances has been slow. More recently, violence associated with crime has become a major social issue. Institutions under pressure and governments facing a myriad of challenges create a situation where crime and violence become a significant drag on economic growth.

El Salvador: Rising from the Ashes of Civil War

El Salvador is the smallest country in Central America in terms of land area and third in terms of population. In terms of GDP per capita it is roughly similar to Guatemala, but far behind Costa Rica and Panama. There are a few key things worth noting about El Salvador as it punches above its small weight in the Western Hemisphere. In most of the region the worst of the political instability settled down in the second half of the 19th century. El Salvador was the reverse. The country was politically stable in the 19th century and then became very unstable. This instability culminated in a brutal civil war that lasted from 1979 to 1992. Against expectations, the country has been a stable democracy since the end of that war. A second point is that El Salvador uses the US dollar as its currency. For a small country in an unstable region this has proven to be a reasonable choice. Representing almost one third of its GDP, El Salvador's industrial sector has shifted from textiles during the rise of the maquila to processed agricultural products and electrical machines for exporting to the United States. Finally, the new motor of the economy is remittances from Salvadorans working outside the country, mostly in the east coast of the United States. The population of the country is about 6.4 million and it is estimated that there are 2.3 million people of Salvadoran origin in the United States. Their remittances back to El Salvador are now approaching $6 billion and account for 22 percent of its GDP. When one thinks of countries that are closely tied to the United States it is normal to think of Mexico, but El Salvador is not far behind.

Nicaragua: A Country as a Family Business

Nicaragua is the country in Central America and in Latin America with the lowest GDP per capita. The sources of this level of development are rooted in history. However, in Nicaragua that history seems very repetitious. Political difficulties began early in the country as there were periodic clashes among the Spanish colonial rulers. Upon independence in the 19th century, the country went through the political instability associated with Central America described above. Furthermore, the possibility of a canal across Nicaragua brought minor incursions by the United States and other foreign powers in the late 19th century. Unfortunately, this was just the beginning. From 1909 to 1933 the United States virtually occupied the country as a possible route for a canal and set up a regime to protect United States interests controlled by the Somoza family. In effect, from 1927 to 1979 Nicaragua was virtually a Somoza family business. Birdsall et al. (2002) describe that the Somoza family wealth in 1979 amounted to about $500 million, roughly one third of Nicaragua's GDP and half of the country's debt. Under this structure, there was not really a comprehensive vision to develop the country. Unsurprisingly, this situation led to a civil war starting in the 1960s that overthrown in 1979 the Somoza regime during the Nicaraguan revolution, and continued for nearly 30 years with intermittent intervention of the United States. Since 1990, political stability has returned to the country but that balance is paramount to preserve to avoid future conflicts. For all of its history, Nicaragua has been agricultural and with relatively low income compared to the rest of the region.

Costa Rica: Unique in a Positive Way

While not obvious from a map, a key characteristic of Costa Rica is its isolation. During the colonial period, it was the outlier province of the region. It was a part of the post-independence federation in Central America but the collapse of that was not a major event for Costa Rica. Land transportation between Costa Rica and the rest of the region is sparse. Perhaps as a result of low links with the rest of Central America, Costa Rica has developed more independently. While the country is formally part of Central America it has always been "different." A distinctive factor was that Costa Rica was not endowed with mineral resources such as gold and silver. The best option was for the Spanish to head to the central highlands and farm the rich volcanic soil. Agriculture in the country did not involve the sort of forced labor common in other countries or the development of large farms. Costa Rica developed an agrarian society much more similar to Canada or the United States. Independence and a short war led to a long period of stability in the 19th century. Civil unrest in the mid-20th century led to a unique national characteristic: the military was abolished. Without any possibility of military rule, the country has been a peaceful democracy since 1948. The demise of the military is also linked to a national strength: education. The military budget was transferred to finance improvements in education. The base was already there as universal primary education had been instituted in 1869. Costa Rica spends nearly 8 percent of GDP on education whereas the average OECD country spends less than 6 percent. This brings up an interesting question. Costa Rica is peaceful, democratic, and has an exceptionally well-educated population. But, why it is not a rich nation yet? For a variety of reasons, the economy has never diversified enough out of agriculture. Historically based on agriculture, the economy only recently transitioned into a more service center with a low participation of the industry. In other words, there are new industries emerging such as tourism and financial services but unfortunately, nothing large enough to push growth to higher levels. In a Central American context, Costa Rica is definitely a strong performer relative to its neighbors. In a wider sense, one wonders why it has not been more successful.

Panama: More than Just the Canal

It is not much of an exaggeration to say that Panama is a distinct country made so by geography. In one of history's dramatic moments, Vasco Nuñez de Balboa made the difficult journey from the Atlantic side of the isthmus to view the Pacific Ocean. For the next 400 years, people and goods moved across the isthmus and as this business waxed and waned so did the fortunes of Panama. However, the emergence of Panama as an independent state is rather recent. After breaking away from Spain in 1821, Panama became a province of Colombia. The country gained its independence from Colombia in 1903 with the support of the United States. There had been two previous attempts to secede from Colombia that created a confluence of interest between Panama and the United States. This partnership led to Panama ceding a portion of its territory to the United States in exchange for the building of the Panama Canal between 1904 and 1914. Panama was characterized as a peaceful democracy until a military coup in the late 1960s lead by Omar Torrijos. This military period was ended in 1989 when the United States invaded Panama. This intervention lasted over a month, after which the National Guard of Panama was dismantled and President-elect Guillermo Endara was quickly sworn into office. The resulting return to democracy was a return to politics as usual for the country, with no sense of any repression.

There are two economic keys to Panama. The first one is the canal. When it opened in 1914, the canal was an engineering marvel that changed the face of world trade with thousands of ships per year making the passage. However, eventually the original project necessitated an expansion that officially began in 2007. The total cost of the expansion and modernization was estimated at almost $6 billion. The expanded canal in 2016 once again changed world trade as it can accommodate much larger ships and lowered transportation costs even further. The impacts of the canal on the Panamanian economy are extensive. Nearly 20 percent of the country's GDP can be tied to the canal. The other key is the financial services sector, enhanced by the use of the US dollar as the domestic currency. The development of Panama as a regional financial center dates to a 1970 law that encouraged foreign banks to set up branches in Panama. The number of international banks rapidly jumped, and Panama became a popular destination where offshore transactions were tax free. New banking regulations in 1998 and after the GFC further strengthened the reputation of the country for financial regulations equivalent to standards in OECD countries. The growth of this industry over the last 50 years has resulted in a financial services sector that is now 10 percent of GDP. Panama is both at the crossroads of world trade and has a fast-growing financial sector. The canal still dominates the economy but the diversification into financial services is giving it an edge in economic growth in the region.

Chapter 8
Looking Towards the Future

Most of the time, you don't need a new road. You just need a new way of walking.

Rubén Galván

The task in this final chapter is to pull together the lessons from the previous chapters. We began the book with a consideration of the history of the region. This chapter starts with a return to that theme. In Latin America, the present is tied to history perhaps more closely than in other regions. Unfortunately, there are many parts of that history that are not positives in terms of economic growth. The first parts of the chapter summarize some of the points covered earlier to put them into the context of moving forward in the 21st century. The story differs from country to country, but the virtually universal result has been the relative economic underperformance. Under the right circumstances and with changes in economic policy, the region could have a much brighter future. The final parts of the chapter consider these changes along with the difficult task of making that happen.

The Relative Underperformance of Latin America

Aside from the Lost Decade, Latin American economic growth has usually been closed to the global average. Two visits to any country spaced 10 years apart will show the changes, often before one has left the airport. The region is almost continually becoming more prosperous. The problem is not a lack of growth but rather the rate of growth. The economic boom of the late 19th century and early 20th has rarely been replicated in any country in the region. This is sort of the missing link in Latin America. One or two decades of rapid economic growth can transform a country. An occurrence in a large economy like Mexico or Brazil could have the potential to transform the entire region. Given the abundance of land, labor, and natural resources in Latin America, the inability to grow at faster rates is a puzzle. It is difficult to make the argument that somehow the workers or business owners are of inferior quality to the rest of the world. Could it be that the slow growth is related to the inability of businesses in the region to capitalize on both the abundance of natural resources and the large amount of labor? Could it be that poverty is a function of the lack of initiative or ability of the workers? A drive through any large city in the region would quickly put all that in doubt. There is business activity in abundance. Nevertheless, if almost everyone is

https://doi.org/10.1515/9783110674934-008

hustling to make a living and produce goods and services, then the slow growth of the region must have its roots elsewhere.

Those roots may not be hard to identify. A large part of the success of any country lies in its ability to produce basic government services. This is almost an indicator of economic success. Every country in the OECD has at least an adequate provision of basic government services. One can debate a bit about the nature of these basics, but in this case one is talking about the fundamentals rather than the relative generosity of the social security system. As Thomas Hobbes pointed out centuries ago, the basic function of government can be summarized by the protection of people's lives and property. The lack of this protection can leave the average person fearful for their personal welfare. Much of the region is now struggling in a much similar way. In the 21st century, crime has slowly become a dominant issue for the average citizen in a Latin American country. No country can sustainably prosper when homicides become commonplace events and average people use *apps* to avoid the violence. By definition, public safety is produced in the public sector. The difficulties to control crime ultimately implies the inefficiency to control the criminal class. If this is the case, then the size of the government does not really matter.

Aside from crime control, the two most often mentioned public sector challenges in the region are education and infrastructure. Until recently, the underperformance of the public education systems of the region was a strong perception. This perception was fueled by high drop out rates and persistent complaints by business concerning the lack of skills of young workers. While illiteracy had been conquered, the sense was that the systems were not producing as much education as the years of schooling data was indicating. Recent advances in international testing of students have confirmed the fears about the state of education in Latin America. Of the nine countries in the region that participate in the testing, three (Chile, Uruguay, and Costa Rica) are in the top 50 in the world in their level of reading. Mexico, Brazil, and Colombia are ranked just outside the top 50. Argentina, Peru, and Panama are closer to the bottom out of 79 countries where tests were administered. The results for the other countries are unlikely to be better. To be fair, educational outcomes are a problem for many, if not most, of the countries of the world. The results from Latin America are not encouraging, but there is a persistent sense that things are not improving much. In a world where the accumulation of human capital is critical to economic success, the lack of progress can be a serious barrier. If governments cannot provide educational opportunities for their young people, then what else could also be missing? A partial answer to that question can be found with the infrastructure. On average, more than 20 percent of the region's roads are not properly maintained or in usable conditions. More seriously, the lack of clean water and sewers is the number one killer of children under the age of 5, according to Ortega-Garcia et al. (2019). With few exceptions in Chile and Uruguay, the infrastructure of the region seems insufficient given its GDP per capita. In general, Latin America invests about 3 percent of GDP in infrastructure. Estache and Fay (2007) estimate that what is needed is about 4 percent, while Coremberg (2018) suggests closer to 5 percent. Moreover, Cavallo and Powell (2019) argue that the effects of postponing this investment on growth are negative and may be lowering it by as much as 2 percent. A final note on infrastructure concerns health care. The 2020 global pandemic highlighted the weaknesses in health care in many of the countries of the regions. While this has been a neglected topic over the years, that may change. While most countries have some form of universal public health care, the quality of that care is very heterogeneous. As the population expands and GDP per capita rises, the strain on public health care systems will only rise. Never waste a crisis is an old saying that, it is hoped, will apply in Latin America.

Of course, these relative challenges of government in most of the countries of the region do not go unnoticed. Foreign direct investment (FDI) in Latin America tends to fall into one of two categories. First, the region was and is a major exporter of commodities. Commodities account for 60 percent of the region's exports. FDI in commodities is invariably tied to where the commodities or the ability to produce them exists. The second common type of FDI is investments aimed at servicing consumer demand in the larger markets such as Argentina, Brazil, or Mexico. The average consumer in Latin America is middle class by global standards. While this "horizontal" FDI is helpful, there is something else not too abundant. Vertical FDI is investment in plant and equipment to make products that flow into global markets. Many of these products are not finished goods, but intermediate products that will be used in other plants higher up the global value chain. Much of the growth difference between Latin America and Asia can be found here. The intuition tells us that crime, below average educational standards, overwhelmed health care, and inadequate infrastructure are serious impediments to this type of investment. Without this sort of FDI, the ability of the economies of the region to diversify out of commodities is limited. Low growth closes the loop. Moving out of this pattern of slow or moderate growth will require both financial resources and the commitment of governments.

While the challenges of government mentioned above are serious problems, firms and workers labor under even more serious problems. Every economy in the world is going to have an informal sector. The only remaining question is how large it is. The global average is in the vicinity of 27 percent of GDP. No doubt the informal sector was much larger in OECD countries in the 19th century then it is today (about 10 percent of GDP). With respect to Latin America, it is useful to keep in mind that GDP per capita in the region is very close to the world average. Medina and Schneider (2018) estimate that the regional average size of the informal sector is nearly 33 percent. As one might expect, the informal sector is 13 percent in Chile, followed by Uruguay and Costa Rica with approximately 20 percent of their GDP. On the other side, it is 48 percent in Bolivia. There are eight countries in the region where it is under 30 percent. As was mentioned earlier, it is not difficult to find the key contributing factors to the sizes of the informal sectors. We return to informality here, as it is one of the main challenges of governments in the region. Most of the problems mentioned above will take both time and resources to solve. Reducing crime, improving education, or building infrastructure are difficult problems for even developed countries. Relatively speaking, reducing informality might be easier to deal with compared to the formers. The sources of informality in Latin America seem to be mainly rooted in the complex business regulations and taxes. When a typical SME cannot possibly deal with this complexity, the result is probably going to be a large informal sector. A large informal sector has many negative effects, but in Latin America there are some that are more pronounced than others. First, the informal sector is a contributor to the lackluster growth that is common in the region. There are inherent limits on the ability of informal firms to grow. Second, governments in the region struggle to provide adequate education or infrastructure due to a chronic shortage of tax revenue. Here is a classic negative feedback loop (a reverse causality issue). The size of the informal sector hinders growth and tax collections. The lack of revenue further hinders growth due to insufficient and sometimes inadequate expenditures on education and infrastructure.

The Heterogeneity of Latin America

Among the world's regions, Latin America is perhaps the most homogeneous. All through this book, or any book, about Latin America this is relatively convenient. In some senses, it is too convenient. Many writers, including the current authors, are frequently guilty of overplaying this homogeneity. In reality, the region is only homogeneous relative to most of the other regions of the world. This relative homogeneity frequently is masking a significant amount of heterogeneity in the region that can be overlooked. This is particularly true with respect to the economies. The GDP data reported in the early parts of the book are a stark example. The difference in GDP per capita between Chile and Nicaragua is more than $10,000. To put that into perspective, $10,000 is an average GDP per capita for the world. In the context of developing countries that $10,000 may mean the difference between having running water or electricity or not. Further, some of these gaps are not closing and instead might be getting wider.

This means that the region is becoming less homogenous and more heterogeneous over time. In most countries there is some form of stable workable democracy and some form of capitalism. In this sense, there is still a lot of homogeneity. The whole region and each of the 17 countries are each in their own way slowly moving on from the past. After the 1980s, growth in the region has been tied to world commodity prices, which are sometimes high and sometimes otherwise. In trying to escape this past, there are clusters of countries that are similar. It is the existence of these clusters that is contributing to the heterogeneity of the region in the 21st century.

Just in an arithmetic sense, the fortunes of the entire region are massively influenced by just three countries: Brazil, Mexico, and Argentina. Together these countries account for nearly two-thirds of the GDP of Latin America. Brazil and Mexico alone account for more than half. If Latin America is to gain the prosperity that it is capable of, it is essential that the economies of Brazil and Mexico begin to grow at faster rates. The barriers to growth are high but hardly insurmountable. In the case of Brazil, the economy has a bedrock of commodity production that can be relied on even when commodity prices are low. The production of iron ore, oil, soybeans, coffee, and sugar are turning to be staples in the world economy of the 21st century. Most of the world still is low to middle income and economic growth in developing countries still leaves considerable room for growth in exports of commodities. The challenge will be increasing the size of the manufacturing sector using the countries' large pool of semiskilled labor. A glimpse of what is possible can be seen in São Paulo. Even with the legendary "Brazil cost" of doing business, the city has become one of the largest and most prosperous in the developing world. It is a vision of what the country could become with a more competitive tax and regulatory environment. However, this is not just an issue for Brazil. For the countries of South America, it is hard to disentangle their fortunes from that of Brazil. A rapidly growing Brazilian economy is almost a necessary, but not sufficient, condition of the overall prosperity of South America. The Mexican economy is almost half the size of the Brazilian economy. However, in so many ways Mexico punches above its weight in both the region and the world. Unlike Brazil, the Mexican economy does not have commodity exports to fall back on. What it does have is easy access to one of the world's largest markets. Going forward the key seems to be capitalizing on that asset. One of Mexico's biggest problems is that there are two Mexicos. The northern and industrial part of the country has leveraged its geographic advantage and has become what much of the rest of Latin America aspires to be: industrial and prosperous. However, the southern part of the country remains mired in almost the 19th-century. The problem going forward will be for the government to assert enough attention to those parts of the country to increase overall economic growth. The fates of Mexico and Central America are intertwined.

It is hard to see an exit from the struggles with poverty of that area without a healthy Mexican economy. Finally, there is Argentina. A hundred years ago, Argentina was comfortably among the top 10 economies of the world. A reasonable comparison is that Argentina and Australia were once very close to each other in economic terms. Let us remember that Argentina was the country that was powering Latin America through its Golden Age. Unfortunately, in the last 100 years, the country has lurched from one political crisis to the next. Overlaid on the unstable politics has been general unsustainable economic policies. Among other things, this has led to periodic bursts of inflation and defaults on the country's debt. Argentina has defaulted on its debt 7 times in the last 100 years. Once again, the current situation in the country is familiar. Inflation is more than 50 percent and yet another default has been narrowly avoided, for now. Argentina's underlying problem can be simplified in the following way. First, the government has struggled trying to achieve a prudent fiscal policy. Revenues are chronically below government expenditures. Unfortunately, the roots of this problem never seem to get fully resolved. Given the low credibility of the government, these deficits have been typically financed issuing debt or by the central bank printing money. Thus, the fiscal tension translates into monetary policy that is frequently inflationary. The second problem is chronically low growth. In the 1930s, the government was an early adopter of ISI. Since then, Argentina has had a harder time than most countries in moving out of those policies. Commodity exports are still nearly 70 percent of total exports. In any period where commodity prices are low, the country is hard pressed to finance its imports and tends to resort to borrowing in dollars. All too often, this foreign debt becomes difficult to repay and leads to either an outright default or some form of assistance from the IMF. As growth has slowed to a crawl over an extended period of time, Argentina moved from being a high-income country to a firmly middle-income country. While Argentina is continuing its slow fade, it is still relatively important in South America. Its relative decline is making it that much harder for the other countries in the area, such as Brazil, Chile, Paraguay, and Uruguay, to develop. What has happened to Argentina is not just a national issue. We could probably argue that if Argentina was now as prosperous as Australia, the fates of these other countries would have probably improved substantially. One can only hope that at some point this decline will halt and reverse.

A look at a brighter future in a Latin American context can be seen in a collection of countries scattered around the region. These countries have two distinctive trends. First, they are growing at or above the average for the region. We are not speaking of rapid growth by global standards but by the more relevant regional standard. Second, and related to the first point, they share relatively prudent economic management. Government budget deficits are typically small.

This gives the central bank room to pursue sound monetary policies with interest rates and exchange rates that are mostly set by market forces. Finally, the burdens of taxation and regulation are at least not getting worse and in some countries are noticeably improving. A convenient way to summarize what is happening is that the environment for potential foreign investors is improving. None of these countries is likely to see a boom in FDI in the near future, but all of them are in far better economic shape than was true at the end of the Lost Decade. This collection of countries includes Chile, Colombia, Costa Rica, Panama, Peru, Paraguay, and Uruguay. Chile is the outlier in both this group and Latin America as a whole. Progress in the 21st century has been slower as the easy gains are in the past. The country now struggles to escape an economic environment dominated by commodities. However, the massive deposits of copper, and now lithium, make this task difficult. Growth has been adequate but a formula for realizing the country's potential has been elusive. Colombia has been one of the region's quiet success stories. In addition to the problem of the Lost Decade, Colombia faced decades of internal strife related to armed opposition to the government and a drug industry that challenged the power of the state. These challenges have led to an example of "that which does not kill me makes me stronger." Since the 1990s, sound economic policy has produced growth and stability. Like the rest of Latin America, the country has the potential for rapid growth. The difference here is that very few countries in the region have had to overcome so many challenges to achieve economic stability, much less solid economic growth. Costa Rica is something of a similar version of Chile and Uruguay. The quantitative difference is that it has not yet been able to achieve the status of a high-income country. While growth has been above the average for Latin America, the country has struggled to diversify a small economy. Costa Rica has moved away from commodities but more into services than manufacturing. As a small market, this sort of diversification is not easy to accomplish. As a former province of Colombia, Panama has always been different. The existence of the canal coupled with the use of the dollar as the national currency contributed to a steady source of income and stability. What has changed the growth trajectory has been the ability of the country to leverage the latter into a rapidly growing international financial center. The country has long passed the point where it is just another tax haven. Another unnoticed success story has been Paraguay. The country has been growing at a nearly 5 percent rate in the 21st century. At 5 percent, GDP doubles every 14 years. At these rates, Paraguay could reach Latin American average GDP per capita in the next decade. The main reasons are familiar: political stability coupled with sound economic policy. Further, the country has a hidden advantage. Industry has been slowly migrating from Brazil in search of lower costs. Peru is a somewhat similar story. The country has achieved a 5 percent growth rate in the 21st century. A favorable external environment, sound policy, and some reforms have turned the country to the textbook example of an average Latin American economy. Given some of the large economic problems the country was emerging from in the late 20th century, this has been no small accomplishment. Finally, Uruguay is almost the forgotten success story in Latin America. GDP per capita is higher than Chile, with similar levels of poverty but less inequality. There are many similarities between the two, but perhaps one intangible difference. Both countries are struggling to escape their commodity-based past, but Uruguay may be somewhat ahead of Chile in this regard.

For the rest of the region, the outlook is less positive. Bolivia, Ecuador, Guatemala, and Honduras seemed to have difficulties escaping the past. Bolivia, like much of Central America, has a long history of commodity-based economic activity punctuated with a substantial amount of political instability. Unfortunately, this chronic instability and its landlocked location in the middle of South America never led to rapid economic growth. Aside from some commodity production, economic activity has been typical for a low-income country. Ecuador, on the other hand, has fewer excuses. It is an oil exporter and has additional exports of agricultural commodities. The ongoing problem for the country is that the oil revenues have never translated into faster economic growth. In the case of Central America, periodic interventions by the US in political affairs did not exactly enhance economic development. Further, these are among the most ethnically fragmented countries of the region. In many cases, Spanish is a second language and the ability of workers to fully participate in the economy can be somewhat limited. These handicaps have contributed to low economic growth and constrained the ability to create the infrastructure and education systems that would increase economic growth. Fortunately, the macroeconomic conditions of these countries are stable. As low-income countries, the promise of faster growth is always there. As the country with the lowest income in Central America, Nicaragua also has the slimmest prospects going forward. Until the 1980s, the country was almost a family business run by a very small elite. A brutal civil war in the 1980s established a more open political system. Unfortunately, that system now seems to have been reverted to the rule of an elite. Economic growth has again been reduced. Sadly, Nicaragua seems like a country that is now what the region once was: agricultural and with relatively low income. Finally, there is the economic collapse of Venezuela. In the last year for which data is officially available, GDP was nearly $500 billion and GDP per capita was nearly $16,000. Since then, it is estimated that the economy may have fallen almost 70 percent. A combination of hyperinflation, a drastic decline in oil exports, general economic collapse, and emigration has taken a massive toll on the economy. Unfortunately, there seems to be no real plan in place to counter this devastating loss.

A Latin American Version of Success

At the end, we need to think of a version of success in terms of Latin America. Most of the countries of the region are now comfortably in the world's middle class. GDP per capita is almost exactly the global average. In that sense, Latin America is already a success. On the positive side, both Chile and Uruguay are now part of the world's high-income countries. By any standard, that would be considered economic success. It shows that this is not just a faint possibility. Optimism has to be kept realistic. Since the Golden Age, there have been few episodes of the type of economic growth that has the capacity to transform a country in a generation. The success stories of East Asia in the second half of the 20th century are unlikely to be repeated in Latin America or elsewhere for that matter. The problem has consistently been that growth is in the 4 to 5 percent range only when commodity prices are high and lower otherwise. Economic progress is being made but it is slow to moderate and inevitably dependent on external conditions set outside of the region. A more realistic goal might be for the region to achieve this higher growth path irrespective of commodity prices. The difference would be quite noticeable. Figures of 2 percent and 5 percent average growth yield a doubling of GDP in 35 or 14 years, respectively. The difference is not much from one year to the next, but the compound effect is striking. While it is not the breathtaking changes that occur with 10 percent growth, it should be achievable for a collection of mostly middle-income countries.

To a large extent this difference is in the hands of the countries of the region. Unfortunately, Latin America still is a relatively challenging place to do business. This alone tends to reduce growth. In some cases, this growth penalty can be potentially reduced by the unilateral actions of the governments of the region. There is progress being made in many countries but it seems painfully slow. This slow pace of change could be accelerated. Why this is not happening is the puzzle. The other barriers to growth are related to this. The slow growth and the size of the informal sector are two sides of the same coin. With a large informal sector, governments of the region are chronically short of the resources to improve either education or infrastructure. Moving a large part of the economy into the formal sector would produce tax revenues that could enhance growth. This path toward higher growth is not particularly mysterious but requires action.

References

Acemoglu, D., and Robinson, J. A. (2006). De facto political power and institutional persistence. *American Economic Review*, *96*(2), 325–330.

Acemoglu, D., Johnson, S., and Robinson, J. A. (2001). The colonial origins of comparative development: An empirical investigation. *American Economic Review*, *91*(5), 1369–1401.

Acemoglu, D., Johnson, S., and Robinson, J. A. (2002). Reversal of fortune: Geography and institutions in the making of the modern world income distribution. *The Quarterly Journal of Economics*, *117*(4), 1231–1294.

Acemoglu, D., Johnson, S., and Robinson, J. A. (2005). Institutions as a fundamental cause of long-run growth. *Handbook of Economic Growth*, *1*, 385–472.

Acosta, P., Fajnzylber, P., and López, J. H. (2008). How important are remittances in Latin America. In P. Fajnzylber J.H. Lopez (Eds.), *Remittances and Development. Lessons from Latin America*, Washington, DC: World Bank, 21–49.

Alix-Garcia, J., Schechter, L., Valencia Caicedo, F., and Zhu, J. (2020). *Country of women? repercussions of the Triple Alliance War in Paraguay* (No. 14752). CEPR Discussion Papers.

Alonso, P. (2018). *Creation and evolution of inflation expectations in Paraguay* (No. IDB-WP -900). Working Paper Series. Inter-American Development Bank.

Amieva-Huerta, J., & Urriza González, B. (2000). *Crisis bancarias: causas, costos, duración, efectos y opciones de política*. Serie política fiscal 180. Santiago de Chile: CEPAL.

Antelo, E. (2000). Políticas de estabilización y de reformas estructurales en Bolivia a partir de 1985. In L.C. Jemio and E. Antelo (Eds.), *Quince Años de Reformas Estructurales en Bolivia: Sus Impactos sobre Inversión, Crecimiento y Equidad*. La Paz, Bolivia: CEPAL-IISEC, 15–98.

Arellano, C., and Heathcote, J. (2010). Dollarization and financial integration. *Journal of Economic Theory*, *145*(3), 944–973.

Argüello, R. (2011). Efectos de la crisis internacional: remesas, comercio y respuesta de política en Colombia. *Perfil de Coyuntura Económica*, *17*, 7–30.

Arias-Ortiz, E., Crespi, G., Rasteletti, A., and Vargas, F. (2014). *Productivity in services in Latin America and the Caribbean* (No. IDB-DP-346). Discussion Paper. Inter-American Development Bank.

Arvis, J. F., Marteau, J. F., and Raballand, G. (2010). *The cost of being landlocked: Logistics costs and supply chain reliability*. Washington, DC: World Bank.

Ayres, J., Garcia, M., Guillén, D. A., and Kehoe, P. J. (2018). *The monetary and fiscal history of Brazil, 1960–2016*. University of Chicago, Becker Friedman Institute for Economics Working Paper.

Bahar, D., and Dooley, M. (2019). *Venezuela refugee crisis to become the largest and most underfunded in modern history*. Brookings Institution. https://www.brookings.edu/blog/up-front/2019/12/09/venezuela-refugee-crisis-to-become-the-largest-and-most-underfunded-in-modern-history/ (accessed September 15, 2020)

Banco Central de Reserva del Peru (2019). *Reporte de inflación 2019*. Marzo 2019. https://www.bcrp.gob.pe/docs/Publicaciones/Reporte-Inflacion/2019/marzo/reporte-de-inflacion-marzo-2019.pdf (accessed August 15, 2020)

Bertola, L. (2005). A 50 años de la curva de Kuznets: Crecimiento económico y distribución del ingreso en Uruguay y otras economías de nuevo asentamiento desde 1870. *Investigaciones de historia económica*, *1*(3), 135–176.

https://doi.org/10.1515/9783110674934-009

Bethell, L. (1996). *The Paraguayan war (1864–1870)*. Research Paper. Institute of Latin American Studies, London.

Birdsall, N., De La Torre, A., and Menezes, R. (2008). *Fair growth: Economic policies for Latin America's poor and middle-income majority*. Washington, DC: Center for Global Development.

Birdsall, N., Williamson, J., and Deese, B. (2002). *Delivering on debt relief: From IMF gold to a new aid architecture*. Washington, DC: Center for Global Development and Institute for International Economics.

Blustein, P. (2006). *And the money kept rolling in (and out): Wall Street, the IMF, and the bankrupting of Argentina*. New York: Public Affairs.

Bonnet, F., Vanek, J., and Chen, M. (2019). Women and men in the informal economy: A statistical brief. International Labour Office, Geneva. https://www.ilo.org/wcmsp5/groups/public/---ed_protect/---protrav/---travail/documents/publication/wcms_711798.pdf (accessed August 15, 2020)

Borensztein, E., and Ruiz-Arranz, M. (2018). Dolarización: desempeño y desafíos. In J. Diaz-Cassou and M. Ruiz-Arranz (Eds.), *Reformas y desarrollo en el Ecuador contemporáneo*. Washington, DC: Inter-American Development Bank, 37–62

Borensztein, E., Piedrabuena, B., Ossowski, R., Mercer-Blackman, V., and Miller, S. J. (2010). El manejo de los ingresos fiscales del cobre en Chile. *Documento de trabajo del Banco Interamericano de Desarrollo*. IDB-PB-193.

Buera, F. J., and Nicolini, J. P. (2018). *The monetary and fiscal history of Argentina: 1960–2017*. University of Chicago, Becker Friedman Institute for Economics Working Paper.

Busso, M., Madrigal, L., and Pagés, C. (2013). Productivity and resource misallocation in Latin America. *The BE Journal of Macroeconomics*, *13*(1), 903–932.

Calvo, G., and Reinhart, C. M. (2001). Reflections on dollarization. In A. Alesina and R. Barro (Eds.), *Currency unions* 39–47.

Calvo, G. A., and Reinhart, C. M. (2002). Fear of floating. *The Quarterly Journal of Economics*, *117*(2), 379–408.

Caputo, R., and Saravia, D. (2018). *The monetary and fiscal history of Chile: 1960–2016* (2018-62). University of Chicago, Becker Friedman Institute for Economics Working Paper.

Carmignani, F. (2015). The curse of being landlocked: Institutions rather than trade. *The World Economy*, *38*(10), 1594–1617.

Carrasco, G. (1905). La poblacion del Paraguay, antes y después de la guerra: Rectificación de opiniones generalmente aceptadas, Talleres Nacionales de H. Kraus, Asunción. Buenos Aires.

Cavallo, E. and Powell, A. (2018). *A mandate to grow*. Washington, DC: Inter-American Development Bank.

Cavallo, E., and Powell, A. (2019). *Building Opportunities for Growth in a Challenging World*. Latin American and Caribbean Macroeconomic Report. Washington, DC: Inter-American Development Bank.

Cavallo, E. A., Powell, A., and Serebrisky, T. (2020). *From Structures to Services: The Path to Better Infrastructure in Latin America and the Caribbean*. Washington, DC: IDB.

Chamon, M. M., Hofman, M. D. J., Magud, M. N. E., and Werner, A. M. (2019). *Foreign exchange intervention in inflation targeters in Latin America*. Washington, DC: International Monetary Fund.

Charotti, C. J., Fernández-Valdovinos, C., and Gonzalez Soley, F. (2019). *The monetary and fiscal history of Paraguay, 1960–2017*. University of Chicago, Becker Friedman Institute for Economics Working Paper.

Chinn, M. D., and Ito, H. (2006). What matters for financial development? Capital controls, institutions, and interactions. *Journal of Development Economics*, *81*(1), 163–192.

Coremberg, A. (2018). *La cuenta satélite de los servicios de infraestructura: una nueva manera de medir la infraestructura en América Latina con base en los casos de Argentina, Brasil y México: fuentes, métodos y resultados*. IDB Technical Note 1502. Washington, DC: Inter-American Development Bank.

Cruces, G., Fields, G. S., Jaume, D. and Viollaz, M. (2015). *The growth-employment-poverty nexus in Latin America in the 2000s: Paraguay Country Study*. WIDER Working Paper 2015/081. Helsinki: UNU-WIDER.

Cruces, G., Fields, G., Jaume, D., and M. Viollaz (2017). *Growth, employment, and poverty in Latin America*. London: Oxford University Press.

Cueva, S. (2008). *Ecuador: Fiscal stabilization funds and prospects*. Country Department Andean Group Working Paper CSI-110. Washington, DC: Inter-American Development Bank.

Cueva, S., and Díaz, J. P. (2018). *The fiscal and monetary history of Ecuador: 1960–2017* (2018–65). University of Chicago, Becker Friedman Institute for Economics Working Paper.

Damill, M., Frenkel, R., and Maurizio, R. (2003). *Políticas macroeconómicas y vulnerabilidad social: La Argentina en los años noventa*. Serie financiamiento del desarrollo 135. Santiago de Chile: CEPAL.

Damill, M., Frenkel, R., and Rapetti, M. (2005). La deuda argentina: Historia, default y reestructuración. *Desarrollo Económico*, vol 45 (178), 187–233.

David, A. C., Pienknagura, S., and Roldos, J. E. (2020). *Labor market dynamics, informality and regulations in Latin America*. IMF Working Papers 20/19.

De Brun, J., and Della Mea, U. (2003). Una aproximación de mercado a la reestructuración de la deuda soberana: Lecciones de la experiencia uruguaya. *Revista de Economía*, *10*(2), 97–142.

De Brun, J., and Licandro, G. (2006). To hell and back – crisis management in a dollarized economy: The case of Uruguay. In A. Armas, A. Ize, and E. Levy-Yeyati (Eds.), *Financial Dollarization – The Policy Agenda*. London: Palgrave Macmillan UK, 147–176.

De Gregorio, J., and Labbé, F. (2011). Copper, the real exchange rate and macroeconomic fluctuations in Chile. In R. Arezki, T. Gylfason, and A. Sy (Eds.), *Beyond the curse: Policies to harness the power of natural resources*. Washington, DC: International Monetary Fund, 203–233.

De La Escosura, L. P. (2007). Inequality and Poverty in Latin America: A Long-Run Exploration. In Hatton, T. J., O'Rourke, K. H., and Taylor, A. M. (Eds). *The New Comparative Economic History. Essays in Honor of Jeffrey G. Williamson*. Cambridge Mass: MIT Press, 291–315.

De Soto, H. (1989). The other path: The invisible revolution in the Third World. New York: Harper Collins.

De la Torre, A., García-Saltos, R., and Mascaró, Y. (2002). *Banking, currency, and debt meltdown: Ecuador crisis in the Late 1990s*. Unpublished manuscript, World Bank.

Diaz J. P. (2018). La historia económica contemporánea de Ecuador, 1972–2015. In J. Diaz-Cassou and M. Ruiz-Arranz (Eds.), *Reformas y desarrollo en el Ecuador contemporáneo*. Washington, DC: Inter-American Development Bank, 7–36.

Dollar, D., and Kraay, A. (2003). Institutions, trade, and growth. *Journal of Monetary Economics*, *50*(1), 133–162.

Dreher, A., and Herzfeld, T. (2008). The economic costs of corruption: A survey and new evidence. In F. Columbus (Ed.), *Economic corruption and its impact*, New York: Nova Science, 115–132.

Duryea, S., and Robles, M. (2016). *Social pulse in Latin America and the Caribbean 2016: Realities and perspectives*. Washington DC: Inter-American Development Bank.

Economic Commission for Latin America and the Caribbean (ECLAC). (2015). *Foreign direct investment in Latin America and the Caribbean*. Santiago, Chile: ECLAC.

Economic Commission for Latin America and the Caribbean (ECLAC). (2019). *CEPALSTAT*. Santiago, Chile: ECLAC.

Estache, A., and Fay, M. (2007). Current debates on infrastructure policy. Policy Research Working Paper Series 4410. Washington, DC: The World Bank.

Faye, M. L., McArthur, J. W., Sachs, J. D., and Snow, T. (2004). The challenges facing landlocked developing countries. *Journal of Human Development*, *5*(1), 31–68.

Ferreira, F. H., Leite, P. G., and Ravallion, M. (2010). Poverty reduction without economic growth?: Explaining Brazil's poverty dynamics, 1985–2004. *Journal of Development Economics*, *93*(1), 20–36.

Fiszbein, A., Cosentino, C., and Cumsille, B. (2016). *The skills development challenge in Latin America: diagnosing the problems and identifying public policy solutions*. Washington, DC: Inter-American Dialogue and Mathematica Policy Research.

Fuentes, J. R., Keymer, B. P., and Calani, M. (2018). Towards efficient taxation of minerals: The case of copper in Chile. In O. Manzano, F. Navajas, and A. Powell (Eds.), *The economics of natural resources in Latin America: Taxation and regulation of the extractive industries*, London: Routledge, 47–77.

Garcia-Escribano, M., and Sosa, S. (2011). *What is driving financial de-dollarization in Latin America?* IMF Working Papers.

Garriga, A. C. (2016). Central bank independence in the world: A new data set. *International Interactions*, *42*(5), 849–868.

Garriga, A. C., and Rodriguez, C. M. (2020). More effective than we thought: Central bank independence and inflation in developing countries. *Economic Modelling*, *85*, 87–105.

Gasparini, L., and Cruces, G. (2010). Las asignaciones universales por hijo en Argentina: Impacto, discusión y alternativas. *Económica*, *41*, 105–146.

Giattino, C., Ortiz-Ospina, E., and Roser, M. (2013). Working Hours. Published online at OurWorldInData.org. https://ourworldindata.org/working-hours (accessed January 20, 2020)

Gomez-Gonzalez, J. E., and Kiefer, N. M. (2009). *Bank failure: Evidence from the Colombian financial crisis. The International Journal of Business and Finance Research*, 3(2),15–31.

Guzman, M. (2020). An analysis of Argentina's 2001 default resolution. *Comparative Economic Studies*, 1–38.

Gwartney, J., Lawson, R., and Norton, S. (2018). *Economic freedom of the world: 2018 annual report*. Vancouver: The Fraser Institute.

Hirschman, A. O. (1968). The political economy of import-substitution industrialization in Latin America. *The Quarterly Journal of Economics*, 82(1), 1–32.

Hofman, A. A. (2000). *The economic development of Latin America in the twentieth century*. Santiago, Chile: ECLAC.

International Monetary Fund (IMF) (2005). *Uruguay: Selected ssues Paper.* IMF Country Report 05/202. Washington, DC: International Monetary Fund.

International Monetary Fund (IMF) (2013). *Peru: Staff Report for the 2013 Article IV Consultation.* IMF Country Report 13/45. Washington, DC: International Monetary Fund.

International Monetary Fund (IMF) (2014). *Panama: Article IV Consultation.* IMF Country Report 14/157. Washington, DC: International Monetary Fund.

International Monetary Fund (IMF) (2015). *Ecuador: Selected Issues Paper.* IMF Country Report 15/290. Washington, DC: International Monetary Fund.

International Monetary Fund (IMF) (2016). *Peru: Selected Issues Paper.* IMF Country Report 16/235. Washington, DC: International Monetary Fund.

International Monetary Fund (IMF) (2020). *Peru: Selected Issues Paper.* IMF Country Report 20/3. Washington, DC: International Monetary Fund.International Monetary Fund.

International Monetary Fund (IMF) (2017). *Nicaragua: Article IV Consultation.* IMF Country Report 17/173. Washington, DC: International Monetary Fund.

International Monetary Fund (IMF) (2018). *Chile: Selected Issues Paper.* IMF Country Report 18/312. Washington, DC: International Monetary Fund.

International Monetary Fund (IMF) (2020a). *Nicaragua: Article IV Consultation.* IMF Country Report 20/59. Washington, DC: International Monetary Fund.

International Monetary Fund (IMF) (2020b). World Economic Outlook database, April 2020. Washington, DC: International Monetary Fund. https://www.imf.org/en/Publications/WEO/weo-database/2020/October (accessed August 15, 2020)

Inter-American Development Bank (2020). Latin Macro Watch. https://www.iadb.org/en/research-and-data/latin-macro-watch (accessed August 15, 2020).

Jácome, L. I. (2004). *The late 1990's financial crisis in Ecuador: Institutional weaknesses, fiscal rigidities, and financial dollarization at Work.* IMF Working paper No. 04/12. International Monetary Fund.

Jácome, L. I. (2008). *Central bank involvement in banking crises in Latin America.* IMF Working Paper No. 08/135. International Monetary Fund.

Jácome, L. I., and Vazquez, F. (2008). Is there any link between legal central bank independence and inflation? Evidence from Latin America and the Caribbean. *European Journal of Political Economy, 24*(4), 788–801.

Jemio, L. C. (2006). Volatilidad externa y el sistema financiero en Bolivia. *Unpublished manuscript.*, La Paz, Bolivia: Corporación Andina de Fomento (CAF)

Jemio, L. C., and Nina, O. (2010). *Bolivia phase 2.* Global Financial Crisis Discussion Series Paper 13. Overseas Development Institute, London.

Johnson, K. (2018). How Venezuela struck it poor. *Foreign Policy,* July, 16.

Kacef, O., and Jiménez, J. P. (2009). *Macroeconomic policies in times of crisis: Options and perspectives* (LC/W. 275). Santiago, Chile: ECLAC.

Kedir, A. M., Williams, C., and Altinay, L. (2018). Services industries and the informal economy: An introduction. *The Service Industries Journal, 38*, 11–12, 645–649, DOI: 10.1080/02642069.2018.1486959

Kehoe, T. J. (1995). What happened to Mexico in 1994–95? In T.J. Kehoe (Ed.), *Modeling North American economic integration.* Dordrecht: Springer, 131–147.

Kehoe, T. J. (2007). What can we learn from the 1998–2002 depression in Argentina? In T.J. Kehoe and E.C. Prescott (Eds.), *Great depressions of the twentieth century,* Minneapolis: Research Department, Federal Reserve Bank of Minneapolis, 373–402.

Kehoe, T. J., and Meza, F. (2011). Catch-up growth followed by stagnation: Mexico, 1950–2010. *Latin American Journal of Economics*, *48*(2), 227–268.

Kehoe, T. J., Machicado, C. G., and Peres-Cajías, J. (2019). *The monetary and fiscal history of Bolivia, 1960–2017*. Working paper No. w25523. National Bureau of Economic Research.

Kiguel, M. A., and Liviatan, N. (1995). Stopping three big inflations: Argentina, Brazil, and Peru. In R. Dornbusch and S. Edwards (Eds.), *Reform, recovery, and growth: Latin America and the Middle East*, University of Chicago Press, 369–414.

Kulesza, M. (2017). *Inflation and hyperinflation in Venezuela (1970s–2016): A Post-Keynesian interpretation* (No. 93/2017). Working Paper, Institute for International Political Economy Berlin.

La Porta, R., and Shleifer, A. (2014). Informality and development. *Journal of Economic Perspectives*, 28 (3): 109–26.

Limao, N., and Venables, A. J. (2001). Infrastructure, geographical disadvantage, transport costs, and trade. *The World Bank Economic Review*, *15*(3), 451–479.

Loayza, N. (2016), Informality in the Process of Development and Growth. The World Economy, 39: 1856–1916.

Loayza N. (2018). *Informality: Why is it so widespread and how can it be reduced?*, Research and policy briefs No. 20, Washington, DC: World Bank.

Loayza N., Oviedo, A., and Serven, L. (2005). The impact of regulation on growth and informality – cross-country evidence. Policy research working paper No. 3623, Washington, DC: World Bank.

Lora, E. (2012). *Structural Reforms in Latin America: What has been Reformed and How to Measure* It *(Updated Version)*, IDB Working Paper – 346. Inter-American Development Bank.

Marandino, J., and Oddone, G. (2018). *The monetary and fiscal history of Uruguay: 1960–2017* (2018–60). University of Chicago, Becker Friedman Institute for Economics Working Paper.

Martinelli, C., and Vega, M. (2018). The *monetary and fiscal history of Peru 1960–2017: Radical policy experiments, inflation, and stabilization* (2018–63). University of Chicago, Becker Friedman Institute for Economics Working Paper.

McCoy, J. L., and Myers, D. J. (Eds.). (2006). *The unraveling of representative democracy in Venezuela*. Baltimore: Johns Hopkins University Press.

Medina, L., and Schneider, F. (2018). *Shadow economies around the world: What did we learn over the last 20 years?* IMF Working Paper No. 18/17. International Monetary Fund.

Melguizo, A., Nieto-Parra, S., Perea, J. R., and Perez, J. A. (2017). *No sympathy for the devil! Policy priorities to overcome the middle-income trap in Latin America*. Working Papers No. 340. Paris: OECD Development Centre.

Meza, F. (2018). *The monetary and fiscal history of Mexico* (2018–64). University of Chicago, Becker Friedman Institute for Economics Working Paper.

Mishkin, F. S. (2004). *Can inflation targeting work in emerging market countries?* Working paper No. w10646. National Bureau of Economic Research.

Mondragón-Vélez, C., Peña, X., and Wills, D. (2010). Labor market rigidities and informality in Colombia. *Economía*, 11(1), 65–101.

Morón, E., Castro, J. F., and Villacorta, L. L. (2009). *The global crisis and the Peruvian labor market: Impact and policy options*. MPRA Working paper No. 22120.

Mussa, M. (2002). *Argentina and the Fund: From triumph to tragedy*. Peterson Institute.

Naím, M., and Toro, F. (2018). Venezuela's suicide. *Foreign Affairs*, 97, 126.

Naranjo, M. (2003). La dolarización de la economía del Ecuador: tres años después. *Cuestiones Económicas*, 19(1–3), 115–155.

National Statistics Republic of China (Taiwan) (2020). National Accounts. https://eng.stat.gov.tw/ (accessed September 15, 2020)

North, D. C. (1990). *Institutions, institutional change and economic performance*. Cambridge: Cambridge university press.

North, D. C. (1991). "Institutions." Journal of Economic Perspectives, 5 (1): 97–112.

Ocampo, J. A. (2017). Commodity-led development in Latin America. In G. Carbonnier, H. Campodonico, and S. Tezanos Vazquez (Eds.), *Alternative pathways to sustainable development: Lessons from Latin America*. Geneva: Brill Nijhoff, 51–76.

Ocampo, J. A., and Parra, M. Á. (2003). The terms of trade for commodities in the twentieth century. *Cepal Review*, 79: 7–35.

Ohanian, L. E., Restrepo-Echavarria, P., and Wright, M. L. (2018). Bad investments and missed opportunities? Postwar capital flows to Asia and Latin America. *American Economic Review*, *108*(12), 3541–3582.

Organization for Economic Cooperation and Development (OECD). (2019). *OECD Economic Surveys, Mexico 2019*. Paris: Organization for Economic Co-operation and Development.

Ortega-Garcia, J. A., Tellerías, L., Ferrís-Tortajada, J., Boldo, E., Campillo-López, F., Van den Hazel, P., ... & Claudio, L. (2019). Threats, challenges and opportunities for paediatric environmental health in Europe, Latin America and the Caribbean. Spanish Association of Paediatrics, 90(2), 124.e1–124.e11.

Pagés, C. (Ed.) (2010). *The age of productivity. Transforming economies from the bottom up*. New York: Palgrave Macmillan.

Pastor, C. (2019). *El mantenimiento como herramienta para conseguir infraestructura de alta calidad y durabilidad*. Washington, DC: Banco Interamericano de Desarrollo.

Perez-Reyna, D., and Osorio, D. (2018). *The monetary and fiscal history of Colombia: 1960–2017*. (2018–61). University of Chicago, Becker Friedman Institute for Economics Working Paper.

Pinon, M., Lopez Mejia, A., Garza, M., and Delgado, F. (Eds.) (2012). *Central America, Panama, and the Dominican Republic: Challenges following the 2008–09 global crisis*. Washington, DC: International Monetary Fund.

Porzecanski, A. C. (2016). The origins of Argentina's litigation and arbitration saga, 2002–2016. *Fordham International Law Journal, 40*, 41.

Potthast-Jutkeit, B. (1991) The ass of a mare and other scandals: Marriage and extramarital relations in nineteenth-century Paraguay *Journal of Family History*, *16*(3), 215–239.

Powell, A. (Ed.) (2013). *Rethinking reforms: How Latin America and the Caribbean can escape suppressed world growth*. Washington, DC: Inter-American Development Bank.

Rapier, R. (2017). How Venezuela Ruined Its Oil Industry. *Forbes*, May, 7, 2017.

Reinhart, C. M., and Rogoff, K. S. (2004). Serial default and the "paradox" of rich-to-poor capital flows. *American Economic Review*, *94*(2), 53–58.

Reinhart, C. M., and Rogoff, K. S. (2009). The aftermath of financial crises. *American Economic Review*, *99*(2), 466–472.

Reinhart, C. M., Rogoff, K. S., and Savastano, M. A. (2003). *Debt intolerance*, Working paper No. w9908. National Bureau of Economic Research.

Restuccia, D. (2018). *The monetary and fiscal history of Venezuela: 1960–2016* (2018–59). University of Chicago, Becker Friedman Institute for Economics Working Paper.

Ríos, G., Ortega, F., and Scrofina, J. S. (2012). *Sub-national revenue mobilization in Latin America and Caribbean countries: The case of Venezuela*, (Working paper IDB-WP-300). Inter-American Development Bank.

Rodriguez, C. M. (2017). The growth effects of financial openness and exchange rates. *International Review of Economics and Finance*, *48*, 492–512.

Salles, R. (2003). *Guerra do Paraguai: memórias & imagens*. Rio de Janeiro: Biblioteca Nacional.

Santos, A. (Ed.) (2009). *Paraguay: Addressing the stagnation and instability trap*. Washington, DC: International Monetary Fund.

Schleicher, A. (2019). PISA 2018: Insights and Interpretations. Paris: OECD Publishing.

Skidmore, T. E., Smith, P. H., and Green, J. N. (2010). *Modern Latin America*. New York: Oxford University Press.

Sosa, S. (2010). *The influence of "big brothers": How important are regional factors for Uruguay?* IMF Working Papers 10/60, International Monetary Fund.

Swiston, A. J. (2011). *Official dollarization as a monetary regime: Its effects on El Salvador*. IMF Working paper 11/129. International Monetary Fund.

Tanzi, V. (2007). *Argentina: An economic chronicle. How one of the richest countries in the world lost Its wealth*. New York: Pinto Books.

UN-World Food Programme (2020). *Venezuela food security assessment*. https://reliefweb.int/ sites/reliefweb.int/files/resources/Main%20Findings%20WFP%20Food%20Security%20As sessment%20in%20Venezuela_January%202020-2.pdf (accessed September 15, 2020).

United Nations Development Programme (UNDP) (2019). *Human development report 2019. Beyond income, beyond averages, beyond today: Inequalities in human development in the 21st century*. New York: UNDP. http://hdr.undp.org/en/content/human-development-report-2019 (accessed July 6, 2020).

United States Energy Information Administration (2020). International energy information. https://www.eia.gov/international/overview/world (accessed August 25, 2020).

United States Geological Survey (USGS) (2019). Mineral commodity summaries. February. https://www.usgs.gov/node/930898 (accessed September 15, 2020).

United Nations Office on Drugs and Crime (UNODC) (2019a). *Colombia. Monitoreo de territorios afectados por cultivos ilícitos 2017*. https://www.unodc.org/documents/crop-monitoring /Colombia/Colombia_Monitoreo_territorios_afectados_cultivos_ilicitos_2017_Resumen. pdf (accessed August 25, 2020).

United Nations Office on Drugs and Crime (UNODC) (2019b). *Global study on homicide 2019. Booklet 4*. Vienna. https://www.unodc.org/unodc/en/data-and-analysis/global-study-on-homicide.html (accessed September 15, 2020).

United Nations Office of the High Representative for the Least Developed Countries, Landlocked Developing Countries and Small Island Developing States (UN-OHRLLS) (2014). *The development economics of landlockedness: Understanding the development costs of being landlocked*. New York: UN-OHRLLS. http://unohrlls.org/about-lldcs/publica tions/the-development-economics-of-landlockedness-understanding-the-development-costs-of-being-landlocked/ (accessed September 15, 2020).

United States Office of National Drug Control Strategy (2003). 2003 National drug control strategy. Washington, DC: The White House.

United States Office of National Drug Control Strategy (2016). 2016 National drug control strategy. Washington, DC: The White House.

United States Office of National Drug Control Strategy (2019). Data on Coca Cultivation and Cocaine Production in Bolivia. Washington, DC: The White House. https://trumpwhite house.archives.gov/briefings-statements/ondcp-releases-data-coca-cultivation-production-potential-bolivia/ (accessed July 15, 2020).

Vegh, C., and Vuletin, G. (2018). *How threatening are fiscal deficits in Latin America and the Caribbean?* Brookings Institution. https://www.brookings.edu/research/how-threatening -are-fiscal-deficits-in-latin-america-and-the-caribbean/ (accessed September 15, 2020).

Vegh, C., Lederman, D., and Bennett, F. R. (2017). *Leaning against the wind: Fiscal policy in Latin America and the Caribbean in a historical perspective.* Washington, DC: World Bank.

Vuletin, G. (2008). *Measuring the informal economy in Latin America and the Caribbean.* IMF Working paper WP/08/102. Washington, DC: International Monetary Fund.

Webb, R. (2000). The influence of international financial institutions on ISI. In Cardenas, M., Ocampo, J, and Thorp, R. (Eds). *An Economic History of Twentieth-Century Latin America* (pp. 98–113). Palgrave Macmillan, London.

Weidemaier, M. C., and Gulati, M. (2014). A people's history of collective action clauses. *Virginia Journal of International Law, 54,* 1.

Weisbrot, M., and Johnston, J. (2012). *Venezuela's economic recovery: Is it sustainable?* Center for Economic and Policy Research. https://cepr.net/documents/publications/venezuela-2012-09.pdf (accessed August 15, 2020).

Wong, S. (2012). *Short-term macroeconomic and poverty impacts of the global economic crisis on the Ecuadorian economy.* Paper presented at IADB-ECLAC 4th Regional Meeting on General Equilibrium Modeling. Guayaquil, April, 19–20. https://ecomod.net/system/files/ Wong_EcoMod_March2012.pdf (accessed August 25, 2020).

World Bank (2018). *Worldwide governance indicators.* Washington, DC: World Bank.

World Bank (2019). *Doing business, 2019.* Washington, DC: World Bank.

World Bank. (2020). World development indicators. Washington, D.C.: World Bank. http:// data.worldbank.org/data-catalog/world-development-indicators (accessed July 6, 2020).

World Economic Forum. (2019). *Global competitiveness report.* Davos, Switzerland: World Economic Forum.

World Trade Organization. (2020). *Trade profiles.* Geneva: World Trade Organization. https:// www.wto.org/english/res_e/statis_e/trade_profiles_list_e.htm (accessed August 15, 2020).

List of Figures

https://doi.org/10.1515/9783110674934-010

List of Tables

https://doi.org/10.1515/9783110674934-011

About the Authors

Cesar M. Rodriguez is Associate Professor of Economics at Portland State University (PSU). He received his PhD in Economics from the University of Pittsburgh in 2009 and a BA (licenciatura) in Economics from the University of the Republic in Uruguay. Before joining PSU in 2013, he worked as an economist at the Inter-American Development Bank in Washington DC. His research focuses on the macroeconomic aspects of international economics and finance, and economic development in Latin America. He has published in several academic journals, such as the *Journal of International Economics*, the *Journal of International Money and Finance*, *Economic Modelling*, the *International Review of Economics and Finance*, *International Economics*, and *Small Business Economics*.

W. Charles Sawyer was the Hal Wright Professor of Latin American Economics at Texas Christian University (TCU). He received a PhD in Economics at the University of Arkansas in 1983 and received both an MA and BA in Economics at St. Mary's University. Before coming to TCU in 2007, he previously taught at the University of Arkansas, LSU, the Helsinki School of Economics and Management, and the University of Southern Mississippi. In addition, he served as a consultant for the United Nations Conference on Trade and Development and the United Nations Industrial Development Organization. He published over 50 articles in leading research journals such as *The Review of Economics and Statistics*, *Economic Development and Cultural Change*, the *Canadian Journal of Economics*, *Economic Letters*, and the *Review of World Economics*. He authored or coauthored five books including *The Demand for Imports and Exports in the World Economy*, *International Economics* (4th edition), *Latin American Economic Development* (3rd edition), and *U.S. International Trade Policy: An Introduction*. His latest book is an edited four volume set, *Latin American Economics*. Recently, he was studying the relationship between institutional quality and economic development in Latin America.

https://doi.org/10.1515/9783110674934-012

Index

https://doi.org/10.1515/9783110674934-013